Mixedblood Messages

◆

American Indian Literature
and
Critical Studies Series
Gerald Vizenor and Louis Owens,
General Editors

Also by Louis Owens

Fiction
Wolfsong (Albuquerque, 1991; Norman, 1995; Paris, 1996)
The Sharpest Sight (Norman, 1992, 1995; Paris, 1994)
Bone Game (Norman, 1994, 1996; Paris, 1998)
Nightland (New York, 1996, 1997)

Nonfiction
John Steinbeck's Re-Vision of America (Athens, Ga., 1985)
(with Tom Colonnese) *American Indian Novelists: An Annotated Critical Bibliography* (New York, 1985)
The Grapes of Wrath: Trouble in the Promised Land (New York, 1989)
(editor) *American Literary Scholarship: An Annual, 1990* (Durham, N.C., 1992)
Other Destinies: Understanding the American Indian Novel (Norman, 1992, 1994)

Mixedblood Messages

Literature, Film, Family, Place

◆

By Louis Owens

University of Oklahoma Press : Norman

Though most have been extensively revised for this collection, versions of several essays gathered here have appeared in the following publications: "The Song is Very Short: Native American Literature and Literary Theory," in *Weber Studies* 12, no. 3 (fall 1995); "Mapping the Mixedblood: Frontier and Territory in Native America" as "Mixedblood Geography: Hybridization in Native American Literature," in *Histoire et Anthropologie: Revue de Sciences Humaines*, Strasbourg 10 (1995); "'Grinning Aboriginal Demons': The End of Tragedy," as "'Grinning Aboriginal Demons': Gerald Vizenor's *Bearheart* and the Indian's Escape from Gothic," in *Frontier Gothic*, edited by David Mogen, Scott P. Sanders, and Joanne Karpinski (Rutherford: Fairleigh Dickinson University Press, 1993); "Apocalypse at the Two-Socks Hop: Dancing with the Vanishing American," as "*D'une disparition a l'autre,*" in *Revue d'études Palestiennes* 55, no. 3 (spring 1995); "Motion of Fire and Form," in *Native American Literature: A Brief Introduction and Anthology*, edited by Gerald Vizenor (New York: HarperCollins, 1995); "Water Witch" in *California Childhood: Recollections and Stories of the Golden State*, edited by Gary Soto (Berkeley: Creative Arts Books, 1992); "The Invention of John Wayne," as "Into the Territory: The Invention of John Wayne," in *Icarus* 10 (spring 1993); "Burning the Shelter" as "The American Indian Wilderness," in *The American Nature Writing Newsletter* 6, no. 2 (fall 1994). Excerpts from "Selling Myself," by Arturo Islas, are used courtesy of Diane W. Middlebrook, Executor of the Literary Estate of Arturo Islas, and Stanford University.

Library of Congress Cataloging-in-Publication Data

Owens, Louis.
 Mixedblood messages : literature, film, family, place / by Louis Owens.
  p. cm. — (American Indian literature and critical studies series ; v. 26)
 Includes bibliographical references and index.
 ISBN 0-8061-3051-2 (alk. paper)
 1. Indians of North America—Mixed descent. 2. Indians of North America—Ethnic identity. 3. Indians in motion pictures—North America. 4. Indians in literature. I. Title. II. Series.
E98.M6309 1998
970'.00497—dc21   98-5361
                                                             CIP

Mixedblood Messages: Literature, Film, Family, Place is Volume 26 in the American Indian Literature and Critical Studies Series.

The paper in this book meets the guidelines for permanence and durability of the Committee on Production Guidelines for Book Longevity of the Council on Library Resources, Inc. ∞

1 2 3 4 5 6 7 8 9 10

This book is dedicated with immense love to my sister, Betty, over whose shoulder I learned to see stories in words and worlds in stories. We have all traveled so far together. Remember all those great cars?

Contents

Illustrations

$\blacklozenge$

All photos are from the author's collection.

Preface: Crow Love

◆

When I was a boy, a friend and I used to keep pet crows. Every spring we would locate places where the flocks nested, and we would watch the eggs until they hatched. We would make friends with the nestlings, visiting them frequently until they were almost ready to fly. Though shy at first, they quickly seemed to anticipate and enjoy our visits, craning their scrawny necks as we climbed up to them. Eventually we would each take two or three—whoever was in the nest—to our homes, where we would put them in cardboard boxes and feed them Gravy Train dog food. They were delightful pets—friendly, extroverted, thrilled to be going on a journey, and apparently ecstatic at the discovery of Gravy Train. They bonded quickly and could be counted on to hang around once they could fly and were released outside. Mine would invariably perch in a dead tree near my family's home and swoop down exuberantly to caw their hellos whenever I appeared in the barnyard. They incorporated us humans into their constant games, hilariously plucking clothespins from the line so that my mother's laundry would flutter to the ground and harassing the dogs at every turn. When migration time came, the crows would sail around above the barn nervously for a few days and then join the great flocks as they went elsewhere. If they returned to nest another year, we never knew it. The next year we would adopt new crows and at the right time they, too, would migrate. For three years we had very fulfilling one-season relationships with our crows. Only one thing darkens the memory for me.

My friend Chuck was a gentle person who loved the natural world. However, his father, a silent man who still ranched the land his great-grandfather had pioneered—land that in his great-grandfather's day had been the home of Chumash Indians—had convinced Chuck that to make crows speak human words it was necessary to split their tongues with a sharp knife. It seemed to be an idea Chuck's father had inherited from his father, but where it had originated was not clear. All that *was* clear was the rancher's firm belief in his theory. Chuck and I argued and even fought over the issue, but finally, one season, I could not convince him to spare his birds' tongues. He wanted desperately to achieve something he thought of as communication with those crows, but strangely, they never did learn to talk. In fact, while my guests would often hurl themselves down from the dead tree with hoarse caws sounding to me very much like "hellos," Chuck's birds appeared to lose even the joy of crow talk and seemed to become sullen and resentful. After that year, Chuck and I lost interest in pet crows. I moved away soon and lost contact with Chuck as well.

Over the years I have often thought about Chuck's crows. I still wince at the memory of the birds, who finally took to the air no longer capable of the glib chatter and easy laughter so important to crows. And I wonder what happened to my friend who loved crows so much, who wanted so terribly to hear his own words spoken back to him. Perhaps, like me, he went on to a career in education.

Many of us have seen something like this story repeated with relatives, friends, and the characters who people literature by writers on the margins. Desperate to give his words to the "other," so that the whole world will ultimately give back the reflected self, the colonizer performs his surgery. The result, as we see again and again in writing by American Indian authors, can be what N. Scott Momaday shows us in the character of Able in the novel *House Made of Dawn*. "Had he been able to say it," Momaday writes, "anything of his own language—even the commonplace formula of greeting 'Where are you going,'—which had no being beyond sound, no visible substance, [it] would once again have shown him whole to himself; but he was dumb. Not dumb—but inarticulate" (57). Echoing Momaday, Sherman Alexie asks in his collection of stories, *The Lone Ranger and Tonto Fistfight in Heaven*, "How can we imagine a new language when the language of the enemy keeps our dismembered tongues tied to his belt?" (152).

But people are not crows, of course. We have the power to heal our tongues and learn to speak in any language on earth or to imagine a new one. When the season ends—even a five-hundred-year season of what the Chippewa writer Gerald Vizenor has called "word wars"— we do not always migrate, though we may have been relocated sometime during that long season. Most significantly, perhaps, we humans have the ability to appropriate and liberate the other's discourse. Rather than merely reflecting back to him the master's own voice, we can, in an oft-quoted phrase, learn to make it bear the burden of our own experience. We can use the colonizer's language, as Momaday demonstrates so brilliantly in *The Way to Rainy Mountain*, to articulate our own worlds and find ourselves whole. This has been the project of Native American writers for a long time.

When I developed and began teaching a course called "The Native American Novel" back in 1982, I had little trouble putting together my syllabus. I could include at least one work by nearly every Indian novelist of whom I knew: N. Scott Momaday, Leslie Silko, Gerald Vizenor, James Welch, Paula Gunn Allen, D'Arcy McNickle, and John Joseph Mathews. I could even include excerpts from works like Ted Williams's hilarious novel, *The Reservation*, or peripheral novels such as Frank Waters's *The Man Who Killed the Deer* or Dan Cushman's *Stay Away Joe*. I knew of John Rollin Ridge, Mourning Dove, and John Milton Oskison, of course, but I was not sophisticated enough to introduce novels as challenging as those authors' into my classroom. I was not sophisticated enough, in fact, to realize what I was getting into with Vizenor's *Bearheart*, a novel that tried my brain cells and a dean's patience, an experience I have written about elsewhere.[1] Never having had the chance to take a course in Native American novels— having, in fact, encountered only one Indian novel in all of my courses through the Ph.D.—Welch's *Winter in the Blood*—I was a self-taught scholar in this particular area with a great deal yet to learn.[2] I had, in fact, been hired as a nineteenth-century American literature specialist and felt very fortunate to be allowed to teach American Indian literature during my first year as a grown-up, tenure-track prof.

A great deal has changed in the world of the Native American novel since that first course. Today when I sit down to plan a syllabus, my quandary is not how to find enough works for a semester but how to select just a handful of novels from the constantly increasing numbers of fine novels by Indian writers. How does one choose whom or what to teach from a list that now includes not just many new works by the above-noted celebrities in the field but also Louise Erdrich, Thomas King, Ronald Querry, A. A. Carr, Anna Lee Walters, Elizabeth Cook-Lynn, Gordon Henry, Jr., Michael Dorris, Linda Hogan, Janet Campbell Hale, Susan Power, Diane Glancy, Betty Louise Bell, Joseph Marshall, Robert Conley, David Treuer, W. S. Penn, Sherman Alexie, Joseph Bruchac, Adrian Louis, Ray Young Bear, Winona LaDuke, and even Louis Owens among others? By the time I have finished writing this paragraph I am sure there will be half a dozen new novels to contend with; two friends have called in the past two days, in fact, to tell me that they have just completed drafts of new books, and I know of at least a dozen in progress.

It is extremely gratifying, to say the least, to see so many new and radically different works emerging from such a broad cross-section of the Native American population. At the same time, critical studies of this literature have multiplied to the extent that the Native American novel seems to have developed its own kind of critical duality between those scholars who embrace contemporary literary theory to one extent or another in their readings and those who prefer a more long-established kind of social-science approach to the field. Kimberly Blaeser, an Anishinaabe poet and scholar, has even contributed the first full-length critical monograph devoted to the works of a single author in her brilliant study, *Gerald Vizenor: Writing in the Oral Tradition* (1996). In the meantime, theses and dissertations on Native American literature are pouring out of graduate programs all over the country as well as in Europe.

Whatever one's critical inclination and one's taste in fiction, today there are likely to be a handful of novels, stories, poems, and critical approaches to satisfy that inclination and taste. And there will be no shortage of debate regarding this material. Today there is more wrangling over diverse issues (identity, authenticity, essentialism, critical colonization, appropriation, and so forth) in this arena of American literature than in any other nook or cranny of contemporary writing. The result is not merely disagreement (a phenomenon perpetually familiar to Indian Country) but more significantly a dynamic energy that brings life to a kind of literature and literary debate that barely existed a quarter century ago—more life and vibrancy, I would argue, than can be found in any other portion of contemporary American literature. I would extend that argument to say that virtually everything that is new and vital and exciting in American literature is coming from the so-called margins—from westerners, from Native American Indians, from the children of Vietnamese "Boat-People" and other Asian immigrants, from the growing richness of Chicano and *mestizaje* literature, from African Americans. I, for one, am more than tired of Iowa Writers Workshop-type stories and books about suburban angst and midlife crises, even when those books win Pulitzer Prizes. Out of boredom the privileged mainstream (mostly male) writers of America turned toward metafiction and so-called neorealism in the sixties, seventies, and eighties. That's over now. New York has pleased its incestuous self with a few narcissistic books about New York (e.g.: the sophomoric *Bright Lights, Big City*) and found more colorful material in fiction about southern white trash—the new "Amos and Andy" caste in a time when it is not quite acceptable to make fun of racial minorities—but this is a sign of the doldrums in contemporary mainstream writing. Despite the puffery of the *New York Times* or *Time Magazine* reviews, everything of interest today is coming from those who are writing back toward that decayed center. Out of this resistance, a new American literature is emerging, and American Indian writing—with all of its anger, humor, bitterness, beauty, feuding, and deep sense of a real subject—is at the heart of this emergence.

The following essays have been gathered from writings I have done over the past several years and months. A few have been published in the United States or Europe, some have been delivered as lectures, and some have never seen the light of day before this; the previously published essays have, almost entirely, been extensively revised and combined to form new wholes. The resulting approach is both informal and personal, and the range is eclectic, including literary analysis, commentary upon film, environmental reflections, and autobiographical musings. My wish is that together these essays should present a consciousness—my own—that arises out of and is concerned with two major issues: questions of mixed heritage and how we articulate those questions, especially in fiction, and the ways in which we relate to the natural world. The autobiographical writings, I hope, will provide a context for the critical and environmental musings, and vice versa.

Acknowledgments

◆

I owe so much to so many for what has gone into this book that it is difficult to single out individuals. First are my family, particularly my eight brothers and sisters, who not only lived much of what is found here but gathered around nearly century-old photographs to wonder, compare, and blend fragments of self-knowledge, and who sat up late sharing stories of alligator sandwiches, innumerable houses, and love. Beyond immediate family are first Gerald Vizenor, whose generosity and genius have helped me and so many others in countless ways; Dale Ann and Marlon Sherman, for kindness, wisdom, and wonderfully quotable prose; Aaron Carr, whose many conversations over fishing poles or coffee have helped clarify so much for me and opened new directions for thought; Alan Kilpatrick, for knowledge and humor; Tom King, for a generous spirit, kind humor, and writing to emulate; Luci Tapahonso, for friendship, serenity, wisdom, and a way with words; Erika Aigner-Varoz, for much aid and insight; Irene Vernon, Larry Smith, and, Jacque Kilpatrick, all of whom helped to shape this volume in important ways; Kim Wiar, the greatest editor and friend a writer could ever find; Sarah Nestor, once again a brilliant editor and polymath; and my wife, Polly, and daughters, Elizabeth and Alexandra, for putting up with me. Finally, this book is a tribute to those people who survived in the poverty of Mississippi and the harshness of Indian Territory to give us all words and the breath to make those words live.

1

Mixedbloods and Mixed Messages

Adventures in Native American Literature

◆

1

Columbus Had It Coming

Crossbloods, Crossreading, and Cultural Survival

◆

Let us begin with the discovery of America, an amusing concept, and with language, the issue most at the heart of American Indian writing as well as the most powerful tool of colonialism. In an early entry in Las Casas's version of the *Diario*, Christopher Columbus considers the native inhabitants of the brave, new world he has discovered. Addressing the Spanish monarchs, Columbus writes, "Our Lord pleasing, at the time of my departure I will take six of them from here to Your Highnesses in order that they may learn to speak" (69). Later, in careful instructions to a subordinate as to how a shipment of Indian slaves to Spain might be rationalized to the monarchs who have forbidden mistreatment of the natives, Columbus echoed this refrain: "Item, say to their Highnesses that because there is no language by means of which this people can understand our Holy Faith . . . thus are being sent with these ships the cannibals, men and women and boys and girls, which their Highnesses may order placed in the possessions of persons from whom they can best learn the language" (69). Columbus's words presage centuries of symbiosis between slavery and silence in the Americas, that long endeavor to eradicate the voices of indigenous peoples and subsume them into the manifest history of what has lately come to be called Euro-America or Euramerica. This sinister symbiosis resembles the process of dehumanizing African Americans described by Henry Louis Gates, Jr., who declared that "logocentricism and ethnocentrism marched together in an attempt to deprive the black human being of even the potential to create art, to imagine a world and to figure it" (*Black Literature*, 7).

But this is old news. Despite the astonishingly ubiquitous commodification currency and profoundly embedded racism represented by the "tomahawk chop" and Washington Redskins and Jeep Cherokees and Mazda Navajos, Columbus at least has been largely exposed. The insidiousness of colonial and federal Indian policies that have sought for several centuries to exterminate Native American cultures in one way or another—through physical and cultural destruction—has also been rather widely acknowledged, even as such policies as removal, relocation, and termination are replaced today by other disastrous strategies such as using reservations as toxic dumping sites.

What is *new* news today, however, is a growing recognition of the subversive survival of indigenous Americans. Five hundred years after Columbus's first voyage, this survival is being illuminated in the United States through a proliferating body of literature by Native Americans demonstrating that the "Discoverer" succeeded beyond his most earnest expectations. The people he mistakenly and unrepentantly called "Indians" have indeed "learned to speak," appropriating the master discourse—including the utterance "Indian"—abrogating its authority, making the invaders' language our language, english with a lower-case *e*, and turning it against the center. Today, together with so-called "marginalized" writers throughout the world, Native Americans are ensuring that, as Robert Young has written, ". . . the First World is now having to come to terms with the fact that it is no longer always positioned in the first person with regard to the Second or Third Worlds" (125). And in helping to reposition this global point of view, Native Americans are beginning, like other writers, to demand that non-Indian readers acknowledge differing epistemologies, that they venture across a new "conceptual horizon" and learn to read in new ways. For many Native Americans even such patronizing terms as First, Second, or Third World demand repositioning to signify not the cultural/historical hegemony of the Western world but rather those paradigmatic, mythic levels that underlie this present world in the origin myths. Today we live not in the first, second, or third, but in the fourth or perhaps fifth world.

A few years ago I was asked to speak at the University of California at Berkeley about something called "cross-reading," which I took at the time to indicate the way in which all of us engage texts across some kind of cultural boundary or conceptual horizon. Because I regularly teach Native American literature to classes with a majority of non–Native American students, and I both create and write about this literature for an audience composed largely of non–Native American readers, crossreading is for me, as it is for countless others, a phenomenon of which I am always conscious. And because I read and write as a mixedblood, a Native American of both Indian and European ancestry, such heteroglossia would also seem, for me, to be the precondition of every utterance. As what the Anishinaabe author Gerald Vizenor would call a "crossblood," embodying a multicultural "torsion in the blood," I believe I experience every thought, every endeavor at utterance, every conceptual encounter, as an experience in crossreading.

Vizenor has written that "we're all invented as Indians . . . and we are stuck in coins and words like artifacts" (Bowers, 47). Recently a student brought to me a facsimile edition of Potawatomi author Simon Pokagon's 1899 novel *Queen of the Woods*, which caused me to recall this declaration by Vizenor. On the overleaf of the edition was a photo of Pokagon, but in the photocopying process the photograph had been emptied out, leaving only the graphically hollow gray outline of a human head and torso with the name, Chief Simon Pokagon, beneath it. I turned to the novel's appendices to find what I remembered from years before as having been there: a copy of a newspaper obituary with the boldface headline, "Pokagon is Dead." It struck me as a finely ironic textual and contextual phenomenon. Like this Pokagon—whose novel, one of the first both by and about an American Indian, has been claimed (rightly or wrongly, the jury is still out, I believe) actually to be the work of the wife of Pokagon's white lawyer[1]—the American Indian in the world consciousness has become not only a static artifact but more importantly, I think, a contested space, a place of signification to be emptied out and reinhabited by Euramerica. For every non-Native inhabitant of the Americas, the outlined space labeled "Chief Simon Pokagon" represents a territory to be reinhabited and remapped, its original inhabitant—the Vanishing American—having supposedly disappeared like Pokagon's narrative authority into the white space. Similarly, we find the Okanogan author Mourning Dove struggling throughout her 1927 novel, *Cogewea, the Half-Blood*, to make her own voice heard over that of her Euramerican editor, Lucullus Virgil McWhorter, whose privileged discourse at times nearly overwhelms the original author to the point that Mourning Dove would eventually say, "I have just got through going over the book *Cogewea*, and am surprised at the changes you made. . . . I felt like it was some one else's book and not mine at all" (*Cogewea*, xv).

To Native Americans, the authoritative discourse of European America, that discourse which, as Bakhtin has pointed out, comes with its authority already fused to it and simply demands allegiance, can inspire both trauma and a tricksterish subversion. A student in one of my Native American literature courses wrote a wonderful essay several years ago in which she recalled a boy in her junior-high-school English class. A member of the Pomo Tribe, the boy always sat in the back of the class and said nothing. One day, however, my student happened to glance at an essay the boy was passing forward. To her astonishment, the handwriting was so minute that she could not read it. When she asked the boy about it, he laughed. "My math teacher has to use a magnifying glass to grade my exams," he added triumphantly. My student, who had spent a term reading novels by Native Americans, recognized the dialogic in retrospect. Like so many Native Americans, the boy who sat wordlessly in the back of the class had been almost silenced, his voice approaching the vanishing point, his inscribed self—the only self recognized within "literate" America—very nearly invisible. In the course of five hundred years of linguistic denigration, of being "taught to speak" by Euramerica, Native Americans, like the protagonists of so many Native American literary works, have often withdrawn into silence. But, although we cannot ignore the terrible pain behind such a story, from his liminal posture the Pomo boy had seized control of the language, finding in his very liminality an empowerment and forcing the authorities to read on his terms. It was, my student recognized, a brilliant, even satirical act of subversion in the splendid tradition of trickster, and I cannot help but think of this as a metaphor for all marginalized writers. Ultimately, the only way to be really heard is to make them read on our terms, though within the language of the colonizer's terminology. On a page of Pomo 'e'nglish, five hundred years had been overturned, Columbus outsmarted. As Vizenor has written, there is unmistakable tragedy in such a story, but not victimization. And there is a tricksterish laughter as well.

Responding in a more ambitious way to the challenge of how one may appropriate narrative authority in English, Blackfoot author James Welch produced *Fools Crow*, a novel set almost entirely in the Blackfoot world of the 1860s and '70s. In an interview, Welch said of this novel:

> I'm staying exclusively with the Blackfeet. I'm trying to write from the inside-out, because most historical novels are written from the outside looking in. My main character is a member of a particular band, and I'm talking a lot about camp life and ceremonial life, those day to day practical things they did to survive-and to live quite decently, as a matter of fact. So I'm writing it from the inside-out. The white people are the real strangers. They're the threatening presence out there all the time. (McFarland, 4–5)

The point of view in *Fools Crow* is that of a Native culture still whole and intact. Throughout the novel Welch attempts the problematic task of conveying the texture and sense of Blackfoot speech not only by insinuating numerous literal "translations" of Blackfoot terms, but also through a careful manipulation of English syntax. Writing in predominantly simple declarative sentences and avoiding complex syntactical constructions, Welch attempts the nearly impossible feat of conveying a feeling of one language through another while simultaneously trying to avoid (without total success, I should say) the clichéd formal pidgin of Hollywood Indians. When, late in the novel, the point of view shifts briefly to that of a young white man, alone on the plains and guarding a whiskey wagon, the prose style, too, undergoes a significant shift as Welch writes, "The rolling prairies were as vast and empty as a pale ocean, and the sky stretched forever, sometimes blue, sometimes slate. The few small groups of mountains, like islands in this sea of yellow swells, only seemed to emphasize its vastness. In the winter, when snow covered the land and lay heavy in the bottoms, the man was filled with foreboding dreams of an even larger isolation" (289–90). Seen through Blackfoot eyes, the landscape has immediate presence; it is intimate and fully inhabited, and its signs are read in direct relation to their interpenetration within the lives of the people and animals. Cold Maker and black clouds have imminent and practical significance for the warm lodges of the Pikuni and for the dogs and horses dependent upon them and at home in this place. In the lyrical rendering of the white man's thoughts, however, Welch suggests the imposition of an aesthetic valorization upon the landscape. For the white man, the landscape is magnificently uninhabited, empty of local significance, mirroring, particularly in the key phrase "foreboding dreams of an even larger isolation," the placelessness that informs the colonial experience.

Having no history, no "place" within the landscape, the European American can only define it in abstract, broadly aesthetic terms that enable him to subsume it into his own romantic narrative. In such an instance, and throughout the acting out of the American metanarrative, the North American continent becomes a kind of deadly theme park in the Euramerican imagination, "free land" as Frederick Jackson Turner would call it, for the manifest imagination in the process of creating its own hyperreality.[2]

In his lyrical response, Welch's naive and doomed character reenacts the symbolic depopulation of the continent ("vast and empty") necessary both as a first step toward appropriation and as a means of making the place accessible to the abstract language that is otherwise so inadequate to the task of description. At the same time, through this lyrically "placeless" language, the white man reenacts the colonial subsumption of the continent into the "manifest" destiny of the invaders. Like the African Americans in Ralph Ellison's *Invisible Man*, the Native Americans become invisible inhabitants of the disturbing Promised Land surrounding the westering Euramerican. Emptiness characterizes this environment: the monochromatic sky stretches forever, while the prairies are a "vast and empty" sea, as if heaven and earth have merged to form an embryonic sea-space within which the romantic imagination may bring forth the new man, the isolate American. Very shortly, however, Indian phantoms will rise up in Welch's novel from that peripheralized reality to murder the young intruder.

If, as the authors of *The Empire Writes Back* argue (and as seems quite obvious), language "becomes the medium through which a hierarchical structure of power is perpetuated, and the medium through which conceptions of 'truth', 'order' and 'reality' become established," the primary structure of power (and epistemology) in the world of *Fools Crow* still belongs to the Blackfeet. The protagonist's world is intact; there is no alienation—yet. However, by manipulating the syntax of the novel, by interpolating literal translations of Blackfoot utterances such as "sticky mouth," "real bear," "Cold Maker," and so on, and by rendering place so fully, Welch makes his reader acutely aware of the "gap" his language attempts to overcome: that "resulting from the linguistic displacement of the pre-colonial language by English" (Ashcroft, 7). Thus, as Welch attempts "to convey in a language that is not one's own the spirit that is one's own," the tensions—dialogism—within the very language of the novel become a radical indicator of the cultural denigration, displacement, even genocide that the novel is meant to demonstrate.

Native American authors such as Welch are accomplishing what might be termed "crosswriting." But what of the reader confronted with the world of *Fools Crow*, or the web of creation in *Ceremony*, or the trickster narratives of Vizenor? How does one on the other side of the cultural line go about the challenge of crossreading, a challenge that for my students often seems enormously intimidating. I once received a phone call from the Literature Board at the University of California at Santa Cruz, where I was teaching at the time. A student in my Native American novels class had requested that my course be accepted for credit as literature in translation. The board wanted to know how I felt about such a request, explaining that the student insisted she had never before been required to penetrate so deeply into a "foreign" culture in any literature course. My first response was to laugh at what seemed a typical Santa Cruz absurdity, but on second thought I was intrigued. Why not recognize the radical appropriation of English and the repositioning of conceptual horizons taking place in American Indian writing and admit that, as Native American novelist D'Arcy McNickle expressed it, this literature comes from and aims toward a different "map of the mind"? It seemed like a good time to barter in the New World fur trade, so I suggested, in turn, that all Native American students should be given foreign literature credit for all non–Native American literature courses. Why not foreign-language credit for Navajo and Lakota and Choctaw students reading Mark Twain, Shakespeare, Emily Dickinson, Milton, Saul Bellow?

To a reader of writing by Native Americans, it will be readily apparent that texts and contexts have changed and that the privileged utterance is refreshingly "other" for the non-Indian reader. To paraphrase Chicano critic Ramón Saldívar, "The truth of the real world that [Native Americans] experience has thus been made to inhabit literature" (5). And just as the oppressively literate modernists felt justified in demanding that readers know a little Greek and Roman mythology as well as the entire literary history of the Western world, Native American writers have begun to expect, even demand, that readers learn something about the mythology and oral histories of Indian America. Dell Hymes, writing about oral literatures, has expressed this point neatly, saying, "As with Beowulf and The Tale of Genji, the material requires some understanding of a way of life" (5). Without an awareness of the nature of traditional trickster narratives, for instance, a reader is likely to be lost and perhaps outraged by Vizenor's Bearheart. Once, however, the same reader has cohabited with Coyote in the oral tradition and watched trickster switch gender to bear the chief's son's children and devour those same children, burn his/her own anus for its failure to guard roasted ducks, and devour his/her own entrails in a deconstructed frenzy of hunger, Vizenor's traditional trickster narratives may be more comprehensible. Similarly, without knowing the story of Yellow Woman from Laguna and Navajo mythology, a reader will fail to comprehend the fullness of Ceremony just as one must recognize the wedded contraries of the Blackfoot trickster-creators, Old Man and Old Woman, to correctly read Welch's Winter in the Blood.

The many sensitive and perceptive responses of my students, who are so wonderfully eager to discover the epistemologically new worlds of Native American literature, tell me that crossreading is both possible and rewarding. I have little sympathy for those who would argue that "outsiders" (i.e., non-Indians) have no business reading or studying Native American literature. To think that poems, novels, stories, or plays written and performed by Native people are not for all audiences is essentialist and absurd. But it takes work; as Grandma says in Leslie Marmon Silko's *Ceremony*, "It isn't easy."

Our responsibilities as readers and writers, as critics and teachers, and as inhabitants of a planet becoming smaller and more fragile by the moment are increasing exponentially. To survive on this globe, it has become clear that we must achieve a transition from egocentrism to ecocentrism. More and more we will be required to read across lines of cultural identity around us and within us. It is not easy but it is necessary, and the rewards are immeasurable. Finally, it is quite clearly the only way the community we call life will survive.

Beads and Buckskin

Reading Authenticity in Native American Literature

◆

Beads and buckskin, sacred pipes, wise elders, prayers to "mother earth," and so on—we all recognize these signifiers of essentialist authoritative discourse in the realm of Native American literature. Although such signifiers have crucial and invaluable meaning to Native peoples, from the Euramerican perspective this is merely a surface discourse established from a cultural glance by the dominant European-American culture over several hundred years of colonization to define the distinct "otherness" of indigenous Americans. To go beyond such facile cultural discourse to the deeper and irreplaceable roles such signifiers play in specific Native cultures would be to recognize the humanity of the colonized, a move certain to make a difficult task of cultural erasure more difficult still. Trying, for example, to somehow fit literacy into his stereotype of an authentic "Indian," a white man is said to have suggested to Sequoyah, inventor of the Cherokee syllabary, that the Great Spirit must have taught him to write. Sequoyah's blunt answer was, "I taught myself," a response that underscores both the dominant culture's desire to impose a delimiting definition upon the Native American and the Native American's insistence upon self-determination and self-authorization.

In literature by contemporary Indian authors, we find characters who constantly face this dilemma of an identity constructed within the authoritative discourse of the non–Indian world. In order to be recognized, to claim authenticity in the world—*in order to be seen at all*—the Indian must conform to an identity imposed from the outside. As Hollywood and every savvy Indian fund raiser knows, there is nothing like traditional regalia and a drum to get the cash flowing. For traditional Indians, however, such shallow commodification is particularly discouraging, because of course specific tribal dress and ceremony still play vital roles in the cultural continuity of Native communities. Furthermore, as Hollywood and the publishing world also know, there is nothing like a drunken Indian tetering on the edge of oblivion to bring immediate recognition from a white audience. The feathered, mystical shaman and the self-destructive drunk are simply two aspects of one side of the European-constructed Noble/Savage stereotype familiar to all. One side is noble and pitiable (shaman-warrior/drunk), while the other (warrior/blood-thirsty obstacle to expansion) is disturbing and threatening. Both sides are supposedly vanishing as the currency of America's self-conception is spent.

For Native Americans, the term "Indian" is a deeply contested space, where authenticity must somehow be forged out of resistance to the "authentic" representation. Chippewa/Anishinaabe author Gerald Vizenor astutely declares that the real "Indian" is the "absolute fake," that which in *Travels in Hyperreality* Umberto Eco calls the "hyperreal." Such simulations, says Vizenor in *Manifest Manners*, "are the absence of the tribal real" (4), since the simulated Native "Indian" is a Euramerican invention. It is the hyperreal simulation that the Native must confront and contest while simultaneously recognizing that only the simulation will be seen by most who look for Indianness. This is a dilemma made more difficult because the simulacrum, or "absolute fake," is constructed out of the veneer of the "tribal real." When a mixedblood named Belladonna Darwin Winter-Catcher, in Vizenor's *Bearheart*, is asked, "What does Indian mean?" the question resounds through all of Native American literature.

Native American writers are unavoidably conscious of this predicament, knowing that in order to be readily recognized (and thus sold) as authentically "Indian" their art must be figuratively dressed in braids, beads, and buckskin. This is why, when Mourning Dove's

Cogewea was finally published in 1927, the publisher insisted on placing an "Indian-looking" photograph of the author at the fore of the book against Mourning Dove's wishes. When in 1899 the Omaha writer Francis La Flesche submitted his manuscript, *The Middle Five*, an autobiographical account of Indian boys in government school, to Doubleday and McClure, the manuscript was rejected. Complaining that La Flesche's Indian boys were too much like other, non-Indian boys (too universally human, that is), the publisher suggested instead "something which would show the actual life of the Indian in his *wilder state*" (xii). In short, the publisher knew what Indians were supposed to be like and knew that his audience also knew. La Flesche, who had been born on the Omaha Reservation and attended a reservation school, apparently did not know how to simulate those "real Indians." Nor did the Indian boys such as La Flesche himself who were busy trying to adapt and survive amidst an invasive foreign culture. La Flesche had made the mistake of believing he could show actual Indian boys adapting to changing cultural circumstances, when the publisher expected a static referent long established in the Euramerican imagination. Similarly, when in 1935 the mixedblood Cree writer D'Arcy McNickle submitted an early draft of his novel *Wind from an Enemy Sky*, his publisher rejected it because, as the publisher said, it did not have enough of *"the Indian"* in it.[1] Again, the publisher knew what was commercially "Indian," while McNickle, who had been born and raised on the Flathead Reservation in Montana where he was tribally enrolled, and who would spend his life working with and for Indian people, obviously did not. McNickle and La Flesche had both made the mistake of confusing the real for the hyperreal, the actual for the "absolute fake."

A recent review of one of my own works, a 1991 novel titled *Wolfsong*, conveniently raises some of the points I have made thus far. The writer begins his review with the declaration, "The larger text of this . . . novel extends beyond 'END' to a following page bearing the author's photograph and biographical sketch. The photo shows a . . . man whose background the caption defines as 'Choctaw, Cherokee, and Irish.' *Wolfsong* is set in Washington state, its protagonist a full-blooded member of a dwindling northwest coast tribe" (Crow, 386).

In response, I want to first stress the fact that all significant art—art that lasts—speaks to the human spirit and therefore clearly transcends the specific culture from and within which it was and is created. How else would we still be reading an oral poet such as Homer in a language other than his own, or Cervantes, or Tolstoy, and so on? We are all human here, and as humans we are astonishingly alike across great cultural and even temporal chasms. Art spans such chasms; that is a crucial aspect of its meaning.

However, with the larger meaning of art being a given that speaks to all of us on shared human levels, and ignoring the reviewer's failure to recognize the author's trick in *Wolfsong* represented by the very word "END," I also want to stress the fact that the reviewer's comment raises the important issue of cultural specificity. Before discussing any aspect of Native American literature, it is important to know what literature we are talking about. For example, James Welch is a contemporary mixedblood poet and novelist of Blackfoot and Gros Ventre ancestry whose work grows out of and deals directly with his tribal heritage. While the shared human characteristics of his fiction will certainly engage us, to be fully involved in his work we should know something about the history and culture of the Blackfoot and Gros Ventre people. In Welch's first novel, *Winter in the Blood*, the unnamed protagonist's grandmother is referred to repeatedly as "Old Woman." Another character, who will turn out to be the protagonist's grandfather, is called "Old Man." If we do not know that Old Man and Old Woman are traditional names for the paired trickster contraries who created the Blackfoot people, we will not understand the novel. Similarly, if we do not know something about Chippewa, or Anishnaabe, trickster stories, or trickster in general, we are not likely to fully comprehend the fictions of either Gerald Vizenor or Louise Erdrich—or many other Native American authors.

However, it is not always as simple as knowing the tribal affiliation of the author, and for illustrations we need not go so far as to invoke the rather infamous case of Jamake Highwater.[2] For example, knowing that N. Scott Momaday is half Kiowa is certainly crucial and unavoidable in reading *The Way to Rainy Mountain*, but to read Momaday's novel *House Made of Dawn* with any effectiveness we must know quite a lot not about Kiowa but about Pueblo and Navajo mythologies, cultures, and histories. What do we do with the fact that D'Arcy McNickle was of mixed Cree ancestry but adopted into the Flathead Tribe and in his fiction was writing about the Salish people he grew up amongst, even when he fictionalized his tribal subject? Similarly, while Thomas King is of mixed Cherokee and European ancestry and grew up in Northern California, to read his novels one had better realize that he is generally writing not about Cherokees but about Blood or Blackfoot peoples in Canada. The same holds for Linda Hogan, a Chickasaw author whose novel *Mean Spirit* is about the Osage, Ronald Burns Querry, who is Choctaw but writes about Jicarilla Apache and Navajo peoples in *The Death of Bernadette Lefthand*, and Adrian Louis, who is part Paiute but writes about Lakota people in *Skins* and elsewhere. What about Mourning Dove, who claimed mixedblood identity like that of her protagonist in *Cogewea* but who, according to biographer Jay Miller, was more likely a fullblood? Is her novel about mixedblood struggles less authentic if her claim to mixed heritage is false?[3] There are plenty of other examples to test this kind of essentialism in varying ways (e.g.: Denton R. Bedford, Charles Penoi, Martin Cruz Smith, Anna Lee Walters, Hyemeyohsts Storm—and what about white author Tony Hillerman, the most successful "Indian" writer of all?).

Do we really need to go beyond "END" and consider photograph and bio-blurb to decide about the authenticity of a fiction? This is a rather large question, of course, one that has the potential to both generate controversy and illuminate a great deal regarding our construction of ethnicity, gender, and social representation. A photograph of Henry James at the end of *The Portrait of a Lady* or *What Maisie Knew* might interest a reader, one suspects, but one also suspects that the reader would not go beyond "END" and turn to that photograph to determine whether James's novel was "authentic." Similarly, a photograph and biographical sketch of Stephen Crane at the end of *The Red Badge of Courage* might suggest that the author was a bit too young to write authoritatively about the Civil War, despite war veterans' insistence that the novel was quite disturbingly accurate.

This is not a trivial question, and it is one that illuminates rather brightly the intensity of the war being waged for half a millennium now for possession of this phantom artifact called "Indian." Why, we must ask, are the rules different for authors who write about Native Americans, whether those authors are of Native American descent or not? Do we disqualify a McNickle, a Momaday, a Hogan, a Querry, a Louis, a King, a Walters, an Owens, or a Dorris because each—although he or she may be of Native American ancestry to one degree or another—has written about a tribal culture that does not happen to be part of that particular author's tribal heritage? Do we shun A. A. Carr because, despite being a fullblood educated in traditional Navajo and Pueblo ways, in his brilliant novel *Eye Killers* he integrates Euramerican characters, themes, and mythologies with deeply felt Navajo and Pueblo beliefs in a novel whose mythological structure is profoundly Native while rejecting the essenialist doctrine of racial purity espoused by a loud minority of other "Indian" writers? Do we criticize Leslie Silko, as Paula Gunn Allen has done, for writing about sensitive cultural and spiritual issues while being, as Silko herself has confessed, an outsider in her Laguna community? Does such a question not grow more complex when we read Allen's own novel, *The Woman Who Owned the Shadows*, and find Grandmother Spider ("Thought Woman") lurking close to the surface of every page and furthermore discover that not only does Allen commit some of the same sins she finds in Silko, but she also does a superb job of inter-twining Western Christian myth with Native American—and not just Pueblo mythology at that? N. Scott Momaday has weighed in on the large issue of authority, declaring very directly, "I've read non-Indians who have written about Indian matters and done it very well, and of course that works the other way around, too. I've also read some things that were very bad *because the writer was simply writing outside his experience*," (Owens, "N. Scott Momaday," 63, emphasis added). A prominent Native American best-selling author, in fact, recently criti-cized Momaday's *The Ancient Child* as not being a real "Indian" book on the grounds that Billy the Kid—one of the mythic centers of the novel—has nothing to do with Indians. To be "really" Indian must a book then deal only with prescribed issues or subjects? Are Native American authors the only artists in America thus straightjacketed?

To raise such difficult issues, and thus challenge a kind of essentializing that has become more common as Indian identity has become more and more commodified, is to underscore the dizzying complexity that is the nature of what we call Native American literature. I am not trying to excuse the professional "Indian" whose fame and fortune depend upon posing as the "absolute fake." Such poseurs may in fact do absolute damage to what Vizenor calls the "survivance" of Native American peoples because the pose can only reinforce the damaging and deadening stereotypes and clichés that make such posing possible in the first place. Indians themselves often fall prey to essentializing stereotypes, applying Euramerican-generated constructions as templates for "authenticity"; and certainly an author of indisputable "Indian" blood may exploit the same destructive clichés found in the works of a Greek poseur, a German "Indian" novelist who has never been to America, a "good-ole-boy" from Oklahoma who writes about Navajos, or anyone else. It is the artifactualization, the stereotyping, the damningly *hyperreal* "Indian" that makes it so difficult for actual living Indian people to comprehend survival, and to adapt and change while holding to cultural identities, amidst the still-colonialist, dominant Euramerican societies of the Americas. Gerald Vizenor emphasizes this point with typical acumen when his hyperreal "absolute fake" Indian in *The Trickster of Liberty*, "Homer Yellow Snow" (a satire very likely aimed at Jamake Highwater) says to his Indian audience, "If you knew who you were, why did you find it so easy to believe in me? . . . because you too want to be white, and no matter what you say in public, you trust whites more than you trust Indians, which is to say, you trust pretend Indians more than real ones" (118).

Perhaps the important point here is the one made by Momaday above: Writing can be destructive and "bad" "because the writer [is] simply writing outside his experience." To read Native American literature means that we had better do our homework and know the cultural specificity of the subject rather than the author, and then make our decisions about the successful representations of the cultures being portrayed. To write this literature, we had better do the same. For example, if Linda Hogan, of mixed Euramerican and Chickasaw heritage, is going to write about Osage people and the brutal experiences of the oil boom in Osage country, when entire families were murdered in their homes, she had better be accurate, because she is dealing with a time and history that irrevocably altered peoples' lives in often horribly painful ways. This represents a great responsibility.[4] John Joseph Mathews, a mixedblood Osage himself and highly respected within the Osage community, faced precisely the same challenge of being culturally, historically, and socially accurate when he, too, wrote of the Osage oil boom tragedy in *Sundown* in 1934. The fact that although Mathews was perhaps one-eighth Osage by blood quantum, educated at Oxford University and in Switzerland, and on a big-game safari in Africa at the time he decided to dedicate his life to his Indian heritage certainly complicates any kind of essentialist picture of what writing within one's ethnicity may mean. If Adrian C. Louis is going to write a novel about Lakota people such as *Skins* (1995), which paints the most despairing and destructive picture of Indian America we have yet seen, he had better be faithful to his actual subjects. Even James Welch, a highly esteemed Blackfoot-Gros Ventre author raised squarely within Blackfoot country and intimately familiar with what it means to be Indian in Montana today, has admitted to not only depending upon family or tribal oral stories but also reading a large number of books about the Blackfeet—books by non-Indian authors—in order to write his historical novel *Fools Crow*. Since he was drawing rather heavily upon writings by white authors for his factual details, does this undermine the "authenticity" of the only historical novel yet written from within an Indian perspective by an Indian author? Are we not caught up in a Borges-like maze of contradictory signifiers when an Indian author must go to white writings about Indians to find out who he or she is or where he or she comes from and then "write back" against the dominant culture? To write "authentically" the "Indian" author must consult constructions of "Indianness" by the dominant non-Indian culture that has always controlled printed discourse. It is enough to drive one mad. All of this points nonetheless toward the unavoidable fact that no matter who we are we had better educate ourselves not about an abstraction called "Indian," but about the particular cultural subjects of particular texts: Blackfoot, Keresan, Navajo, Osage, or whatever. And it would be wise not to rely merely on essentialist claims of "real Indian" blood or a convincing photograph beyond "END" for our authority if we are going to continue constructing familiar clichés and stereotypes of Indianness.

Just as modernists such as Pound, Eliot, and Joyce required a great deal of erudition on the part of their readers—one cannot get very far beneath the confusing surface of *Ulysses*, for example, without first reading the *Odyssey*, and much, much more; nor can one comprehend much at all of *The Waste Land* without a rather encyclopedic education in Western art and culture—contemporary Native American authors are requiring that readers cross over the conceptual horizon into an Indian world. In addition to Roman and Greek mythology, today it helps a great deal if a reader knows Choctaw, Chippewa, Navajo, or Blackfoot mythologies in order to read Native American works. In addition to the history of ancient Rome, the reader must know the history of Native America. A different kind of sophistication is being required and expected. To cite an example with which I am intimately familiar, a reader should know something about both European and Choctaw mythologies and cultures to understand what to make of a mixedblood character significantly named Attis McCurtain who, while spinning in a black river, encounters tribal bone pickers in my second novel, *The Sharpest Sight*. In a multicultural world, both the name Attis and the traditional bone pickers have significance. If we miss one, we miss the whole. This, of course, is not to say that such a novel cannot be read simply for character and plot, with the sub-surface drama left to subliminal effects.

But to return to the most important point made by the above reviewer of *Wolfsong*: "Owens . . . boldly insists upon his privilege to write of experience outside of his immediate ethnic heritage. We are led to difficult questions about authenticity, about common bonds which Native Americans of very different, or mixed, background, may be in the process of discovering" (Crow, 386). Difficult questions about authenticity, of course, are the hallmark of the postmodern condition. But this reviewer is writing of a more narrowly defined kind of authenticity, I suspect, the kind that has to do with a constructed absoluteness. Like other Native American authors noted above, I do indeed insist upon my privilege to write of experience outside my immediate ethnic tribal heritage and outside my gender as well. Characters in my novels are fullblood and mixedblood, Indian and Anglo American and Chicano and African American, male and female. (Following this reviewer's line of thought, we might wonder if anyone has pointed out that Willa Cather "boldly" insisted upon her privilege to write of experience beyond her immediate gender with a male narrator in *My Ántonia*, that Henry James "boldly" wrote *What Maisie Knew* from the point of view of a young girl, that the Cherokee author John Rollin Ridge boldly wrote about a Mexican-California bandit, and so forth.)

In *Wolfsong*, the novel in question, I wrote about a fictionalized tribe based closely upon a small Native American community in a North Cascades valley where I lived and worked for a number of years. While I fictionalized the name of the tribe to avoid embarrassing anyone, I also took pains to be as faithful to a specific culture as possible, a culture I learned about through talking with people over several years as well as reading everything I could find. What T. S. Eliot would have called the mythological structure of the novel arises out of a specific tribal culture; it is not pan-Indian or Choctaw or Cherokee. While the story can be read as a character/action thriller of sorts, with no knowledge required beyond what is offered in the text, to get to a deeper and more rewarding level a reader would do well to note where the novel takes place and familiarize him- or herself with the indigenous (Salish) culture in that area.[5] At the same time, that novel involves concerns common to Native American experiences across tribal boundaries, and in retrospect it is clear to me that I incorporated aspects of both form and content that might be considered representative of fiction by Native American authors. Foremost among these is precisely the complex and often torturous question of identity and authenticity—who are we, fullblood or mixed, in contemporary America? Second is the question of how we bring together the nearly schizophrenic parts of the self into a coherent personal identity while resisting the "absolute fake" self that is thrust so powerfully upon us from the dominant culture that has constructed the Indian, and how do we find a voice to articulate that coherence? Finally, how do we preserve the earth that is so integral to self-definition and that has been so rapidly and ruthlessly destroyed on this continent? In fact, in my mind the true protagonist of *Wolfsong* is the so-called wilderness itself, a place I felt and still feel that I knew as well as anyone alive.

These are questions that form common bonds for Native American writers, questions that both haunt and inform Native American writing today. Obviously, they are also questions that absorb a wide swath of contemporary writers, whether we are talking about Saul Bellow or Joan Didion, Pam Houston or Leslie Silko. What sets Native American fiction apart, however, is among other qualities an insistence upon the informing role of the past within the present, a role signified by the presence of Native American myth and history reflected in both form and content. What the above reviewer seems to have missed is that *Wolfsong*, like all novels, is an *authentic fiction*. It is a tropical figuration, not the "real" thing. Were it to pretend to be essentially and absolutely a representation of a fixed reality that exists beyond the boundaries of the text—a kind of "global adjective" of Indianness—it would not only cease to be art but would also necessarily conform to readers' notions of the "authentic" or "hyperreal" fake. The only "real" Indians in writing by Native authors are clichéd representations of the Euramerican-constructed Indian, and as Vizenor has pointed out, the presence of such authentic representations signifies the absence of the "tribal real." Despite the fact that I wrote *Wolfsong* with a didactic intent—to illuminate an actual multinational mining corporation's plans to mine the heart out of an actual wilderness—the novel, like all stories, exists nonetheless only in the telling. As a signifier, it answers to no static referent. It is a story that must be made and remade by the reader.

It has taken Native American writers a long time to find a voice, or voices, within the discourse of literate America. Initially, it was necessary to learn to imitate the master language. Thus the original Native writers in English were constrained to subversion. The first

Native American novelist, John Rollin Ridge, for example, had to disguise his outrage deeply in *The Life and Adventures of Joaquín Murieta, the Celebrated California Bandit* in 1854. Another early Native American novelist, Simon Pokagon, may have had his voice stolen utterly. Another, Mourning Dove, saw her novel *Cogewea, the Half-Blood*, half-appropriated by her Euramerican editor, Lucullus Virgil McWhorter. It was not until the 1930s, when the Osage writer John Joseph Mathews and his contemporary, D'Arcy McNickle—both Oxford students for a brief time—began to publish that Native American writers moved more fully out of the arena of subversion and began to openly confront the dominant culture on its own textual grounds.

Since the 1930s, there has been an impressive increase in the quantity and quality of literary works by Native American writers, an increase that became a flood after N. Scott Momaday received a Pulitzer Prize for *House Made of Dawn* in 1969. Today I think we are on the verge of a new wave of Native American literature as poets, fiction writers, and playwrights are beginning to emerge in greater numbers from deep in the heart of "Indian Country," both urban and reservation. Poets such as Luci Tapahonso, Rex Lee Jim, and Laura Tohe, for example, are publishing in both English and their native Navajo language. Playwrights such as William Yellowrobe and E. Donald Two-Rivers are bringing new life to urban Indian theater. Native American literature, which from its inception as a written literature has been the domain of the mixedblood, is changing. Native teachers and writers are stirring up Native American communities, making young Indian students aware that they can have a voice. As we move into a new century and a new millennium (according to the arbitrary linear dating of Western civilization), the voices from the margin are beginning to surround if not engulf the center, albeit against signficant obstacles, and they are changing the way we conceive of ourselves as a people and a nation. Native American writers are insisting that rather than "use" Native American literature, the world must enter into dialogue with that literature and make it profoundly a part of our modern existence, just as Native Americans have for centuries made

European literature a part of Native America. And they are insisting that rather than looking to this literature for reflections of what they expect to see—their own constructed Indianness—readers must look past their mirroring consciousness to the other side.

Mapping the Mixedblood

Frontier and Territory in Native America

◆

The life of the Native halfbreed in Euramerican fiction has ever been nasty, brutish, and short. With few exceptions, in the literature of white America, from Mark Twain's pathological Injun Joe in *Tom Sawyer* to Larry McMurtry's psychopathic Blue Duck in *Lonesome Dove*, the tortured and torturing "breed" has served as a matrix for the conflicted terrors of Euramerica, the horror of liminality that is the particular trauma of the colonial mind. In the narratives of the dominant, colonial culture—and after half a millennium indigenous American tribal cultures, as we near the twenty-first century, remain colonized—the mixedblood is a mirror that gives back a self-image with disturbing implications, like the reflecting forest of Hawthorne's darkest fiction. The instinct of the dominant culture, facing evidence of its own uncontained mutability, is to rewrite the stories, eradicate the witness, and break the mirror. This long project of erasure is what the mixedblood reader sees when he or she looks into the pages of American literature: images of otherness and doom. Such images would not change until the other began to write back and mixedblood literature was born.

In today's classrooms it is an accepted commonplace that discourse exists within what Mikhail Bakhtin defined as "dialogically agitated space" and that communication between cultures takes place within what Mary Louise Pratt calls those "social spaces where disparate cultures meet, clash, and grapple with each other" (4). Such seams constitute what I prefer to call "frontier" space, wherein discourse is multidirectional and hybridized. Within the language of the colonizer the term "frontier" may indeed, as Pratt argues, be "grounded within a European expansionist perspective" (7)—and thus bear the burden of a discourse grounded in genocide, ethnocide, and half a millennium of determined efforts to erase indigenous peoples from the Americas. I want to suggest nonetheless that when one is looking from the "other" direction, "frontier" is a particularly apt term for this transcultural zone of contact for precisely the reason Pratt cites. Because the term "frontier" carries with it such a heavy burden of colonial discourse, it can only be conceived of as a space of extreme contestation. Frontier, I would suggest, is the zone of trickster, a shimmering, always changing zone of multifaceted contact within which every utterance is challenged and interrogated, all referents put into question. In taking such a position, I am arguing for an appropriation and transvaluation of this deadly cliché of colonialism—for appropriation, inversion, and abrogation of authority are always trickster's strategies. "Frontier" stands, I would further argue, in neat opposition to the concept of "territory" as territory is imagined and given form by the colonial enterprise in America. Whereas frontier is always unstable, multidirectional, hybridized, characterized by heteroglossia, and indeterminate, territory is clearly mapped, fully imagined as a place of containment, invented to control and subdue the dangerous potentialities of imagined Indians. Territory is conceived and designed to exclude the dangerous presence of that trickster at the heart of the Native American imagination, for the ultimate logic of territory is appropriation and occupation, and trickster defies appropriation and resists colonization.

It is certainly no accident of the American metanarrative that 1890, the year Frederick Jackson Turner chose to mark the death of the frontier, is also the year of perhaps the most notorious of the countless massacres of indigenous people—Wounded Knee, where nearly three hundred unarmed people, two-thirds women and children, were murdered by U. S. troops. That dimension of the colonial American experience which Turner defined as one of "perennial rebirth . . . fluidity . . . new opportunities," seemed to vanish once the Native

inhabitant's capacity for militant resistance was convincingly elimi-
nated and the Indian either killed or securely confined to clearly
demarcated reservation space. Frontier, a dangerously unstable space,
had become stable and fully appropriated territory, its boundaries
marked and known in the Euramerican imagination, with Turner's
proclamation of "the closing of a great historic movement" (662).
Official Indian Territory, for which Huck Finn would light out ahead
of the rest and within which John Wayne's Hollywood characters
would indulge anachronistic and anarchic fantasies, was given body
between 1830 and 1860 largely in what is today Oklahoma. Ultimately, of course, like the rest of the continent (what Turner called
"free land"), Indian Territory was simply space to be emptied and
reoccupied by the colonial power. Indian Territory, however, transcends geographical location. This formalized space, to borrow from
and paraphrase Jean Baudrillard in *Simulacra and Simulations*, both
"precedes the map, [and] survives it."[1] Today, as was suggested
above, Euramerica remains involved in an unceasing ideological
struggle to confine Native Americans within an essentialized territory
defined by the authoritative utterance "Indian." Native Americans,
however, continue to resist this ideology of containment and to insist
upon the freedom to reimagine themselves within a fluid, always
shifting frontier space.

For those of us who, like most of the authors we recognize as
Native American, are mixedbloods, the hybridized, polyglot, transcultural frontier is quite clearly internalized. For all of us, however,
territory remains a constant threat, an essential fiction of the colonial
mind, that realm of authoritative discourse arriving endlessly and
indissolubly fused, as Bakhtin pointed out, "with its authority—with
political power" (342). Territory, thus conceived, would become an
"other" space infinitely permeable from the privileged outside but
safely containing that which is already within. From the very beginnings of European relations with indigenous Americans, the goal of
the colonizer has been to inhabit and erase an ever-moving frontier
while shifting "Indian" to static and containable "territory"—both
within the trope of the noble and vanishing red man and within the
more effective strategy that equated good Indians with dead ones.

When Frederick Jackson Turner conveniently declared the "frontier" closed, he imagined for America that the Indian had been effectively subsumed into the national metanarrative. A century later, we know Turner and America were wrong; the Indian continues to "light out" from the territory ahead of the rest toward new self-imaginings, continual fluidity, and rebirth.

American Indians recognized very early that their role in the American metanarrative was imagined as inexorably tragic, and as Bakhtin has suggested, outside of his tragic destiny "the epic and tragic hero is nothing; he is, therefore, a function of the plot fate assigns him; he cannot become the hero of another destiny or another plot." This is the hero who, according to Bakhtin, "by his very nature, must perish" (36). Perhaps the first Native American novel to effectively turn the mirror back on Euramerica and to make the mixedblood the embodiment of frontier space was Okanogan author Mourning Dove's *Cogewea, The Half-Blood: A Depiction of the Great Montana Cattle Range*, published in 1927.[2] *Cogewea*, the novel's protagonist, is the daughter of an Indian mother and a white father. With her mother dead and her father having abandoned his children for the "ghastly whiteness" of the Alaskan Yukon, Cogewea is left more or less to her own devices to decide who and what she is. Profoundly conscious of spatial politics, from the first paragraph Mourning Dove's narrative confronts us with the novel's central issue: "Of mixed blood, was Cogewea; a 'breed'!—the socially ostracized of two races. . . . Regarded with suspicion by the Indian; shunned by the Caucasian; where was there any place for the despised breed!" (16–17). Cogewea rebels against all attempts to define the space of the mixedblood. We are told that "Her longings were vague and shadowy; as something not to be attained within the narrow limits of her prescribed sphere" (22). Cogewea herself articulates the mixedblood's difficult interstitiality: "Yes, we are between two fires, the Red and the White. Our Caucasian brothers criticize us as a shiftless class, while the Indians disown us as abandoning our own race. We are maligned and traduced as no one but we of the despised 'breeds' can know"(41).

Cogewea's mixedblood space is defined by the parameters of her white brother-in-law's acutely hybridized cattle ranch. Married to a half-Indian wife, the apparently prosperous brother-in-law ranches allotted Indian land on what had been the Flathead Reservation of northern Montana. The cowboys on his ranch are predominantly mixedbloods, symbolically if not literally the heirs of those from whom the land was taken, now reduced to the status of retainers on that same land. Within the boundaries of the ranch, however, the mixedblood world is a carnivalesque scene of teasing banter and sardonic deceptions.

The Horseshoe Bend Ranch is a polyglot space containing a richly hybridized assortment. Cogewea and her two sisters represent a careful spectrum of responses to mixed and relational identity. For Cogewea, her Indian and white selves are in constant struggle with one another, a struggle that forms the primary plot of the novel. In contrast, Cogewea's sister Mary, who is marked by fair skin and blue eyes, is paradoxically the most traditionally "Indian" of the sisters and apparently comfortable with that sense of self. The third sister, Julia, is married to the white rancher and clearly identifies with the white half of her own ancestry. When a conspiring tenderfoot easterner named Densmore invades the space of the ranch, Cogewea is alternately strongly attracted to him and deeply suspicious of him, Mary is unremittingly hostile, and Julia views the potential union of Densmore and Cogewea very favorably.

Surrounding Cogewea is a wonderful assortment of hybridized cowboys: the half-blood hero of the novel, James LaGrinder, who speaks both his Okanogan language and the colloquial English of the range, and who dances traditionally in a "borrowed costume" at the Indian celebration and at the same time maintains throughout the novel an impressive imitation of the strong, silent hero of conventional Westerns; Rodeo Jack, a blond, quarter-blood Texan of "uncertain qualities"; Celluloid Bill, a "light-complexioned half-blood Cheyenne" who "got his range sobriquet wearing a white celluloid collar when he first came to the ranch"; and Silent Bob, a white West Virginian who has found a home with the mixedbloods. Into this mix soon come Frenchy, a French aristocrat who shows up playing the role of cowboy and, with a strong French accent, speaking awkward English learned from a Chinese cook, and Densmore, the serpentine easterner whose formal English signifies privilege.

The mixedbloods of the ranch have defined a borderland space for themselves between Indian and white worlds. When the big Fourth of July celebration comes along, the mixedblood cowboys are eager to enter the bronc-riding competition and see the "great Injun war dance" that will be held by the traditional Indians, and they eagerly look forward to gambling with and getting the best of the Indians. For Cogewea, the Fourth of July festivities provide the perfect opportunity to force the issue of her mixed identity as she determines to enter both the "Squaws" race for Indians and the "Ladies" race for whites. "I'm part Injun and can participate in that as well as in the ladies race," she tells Jim. "They can't stop me from riding in both races, can they? . . . I am going to *pose as both* for this day" (58–59, emphasis added). To pose as an Indian, Cogewea rents a costume from the fullbloods; however, the inevitable outcome is that she is disqualified from both races.

When the easterner, Densmore, chances upon this hybridized world, he is appalled by the mixed nature of it: "Where were those picturesque Indians that he was promised to meet: Instead, he had been lured into a nest of half bloods, whom he had always understood to be the inferior degenerates of two races" (49). Expecting an Indian *territory*, Densmore has stumbled upon a mixedblood *frontier*, a space wherein his privileged status will be challenged and his authoritative language disputed.

Not only does Mourning Dove appropriate the conventional frontier genre of the western romance for her own subversive novel, but to insure that we do not miss this maneuver she includes a scene in which Cogewea reads a western romance sounding much like an inversion of the one we are reading. Titled *The Brand*, this novel, according to Cogewea, "does nothing but slam the breeds! as if they were reptiles instead of humans" (89). The halfblood hero, she comments, "was doomed to a malarial death amid the brackish pools flowing from the quill of this neoteric writer" (92). In the same scene,

Cogewea reflects yet again upon her mixedblood status: "The Indian is a peculiarly mysterious race; differing from all others. . . . We breeds are half and half—American and Caucasian—and in a separate corral" (95).

As Cogewea is reading *The Brand*, she is startled "by a shadow falling across her lap. The broad shoulders of Densmore barred the rays of the low hanging sun" (92). Throughout the novel, Cogewea engages in frequent code-switching, using the heteroglossia that comes with her transcultural identity as a political tool, leveling proper "schooled" English at the mixedblood cowboys when she wants to assert her authority, and using the convoluted cowboy lingo of the range to destabilize Densmore. In this scene, as she is interrupted in the midst of a reverie about how "her race" had "suffered as much from the pen as from the bayonet of conquest," Cogewea responds to Densmore's intrusion by turning language even more sharply against the easterner, calling Densmore "Shoyahpee," the Indian name for whites among her tribe, which we are told is a "not altogether friendly greeting." The easterner responds to her challenge by suggestively mispronouncing her name: "Cage— Cogcwca." And when, a page later, he says to Cogewea and Jim, "But has it ever occurred to you that you may be standing in your own light—casting shadows over your own road to progress?" we are reminded that it was Densmore who "barred the rays of the . . . sun"—coming between Cogewea and the word—earlier in the same scene. Later, in trying to seduce and defraud her, Densmore will say, "You are as much of one race as the other! How can you consistently choose the one over the other?" and Cogewea's reply will be, "Of the two, I prefer the one of the highest honor, the Indian! But why not stay in my own class, the mixed-blood?" (232).

Even Cogewea's grandmother, Stemteemä, a fullblood whose tepee sits on one margin of the mixedblood ranch while the nearby white town rests in opposition on the other, acknowledges her granddaughter's liminal status as an "other" class. "If you marry in your own class, the mixed blood," the grandmother says, "I will gladly bless you with the Great Indian Spirit. . . . But if you take this Shoyahpee, I will forget that I ever had a grandchild" (250).

To Densmore, Cogewea embodies the American frontier, that "hither edge of free land" as Turner called it, the "meeting point between savagery and civilization" (662–63) that is the rightful spoil of the adventuring Euramerican. Mourning Dove's consciousness of the romantic discourse of Indianness achieves a fine satirical edge when, upon discovering that Cogewea owns almost no land or extractable resources, Densmore steals what little money she has, ties her to a tree, and mocks her in a splendidly parodic moment: "O statuette in bronze with a wild-wood setting! How superb! and the sun fast sinking to rest" (265). With wonderful irony, Densmore's language must remind Cogewea that she is indeed the victim of a privileged discourse that has rendered her powerless at that moment.

When Jim learns of Densmore's betrayal, he rides furiously to Cogewea's rescue. Throughout the novel, Jim has self-consciously played the conventional role of the strong, silent western hero, the "best rider of the Flathead" with a potentially quick trigger finger. The narrative has, in fact, consistently sidestepped his vassal status on the ranch while portraying him as the man of action and few words whom it is dangerous to cross. When Jim sets out to rescue Cogewea and punish the white intruder, however, the falseness of his self-conception is illuminated by the mocking laughter of trickster as Mourning Dove writes, "He did not notice the mocking twitter of the magpie" (275). It is trickster's role in traditional Native American literature to mock and taunt us into self-knowledge, illuminating the absurdity of our pretenses, postures, and false gestures. Here, trickster magpie clearly mocks Jim's groundless belief in his own power. While Jim tries to assume the stereotypical dime-novel role of savior of womanly virtue and avenger of wrongs, as a "breed" he is incapable of meaningful action against the privilege represented by Densmore. Very soon Jim will himself acknowledge his own impotence when he tells Cogewea that "it ain't no use tryin' to get back your dough. . . . No laws of recovery like this here case is for our kind!" (278). Shortly thereafter, Cogewea will echo Jim when she explains to the angry collection of mixedbloods that because they are mere "breed Injuns," an appeal to justice "would be of little or no avail" (279). They can do nothing but accept the injustice.

Mourning Dove's novel ends in good romantic fashion as, two years after her betrayal by Densmore, Cogewea accepts Jim LaGrinder's proposal of marriage. The scene of romantic closure, however, is complicated by this mixedblood pair's shared sense of who and where they are. "We despised breeds," Cogewea says to Jim, "are in a zone of our own and when we break from the corral erected about us, we meet up with trouble. If only the fence could not be scaled by the soulless creatures who have ever preyed upon us." Jim responds: "S'pose we remain together in that there corral you spoke of as being built 'round us by the Shoyahpee?"

The "zone" Cogewea and Jim try to imagine for themselves is a frontier space where white and Indian worlds collide. Paradoxically, they imagine somewhat wistfully the possibility of appropriating a territory, of turning the white world's "corral" into a protective barrier against the privileged center. However, everything in this novel has indicated that such a contained territorial space is an impossibility. Their hybridized world, by its very unstable, tricksterish nature, will always be permeable for a Densmore, will always leave them exposed to the dominant white world. Transcultural space is always vulnerable, easily penetrated, and in endless flux, and within this instability lies its vitality. The irony of this mixedblood pair's dilemma is driven home when, in one of the novel's final utterances, Cogewea exclaims, "*Isn't* this a splendid world?" and Jim replies, "Yes! It is jus' 'bout right—when not too cold nor too hot-nor nothin' wrong with the corral fencin'." *Cogewea, The Half-Blood* ends with fine ambiguity. The liminal terrain of the mixedblood remains both "other" and unstable, as does the entire, constantly shifting space where Indian and Euramerican cultures collide and deal with one another. Jim and Cogewea will undoubtedly marry and have children who, like their parents, will be half-bloods. The next generation will remain balanced precariously in that transcultural zone.

Despite the uncomfortable implications of her novel's conclusion, Mourning Dove depicts in *Cogewea* a mixedblood world that is vibrant, exciting, infinitely mutable, and rich with life. Regardless of what lies on the edges of their borderland world, Mourning Dove's mixedbloods have claimed the frontier as their space, and within that space they thrive with humor and mutual respect. Following Mourning Dove, the depiction of the world of the mixedblood would change significantly in such novels by Native American authors as John Joseph Mathews's *Sundown* (1934) and D'Arcy McNickle's *The Surrounded* (1936). In *Sundown*, Mathews's protagonist, Chal Windzer, is the son of a fullblood mother and mixedblood father. While the mother holds fast to traditional Osage values, the father believes in acculturation and assimilation to the values of the white world rapidly encroaching upon Osage culture. Caught in this transcultural frontier, Chal suffers from a kind of terminal indeterminacy that the novel does not resolve. Gone are the boisterous code-switching and teasing humor of Mourning Dove's frontier world. In their place is a torturous struggle for language and a coherent identity that ends in only the faintest of hope. Heteroglossia is overtly desired but seemingly denied in Mathews's novel.

Like Mathews's Chal Windzer, McNickle's half-Indian protagonist, Archilde Leon, returned home to his Euramerican father's ranch, finds himself straddling a seam between Indian and white worlds, with seemingly no possibility for the maintenance of a hybridized or heterogeneous reality that would span the two. McNickle's novel is set in the same Flathead country of which Mourning Dove wrote, and like Mourning Dove, McNickle presents this place as a richly hybridized zone of cultural contact. However, more sharply than either Mourning Dove or Mathews, McNickle demonstrates the power of the Euramerican consciousness to essentialize what it calls "Indians" and to consign people thus designated to a kind of territory that is both marginal and clearly "other." Between that Indian territory and the authoritative white world there appears to be no possibility for a viable and inhabitable transcultural frontier. Archilde is made to choose one authorized space or the other, and in the process he is rendered powerless and voiceless, so that the novel's final words are "Archilde, saying nothing, extended his hands to be shackled" (*The Surrounded*, 297). McNickle effectively presents us with an ideological struggle in which the Indians—most particularly the mixedbloods like Archilde—attempt to live within a fluid, ever-changing reality while the Euramerican world, with its fixed, authoritative discourse, attempts to deny such possibilities. The Indians would live within a frontier world of possibility and change, while the Euramericans would force Indians into static, fixed, and terminal territory.

It would not be until the fictions of Gerald Vizenor and Leslie Marmon Silko in the 1970s that characters in Native American novels would begin to successfully inhabit the kind of frontier space first explored by Mourning Dove. Silko's *Ceremony* (1977) delves into the realities of a protagonist who is half Pueblo and half white and who seemingly finds himself in the terminal condition of a Chal Windzer or Archilde Leon. Silko, however, inverts the tragic image of the halfbreed, constructing a novel that argues for hybridization and heterogeneity as sources of power and rich potential. "Things which don't shift and grow are dead things," a mixedblood medicine man in the novel explains. Those forces that seek to fix, to separate and contain discrete parts of the world, are labeled "witchery" in this novel, with the ultimate symbol of destruction being a piece of uranium ore—a portion of the earth that, when separated from the earth and broken down into its smallest parts, becomes the most destructive force ever known. In the end—which announces itself as not-an-end—Tayo, *Ceremony*'s protagonist, has become an animate transcultural space and a rich resource for his Indian community. Descending into the sacred kiva at the heart of his Pueblo community in order to tell his story, Tayo is able to articulate, to make whole and heal, his split self, community, and world.

Despite the romantic coherence of its conclusion, however, *Ceremony* bears a very interesting resemblance to Mourning Dove's novel. In *Ceremony*, Silko not only celebrates mixed and relational identities but, unlike Mourning Dove, takes her mixedblood protagonist back to the core of his Indian world. On the one hand the "corral"—or appropriated territory—imagined by Cogewea and Jim appears to have vanished, but on the other hand Tayo's reintegration into a coherent, centered Pueblo world that is very carefully bounded by sacred demarcations within the landscape suggests provocatively that once again the Euramerican notion of a fixed, known "territory" imagined to contain Indians has been appropriated and inverted. In fact, Tayo's fully imagined Pueblo world, which he has traversed in

seven sacred directions and effectively "lived into" through his cere-
monial/mythic journey, suggests that Native American cultures are
capable of an appropriation and transvaluation of territory, making of
it a richly hybridized frontier space. In short, Tayo succeeds in
accomplishing what Cogewea and Jim could only wistfully imagine.

It would fall to the Chippewa writer Gerald Vizenor, whose work
will be discussed in more detail below, to exuberantly declare the
mixedblood to be a sign not of naturalistic despair but of limitless
possibilities and excitement. Mixedbloods, Vizenor has written,
"loosen the seams in the shrouds of identities." For a sense of the
astonishing barriers Vizenor and all Native American writers are up
against in their attempts to be heard by the critical center in this
country, we need only take a cursory glance at several fairly recent
and prominent publications. In *Culture and Imperialism*, Edward Said
declares that, "If the Japanese, East European, Islamic, and Western
instances express anything in common, it is that a new critical consciousness is needed." Said goes on to state: "Instead of the partial
analysis offered by the various national or systematically theoretical
schools, I have been proposing the contrapuntal lines of a global
analysis" (330). Said's "contrapuntal lines of a global analysis" clearly
do not include the voices or consciousnesses of Native Americans,
however, for in the same recent study, Said reduces all writing by
indigenous Americans to what he condescendingly terms "that sad
panorama produced by genocide and cultural amnesia which is
beginning to be known as 'native American literature'" (304). What is
one to make of such a statement if one is aware of the rich and
complex legacy of Native American writing? It is, in fact, precisely the
tragic assumption underlying Said's clichéd and abysmally unin-
formed utterance that Vizenor and other Native American writers
have spent years attacking.

Examples of such ignorance of Native American voices are dis-
tressingly abundant. Werner Sollors, for example, in *Beyond Ethnicity*,
provides a plentiful assortment of representations of American Indians
by Euramerican writers but in nearly four hundred pages devotes only
one phrase—not even a full sentence—to texts authored by Native
American Indians. Sollors's sole nod to actual Native writers is to

note, as an aside, one title each by N. Scott Momaday (a Pulitzer Prize winner for *House Made of Dawn*), Leslie Silko, and that other major figure in American Indian literature, Hyemeyohsts Storm. The reference list for Sollors's book includes works by African American and Asian American authors and studies of Native Americans by Euramerican authors but does not include a single title by an American Indian author. Indian writers, we are left to assume, must be out "there" in the territory somewhere, incapable of being taken seriously or even heard at the metropolitan center of multicultural posturing.

It is not only the male mainstream of critical privilege that serves to silence Native American voices. In *Playing in the Dark*, her less-than-penetrating examination of what she calls "Whiteness and the Literary Imagination," Toni Morrison shows a surprising refusal or inability to acknowledge the Native American presence in the figuration of whiteness in racialized America. Morrison's first chapter opens with the declaration, "I want to draw a map, so to speak, of a critical geography and use that map to open as much space for discovery, intellectual adventure, and close exploration as did the original charting of the New World." (3). The unmistakable discourse of colonial discovery and appropriation clearly marks this strange beginning, making it difficult for any reader to ignore the significance of Indianness in this New World figuration. Throughout her book, however, Morrison simply ignores the Native "red" presence that shadows her critical map. Although she does pause to ask rhetorically if America might be seen as "raw and savage" "[b]ecause it is peopled by a nonwhite indigenous population," she answers herself with a quick and simple "perhaps" before proceeding to ignore entirely the implications of her own question. She refers several times in her text to Melville and racial difference without once noting the existence or implications of characters named Queequeg or Tashtego or a ship called the *Pequod*—or the fact that Melville's narrator and protagonist, Ishmael, having begun the novel in bed with a Native, ends the novel floating on the same Native's empty coffin. Morrison interrogates what she calls Hemingway's "Tontos," who, she says, "are almost always black," but she ignores entirely the implications and problematics of this discourse of Indianness within her own text. Throughout the "discovery" and "exploration" charted in *Playing in the Dark*, the Native American presence is implicitly invoked and routinely erased.

Fortunately, a few serious critics of Native American writing—who actually notice the presence of Native voices—do exist. Foremost among these is Arnold Krupat, whose *The Voice in the Margin* (1989), *Ethnocriticism* (1992), and, most recently, *The Turn to the Native* (1996) have struggled admirably, if at times in less than profitable directions, not only to bring European theory into some kind of meaningful relationship with Native American writing, but also—most particularly in *Ethnocriticism*—to formulate a new theoretical discourse that may encourage dialogue with this literature rather than merely overlaying it with an authoritative and ill-fitting European theory-grid. "Ethnocritical discourse," Krupat explains, "in its self-positioning at the frontier, seeks to traverse rather than occupy a great variety of 'middle grounds,' both at home and abroad." Wisely, Krupat points out: "In every case, the danger the would-be practitioner of ethnocriticism must try to avoid is . . . to speak for the 'Indian,' 'interpreting' her or him . . . to a dominative discourse" (*Ethnocriticism*, 25, 30). If the heteroglossia that is the discursive home of the mixedblood writer is to be engaged in any significant way in this area, it will be due to the work of critics such as Krupat within the metropolitan center and Vizenor from the frontier zone of the Native trickster.

If the mixedblood is a tragic mirror for Euramerica, giving back a disturbing reflection, the Euramerican in turn would seem to offer no reflection at all for the mixedblood who gazes back. Native American novelists, nearly all of whom are of mixed descent and write about the complications of mixed identity, are excluded from the dominant critical discourse, and in the dominant discourse the Indian continues to be reduced to Vizenor's "occidental invention that became a bankable simulation." What the Euramerican consciousness clearly desires is a Native America safely consigned to a known and unchanging territory defined by the authoritative utterance "Indian"; that Native America can continue to function as a kind of natural resource to be mined at will by Euramerca for such projects as the films *Dances with Wolves* or *The Last of the Mohicans*. Faced with this reality, the temptation is to conclude that the world out "there" remains securely in the control of Densmores, and to reimagine Mourning Dove's territorial corral or reexamine the muteness of a Chal Windzer or Archilde Leon. Despite the unreflected gaze, and though unheard at the center, however, contemporary mixedblood authors continue to celebrate their freedom, in the words of Vizenor's *Manifest Manners*, to "oust the inventions with humor, new stories, and the simulations of survivance" (5).

Of the novel, Bakhtin has written:

> Everything that makes us laugh is close at hand, all comical creativity works in a zone of maximal proximity. Laughter has the remarkable power of making an object come up close, of drawing it into a zone of crude contact where one can finger it familiarly on all sides, turn it upside down, inside out, peer at it from above and below, break open its external shell, look into its center, doubt it, take it apart, dismember it, lay it bare and expose it, examine it freely and experiment with it. Laughter demolishes fear and piety before an object, before a world, making of it an object of familiar contact and thus clearing the ground for an absolutely free investigation of it. (23)

This "crude zone of contact" is the frontier space of trickster and the shifting space of mixedblood identity. As early as the second decade of this century, writing in a tent after working as a farm laborer all day, Mourning Dove sought to enter that space and expose the false representations of mixedblood identity in Euramerica. As late as the final decade of the same century, Gerald Vizenor, writing from a professorship within the University of California, is still exploring this zone—the zone of the Native American trickster, s/he who brings the world close and directs this "comical operation of dismemberment," laying bare the hypocrisies, false fears, and pieties and clearing the ground "for an absolutely free investigation" of worldly fact.

In *Imperial Eyes: Travel Writing and Transculturation*, Pratt defines "autoethnography" as "instances in which colonized subjects undertake to represent themselves in ways that engage with the colonizer's own terms," and adds that "autoethnographic texts are those the others construct in response to or in dialogue with those metropolitan representations" (7). Native American novels are such autoethnographic texts, though we must qualify this distinction by pointing out that, inhabiting both sides of the frontier plus the middle, the mixedblood text also writes back to itself. The discourse of this mixedblood space and of Native American literature is, as Krupat has suggested, oxymoronic, the oxymoron being "that figure which offers apparently oppositional, paradoxical, or incompatible terms in a manner that nonetheless allows for decidable, if polysemous and complex, meaning" (*Ethnocriticism*, 28).

Mixedblood characters in novels by Native American authors, whether Mourning Dove's Cogewea, McNickle's Archilde, or Vizenor's Bearheart, are not, I would suggest, what ethnohistorians are fond of calling "cultural brokers." In one recent and very interesting study, such brokers are defined as "cultural intermediaries—the people between the borders—[who] juggle the ways of different societies with apparent ease" (Szasz, 3). The concept and language are drawn from Robert Paine's "patron-broker-client" theory, which offered four stages of cultural brokerage defined by varying kinds and degrees of remuneration (Szasz, 11). However, although the mixedblood in Native American novels does indeed live between, or within, borders and often shapeshifts across that space with tricksterish dexterity, the mixedblood in literature by mixedblood authors does not conform to this strangely mercantile and Eurocentric concept. Within its unmistakable discourse of cultural commodification, such a perspective seems to arise out of what Vizenor defines in *Manifest Manners* as the false and deadly Euramerican sign of Indianness when he states: "The Indian was an occidental invention that became a bankable simulation; the word has no referent in tribal languages or cultures" (10). Culture, within the imagined context of cultural brokerage, would seem to have become "a bankable simulation," an invented commodity somehow capable of decontextualization and travel.

Cultures can and indeed cannot do otherwise than come together and deal with one another, not only within the transcultural regions of frontiers or borders but also within the hybridized individual, Vizenor's "crossblood," who internalizes those frontier or border spaces. As conceived by Vizenor, and by Native American authors generally, however, the mixedblood is not a cultural broker but a cultural breaker, break-dancing trickster-fashion through all signs, fracturing the self-reflexive mirror of the dominant center, deconstructing rigid borders, slipping between the seams, embodying contradictions, and contradancing across every boundary. The Indian has appropriated and occupied the frontier, reimagining it against all odds. A century after Frederick Jackson Turner's famous pronouncement, the frontier appears to be moving once again, but this time it is a multidirectional zone of resistance.

Multicultural Tourism

Native American Literature, Canon, and Campus

◆

To write about "crossreading" and the presence of Native American literature in the classroom is to raise issues of representation and what I have come to think of as a kind of literary tourism. Too often, that is, not only students in our classes but readers at large (and, of course, publishers) want not literature that challenges them to think and feel in new ways but literary works that provide a comfortable, easy tour of colorful Indian Country. Crossing conceptual horizons can be, and in fact must be, hard work. Perhaps one way of approaching this dilemma is to consider briefly the classroom and Native American literature as something like the territory and frontier defined above.

By "territory," again, I am referring to the concept of contained and boundaried space represented in the notion of "Indian Territory"—a literal and imagined space constructed to contain and neutralize Indians. By "frontier" I mean what Mary Louise Pratt has labeled a "zone of contact" or James Clifton has called that place where cultures come together and "deal with" one another. Powerful social and historical forces conspire to turn Native American literature, and the Native American classroom, into a kind of safe territory that, like a colorful but dubious relative, can be visited but does not threaten to return the favor. In contrast, it is in our interest and the interests of our students to conceive of this literature and our classrooms not as contained territory but as frontier space, which, as I suggested above, is multidirectional, uncontained, unstable, and always plotting return visits.

In the *New York Times Book Review* for May 3, 1992, a front-page essay broadcast in bold heading the question, "Who Gets to Tell Their Stories?" In this review of more than a dozen publications by and about Native American Indians, the author of the piece, James R. Kincaid, asked important questions: "How do our stories of what is past, passing or to come get to be manufactured, circulated and understood? Whose stories are they? Who gets to make and tell them?" Finally, he asked, "Who is listening—and how well?" Kincaid was identified in a biographical statement as "the author of books about Dickens, Tennyson and Trollope" (Kincaid, 24–29).

This *New York Times* essay tells us a great deal about how our stories get to be manufactured, circulated, and understood, and, more importantly perhaps, both who gets to tell them and who is listening. Professor Kincaid is undoubtedly a perceptive and talented scholar, a man of insight and compassion. But I am sure many readers were somewhat curious about the process that led the *New York Times* to invite a scholar of Victorian literature to write a mass review of Native American works. I can only conclude that an editor at the newspaper found him- or herself faced with a pile of books that looked more or less authentically "Indian," put those miscellaneous volumes into a box, and made a phone call or two to find a critic willing to do such a review. Kincaid's highlighted questions suggest that he at least suspected the awkwardness of his undertaking. Those of us with particular interest in Native American literature were pleased to see a front-page review of this work but were left to wonder, nonetheless, why a specialist in Native American literature was not invited to do the review. There are a number of highly qualified individuals around the country—both Native American and Euramerican—who know this field and could have written an informed review. Why choose a Victorian scholar? I suspect that the *New York Times*'s answer to this question would be, "Why not? Anybody can write about this stuff." A more acute editor might have responded with, "Why not? Anybody can write about this stuff since we invented Indians in the first place." Because, as far as I know, the *Times* neither printed nor responded to letters by Native Americans or anyone else raising this question, we can only speculate. We might suspect, however, that the *Times* would not have felt so comfortable in asking Norman Mailer to review a box full of writing by and about women or a white reviewer to write on African American works. And I doubt strongly that the same publication would select a specialist in Native American literature to review Victorian novels. That being said, those of us who have been writing for some time about the special demands made by Native American writing can only read Kincaid's question, "Who is listening—and how well?" and conclude that, while we listen to one another, the privileged literary center represented by New York reviews and Victorian scholars is not listening at all, though occasionally lecturing.

Such an ignorant and arrogant act by the most prominent literary review in the nation underscores a frustrating dilemma facing Native American writers and scholars. For the rest of the world, Native American Indian literature too often constitutes a kind of literary Indian Territory to which students can be sent briefly for a semester's touch of the exotic. While campuses often like to have one or two "authentic" Indian faculty members to validate the essential ethnographic exotica of this material, as literature the writing is not supposed to be difficult or particularly challenging.

As we all know, losing one's voice and one's stories is an old and familiar experience for indigenous Americans as well as others on the margins of U.S. society. We need only consider the long tradition of blackface, or the success of the Charlie Chan novels of Earl Biggers, or the recent success of a white supremacist in pawning off *The Education of Little Tree* as a genuine Indian autobiography (the "absolute fake").

However, it is the distinction between "territory" and "frontier" that I wish to pursue. And I want to recuperate the history-laden term "frontier" in the process. Seen from the stock Euramerican perspective, frontier is the cutting edge of civilization. Beyond the frontier is the incomprehensible "other." To inhabit that frontier is to somehow accommodate a radical alterity, the internalization of which leads dangerously in the direction of psychic disintegration or schizophrenia. To make that space inhabitable, it is necessary to map it—that is, figuratively to appropriate it and imagine fixed boundaries, make it conform to a metanarrative. In the American imagination, the Indian still inhabits, and represents, Indian Territory. This territory is the West of unlimited potential for the Euramerican imagination, where the past can be cast aside and the self reimagined in relation to a vast landscape, as we saw in Welch's *Fools Crow*. Most importantly, however, it is a safe place, not the wilderness realm of psychic disintegration illuminated by Hawthorne but a region bounded by discourse, articulated and controlled. Like the Indian, the territory participates in a kind of "discourse of nature." However, because its borders can be known and marked—because, after all, it was initially created to contain wild Indians– -it is safe. Ultimately, it can be not only imaginatively reoccupied and appropriated, but cleansed of Indians, a pattern that we see in the many westerns of John Wayne, wherein Indian Territory figures prominently from beginning to almost the end. In the end, however, the Indian has vanished, leaving, in Wayne's *The Cowboys*, for example, not cowboys and Indians but only cows and deadly boys and finally, in *The Shootist*, only the isolate American hero, a man most appropriately named Books, with not a trace of the Indian. But more of John Wayne in a later chapter.

It is finally the signifier "Indian" that Euramerica seeks to subsume. Ultimately the "Indian" story has nothing at all to do with the actual people who are native to this continent. Only from such a perspective could Euramerica feel so utterly comfortable in reimagining Indians and speaking for Indians as we see evidenced in *New York Times* book reviews. And within such a perspective the multicultural reality of Native American identity has no place, for what David Murray calls a "discourse of Indianness"—the kind of essentializing necessary for the subsumption of Indian identity into the national metanarrative— can allow for no stress on the radical specificity of Native American tribal identities. There can be no such thing as Blackfoot literature, or Choctaw literature, or Pueblo literature, but only "Indian" literature.

Within a territory the only possible voice for the Native is that of subversion, for, as Carolyn Porter has suggested, subversion can exist only as a resistance "from within power's domain." We see the subversive voice clearly in such important early Native American writers as William Apes and Samson Occum and in such novels as John

Rollin Ridge's *The Life and Adventures of Joaquín Murieta, the Celebrated California Bandit*, published in 1854.

From the Native perspective, however, the trope of territory is rejected in favor of that of frontier. Seen from the "other" side, a frontier cuts both ways. And given the fact that almost all of the more than sixty novels by Native American authors are by writers of mixed Native and European descent—mixedbloods who embody the frontier, transcultural experience—I would suggest that the Native American novel is the quintessential postmodern frontier text, and the problem of identity at the center of virtually every Native American novel is the problem of internalized transculturation.

It is our responsibility, as writers and teachers, to make sure that our texts and our classrooms are not "safe" spaces from which a reader or student may return unchanged or unthreatened. While a fictional territory—a safe, unthreatening space inhabited by cuddly, colorful Natives—may guarantee million-dollar advances in New York and glowing student evaluations, we have to remember the immortal words of Gerald Vizenor: "Some upsetting is necessary." Literary terrorism is preferable to literary tourism.

This, however, is not what Euramerican readers want to see in Native American writing. For European Americans, contact with Native America in whatever form retains powerful traces of the desire for a mythical moment of encounter with the absolute other that defines first contact. When Kincaid begins his review by asking, "What can it mean to go one-on-one, white on red, with the large number of important recent works by and about American Indians?" he suggests this essentialist attitude rather quickly. And just as quickly, he inhabits the role of interpreter, the intermediary who "translates" what Derrida calls the "voice of Nature," and thus supplies nature's lack. In his book *Forked Tongues: Speech, Writing and Representation in North American Indian Texts*, David Murray suggests that "once it has been decided that not all human beings are equally cultural (and, for that matter, natural) in having language, and societies, then the idea of development becomes as much about drawing distinctions as about establishing continuities" (611). Clearly, Native American writing is not equally "cultural" for the *New York Times*, and just as clearly, distinctions must be drawn. What is required then is a reviewer who will perform somewhat like a salvage anthropologist, who can go into textual Indian Territory and come back to tell civilization about the experience. As Murray has also pointed out, for such intermediaries, "The degree of immersion in native life, the degree of the loss of white Western subject in the object being studied is . . . always controlled by the need to come back, to re-establish objectivity, and to this end the writing down and recording is crucial" (133). The reviewer goes into the territory of the Indian text and returns to the objective pages of the *Times* to write down the experience—just as John Dunbar in Kevin Costner's film *Dances With Wolves* must return from the realm of the doomed Sioux, bearing both the stamp of otherness and the reclaimed white woman, before he writes the experience down.

After Ridge in 1854, the Native American novel becomes ideally not a territory but a frontier, a space of resistance—or what Vizenor would call "survivance"—where hegemony is not acknowledged. Beginning with *Cogewea, the Half-Blood* in 1927, the Native American attempts not merely to subvert but to confront the dominant discourse in a clear dialogic. It becomes a place of contact between cultural identities, a bidirectional, dynamic zone of resistance. Within that zone, we are the ones who get to "make and tell" our stories. The question that remains, however, is the other crucial question raised by the *New York Times* review: "Who is listening—and how well?" It is our job in the classroom to answer both of those questions as effectively as possible. It is our job as teachers and writers to make people listen well, to disrupt the discourse of dominance, to challenge and discomfit the reader, to ultimately startle that reader into real knowledge.

"The Song Is Very Short"

Native American Literature and Literary Theory

◆

I've taken my title—"The Song Is Very Short"—from Maria Chona's famous explanation in *The Autobiography of a Papago Woman*: "The song is very short because we understand so much." I think we need to pay attention to the implications of this Tohono O'odham woman's words regarding cultural knowledge, for her words raise important issues. For example, who are "we" who understand so much, and how do "others"—the "not-we's"—attend to the brief utterance of song shadowed by such cultural complexity and depth? When the song is sung beyond the circle of "we," how is communication achieved—if, indeed, it is achieved at all? Or is it inevitable that what takes place within the transcultural frontier—as the indigenous "text" is "read" by those in power—may be mere surface appropriation, a shadow borrowing and simulacrum of tribal culture? In such circumstances, the short song may appear in ethnographic anthologies, most probably in translation, while that which it signifies remains locked away in cultural distance. Can or should critical theory attempt to enable the "not we" to access the "so much" that lies beyond the song simulated in English or beyond the song heard even in the original tongue by the linguistically adept outsider? More crucially yet, can such theory illuminate transcultural zones in such a way that the "dialogically agitated space" becomes a matrix within which communication and comprehension are indeed multidirectional and multireflexive? Finally, what dangers must we keep in mind when we pose as intermediaries in this critical process?

With the recent interest in what Arnold Krupat calls the "voice in the margin," there seems to be a widespread sense that a new kind of critical-theoretical approach is needed if multiculturalism is to be more than another aspect of the familiar discourse of dominance, what has been called "critical imperialism." As part of this argument, Gerald Vizenor has written that "academic evidence is a euphemism for linguistic colonization of oral traditions and popular memories" ("Socioacupuncture," 183). More than any other Indian writer, however, Vizenor liberally sprinkles his texts with academic evidence, quoting and paraphrasing theorists to an extraordinary degree, gathering fragments of authoritative critical discourse the way a trickster magpie gathers the shiny and curious debris of civilization and weaving these shards into the fabric of his own prose. It would seem, to Vizenor at least, that critical discourse is a fruitful target for appropriation, abrogation, and rearticulation. In fact, Vizenor has even edited *Narrative Chance*, the only collection of critical essays to self-consciously seek a "postmodern" theoretical approach to Native American writing. Among the essays in *Narrative Chance* the reader will find a Lacanian reading of Silko's *Ceremony*, a reader-response approach to D'Arcy McNickle's *The Surrounded*, and a Bakhtinian analysis of Vizenor's own work.

Elaine Jahner has echoed Vizenor's initial concern, writing that "'critics need to be aware that conventional approaches and vocabulary are as likely to obscure as to illuminate' both the form and the content of Native literature" (Jahner, 212). Elaborating upon the dangers of critical imperialism, Krupat has further argued that

> postmodern positions, regardless of what they call themselves . . . are all based upon models both of Western "scientific," "social-scientific," "rational," "historical" modes of thought, and of non-Western "religious," "biogenetic," "mythic," or vaguely specified "Indian" modes, that are grossly overgeneralized—overgeneralized, so that they may be reified as categories presumptively in (binary) opposition to each other. (*Ethnocriticism*, 5)

Having coined the word "ethnocriticism" to define his version of multicultural critical discourse, Krupat goes on to confess: "But inasmuch as the conceptual categories necessary to ethnocriticism—culture, history, imperialism, anthropology, literature, interdisciplinarity, even the frontier—are Western categories, the objection may be raised that ethnocriticism is itself no more than yet another form of imperialism, this time of a discursive and epistemological kind" (*Ethnocriticism*, 5). Like Krupat, Edward Said apparently feels a need for a new critical discourse, writing in Culture and Imperialism, as I noted above, that "If the Japanese, East European, Islamic, and Western instances express anything in common, it is that a new critical consciousness is needed." Said's statement that "Instead of the partial analysis offered by the various national or systematically theoretical schools, I have been proposing the contrapuntal lines of a global analysis" (330) strikes me as not far from Krupat's argument for "ethnocricism."

As Krupat amply demonstrates in the introduction to his volume titled *Ethnocriticism*, we could easily find any number of other writers arguing for the necessity of new theoretical approaches to multicultural literature. However, given the truth of Houston Baker's recent statement that "it took more years than anyone could possibly have imagined for the earth to move in the world of American literary and cultural studies" (5), it may be that we will have a long time to wait.

But what are the obstacles we face in thus moving the critical earth? One of the foremost, I would suggest, arises from a twofold kind of resistance: the resistance of the so-called "other," who very rightly suspects and frequently rejects the critical discourse of the metropolitan center as little more than further colonialism or cultural imperialism, and the resistance of the privileged center itself, which continues, in the face of what strikes me as often hypocritical posturing, to ignore the voices of Native Americans who would seek to construct and represent themselves.

As I have discussed earlier, examples of this refusal to hear or recognize Native American voices are astonishingly and depressingly easy to discover. How else can we explain, for example, the fact that such a perceptive study as *The Empire Writes Back: Theory and Practice in Post-Colonial Literatures*, published in 1989, considers Euramerican literature within its discussion of post-colonial writing but ignores entirely the impressive body of literature written by American Indian authors? Is writing by an American Indian less post- or neocolonial than that by a native Nigerian or by those other Indians from India? How could such an oversight have occurred? Were the authors of this study simply unaware of writing by American Indians, or did they for some reason deem such writing insignificant? The authors might have made the very interesting point that in fact Native American writing is not postcolonial but rather colonial, that the colonizers never left but simply changed their names to Americans; but the editors do not make such a point. The basic problem seems to be that the center, even when it begins to define itself as something ambiguously called "multicultural," still does not always hear more than the echo of its own voice or see very far beyond its own reflection.

And this point brings me to the first kind of resistance I mentioned above: the suspicion by Native Americans that critical theory represents little more than a new form of colonial enterprise. Why should people who have borne the brunt of authoritative discourse for five hundred years participate in a theoretical discourse that originates from the very center of colonial authority? Why should Indians attend to what Aldon Lynn Nielsen has called the "language of white thought," which in Nielsen's words "has had to create the boundaries of its existence and to determine what will not be allowed inside"?[1] We are disheartened not only by examples such as those above, but on a different level when, for example, the *New York Times Book Review* finally decides to notice American Indian voices in a front-page review titled "Who Gets to Tell Their Stories?" and assigns the review to a professor identified in a biographical statement as "the author of books about Dickens, Tennyson and Trollope."

More than a little tired of being what Vizenor has called "a bankable simulation" (*Manifest Manners*, 11), a construction useful when Euramerican or Western intellectuals require a reflecting "other" to give them back culturally enhanced shadows of the self, the Indian may opt out and, in the words of M. Annette Jaimes, call ambiguously for "an autonomous Indian tradition of intellectualism" or take the approach of Robert Warrior in suggesting a poorly defined kind of Indian "intellectual sovereignty" arising from direct attention to a community of Indian intellectuals.[2]

Such separatist intellectual sentiments are easy to understand but difficult in the end to ratify entirely. The real problem is that we do not have the luxury of simply opting out because, whether or not we are heard by Said, Sollors, or others, we already function within the dominant discourse. To think otherwise is naive at best, for the choice was made for all of us generations ago. Half a millennium of Euramerican attempts to both eliminate and reimagine the Indian has resulted in a hybridized, multicultural reality clearly recognized in fiction as long ago as the 1920s and '30s by such Native American writers as Mourning Dove, McNickle, and Mathews. As Krupat has accurately written, "from 1492 on, neither Euro-American intellectuals nor Native American intellectuals could operate autonomously or uniquely . . . in a manner fully independent of one another" ("Scholarship and Native American Studies," 88). The very act of appropriating the colonizer's discourse and making it one's own is obviously collaborative and conjunctural. We have long since entered inescapably what Pratt terms a "contact zone" and what I prefer to call a "frontier," in James Clifton's definition, "a culturally defined place where peoples with different culturally expressed identities meet and deal with each other."[3]

Vizenor, the most aggressively intellectual of Native American writers, has illuminated Native Americans' problematic but unavoidable participation in this dialogically agitated discourse, writing that "The English language has been the linear tongue of colonial discoveries, racial cruelties, invented names, the simulation of tribal cultures, manifest manners, and the unheard literature of dominance in tribal communities; at the same time, this mother tongue of paracolonialism has been a language of invincible imagination and liberation for many tribal people in the postindian world." Vizenor adds, "English, that coercive language of federal boarding schools, has carried some of the best stories of endurance, the shadows of tribal survivance, and now that same language bears the creative literature of distinguished postindian authors in the cities" (*Manifest*

Manners, 105–106). The Eurocentric consciousness that dominates Graduate Records Exams, the publishing world, and the realm of critical discourse may hear only the short part of Maria Chona's song, or it may hear nothing more than its own voice echoed back, but it behooves the rest of us to liberate as much as possible "this mother tongue of paracolonialism." However, a very real danger faced by the Native American, or any marginalized writer who would assume the role of scholar-critic-theorist, is that of consciously or unconsciously using Eurocentric theory merely as a way of legitimizing his or her voice—picking up the master's tools not to dismantle the master's house but simply to prove that we are tool-using creatures just like him and therefore worthy of intellectual recognition. It is tempting to believe that if, like my friend Chuck's crows, about whom I wrote in the preface, we learn to say Lacan or Derrida, we may be heard at the distant center. The result of such a contrived pose may be, of course, a split that will not heal.

Given all of the above, the odds that an American Indian scholar will emerge to enter the critical dialogue are slim at best. Collaboration with the enemy's discourse represents a difficult goal even if one should decide to undertake it. Krupat has defined the concomitant danger for the Euramerican or Eurocentric critic rather well, confessing that "the danger I run as an ethnocritic is the danger of leaving the Indian silent entirely in my discourse" (*Ethnocriticism*, 30). As we have seen, such silence is not uncommon.

A danger seemingly inherent in much contemporary critical discourse concerning minority literatures, or multiculturalism, is a tendency to move in the direction of the binary structures postmodern theory so loathes. In *Resistance Literature,* for example, Barbara Harlow writes: "Resistance literature calls attention to itself, and to literature in general, as a political and politicized activity. The literature of resistance sees itself furthermore as immediately and directly involved in a struggle against ascendant or dominant forms of ideological and cultural production" (28–29). In her book *Imperial Eyes: Travel Writing and Transculturation,* Pratt defines "autoethnography" as "instances in which colonized subjects undertake to represent themselves in ways that engage with the colonizer's own terms," and adds that "autoethnographic texts are those the others construct in response to or in dialogue with those metropolitan representations" (7).

I would define literature by Native American authors about Native American concerns and informed by Native American cultures as undeniably both a deeply politicized literature of resistance and an example of autoethnography according to Pratt's term. And I find no disagreement with the principles articulated by Harlow and Pratt. However, as a writer, critic, and teacher of something called Native American literature, I feel oddly uncomfortable with these definitions. Perhaps my discomfort comes from the derivation of the very word "define": that is, "to set a limit to, [to] bound." Perhaps it stems from a reluctance to be so firmly "othered." I suspect that Native American written literature—a literature produced almost exclusively in English by predominantly mixedblood authors steeped in Western education—well beyond its involvement "immediately and directly . . . in a struggle against ascendant or dominant forms of ideological and cultural production," like all multicultural literatures, must actually participate in myriad ways within that same process of ideological and cultural production. We must be careful of the tendency Henry Louis Gates, Jr., recently pointed out when he wrote that "under the sign of multiculturalism, literary readings are often guided by the desire to elicit, first and foremost, indices of ethnic particularity, especially those that can be construed as oppositional, transgressive, subversive" ("Beyond the Culture Wars," 8). Gates quotes John Guillory to the effect that "The critique of the canon responds to the disunity of the culture as a whole, as a fragmented whole, by constituting new cultural unities at the level of gender, race, or more recently, ethnic subcultures, or gay or lesbian subcultures" (8). In the same journal, Susan Stewart writes: "If scholars in our discipline constantly examine the relation between dominant and minority cultural forms as one of a colonizing appropriation and borrowing by the dominant, they end up, as nineteenth-century folklorists did, turning minority forms into something like nature—that is, a reservoir of spontaneity bereft of particularity and agency." Stewart goes on to write that "Narrative closure, cultural fixity, bounded knowledges are bought at the cost of tremendous violence to the possibilities of thought and action" (13). David Murray defines the challenge well, writing that "difference, rather than being essentialised, [must be] seen to be in constant interplay with cross-cultural unities and continuities" (3).

It is important to heed such warnings. In our desire to imagine an oppositional, culturally unified "other"—whether from an indigenous perspective or that of the "paracolonial" center—we run the risk of constructing what Vizenor has called "terminal creeds": those mono-logic utterances that seek to violate the dialogic of trickster space, to fix opposites and impose static definitions upon the world. Terminal creeds occur, says Vizenor, "in written literature and in totalitarian systems."[4] "Narrative closure, cultural fixity, bounded knowledges," as Stewart calls them, would terminate the possibilities that energize the multicultural frontier, opposing directly what Vizenor labels both "trickster discourse" and the literature of "survivance," and, as I read her, what Pratt defines as "survival literature."

A way of avoiding this critical dead end may be to pay careful attention to the admonitions of Vizenor, whose "trickster discourse" insists upon and celebrates the boundless zone of transculturation from a perspective beginning deeply within the traditional trickster narratives of Native America. Vizenor, I would suggest, has long been involved in an effort to move Native American studies in the direction of what Krupat has called the "project of ethnocricism," a critical enterprise Krupat defines as "not only at but of the frontier." Krupat goes on to argue that the "trope most typical of ethnocritical discourse . . . is the *oxymoron*, that figure which offers apparently oppositional, paradoxical, or incompatible terms in a manner that nonetheless allows for decidable, if polysemous and complex, meaning" (*Ethnocriticism*, 28). Despite his tedious, at times gratuitous-seeming, use of Latin tropes to organize his discussion of American Indian writing—a very familiar appeal to authoritative discourse—and despite his failure to come to terms in any meaningful way with Vizenor's concept of trickster discourse, Krupat seems nonetheless to be breaking important ground in his search for a way of talking about this literature.[5] Breaking even more impressive ground in the area of critical studies is the Chippewa poet and scholar Kimberly Blaeser in *Gerald Vizenor: Writing in the Oral Tradition*. Blaeser, from the same

White Earth Anishinaabe reservation as Vizenor, does a brilliant job of illuminating the traditional foundations of Vizenor's work while simultaneously critiquing the presence and influences of poststructuralist theory in that work. The scope of Blaeser's study is unequaled thus far in any work dedicated to a single Native American artist.

In the end, some songs, in Maria Chona's words, will remain very short, and some understandings will remain the domain of deep cultural response. To paraphrase David Murray, however, the challenge facing the critic is to avoid the error of imagining the encounter with Native American texts as a "meeting with the untouched and unknowable other" and to simultaneously escape the temptation to believe in the "unproblematic translatability, and . . . transparency" of texts and cultures" (Murray, 2). Those of us who write, teach, and critique Native American literatures, whether we identify as American Indian, Euramerican, both, or neither, face the complex challenge of attempting to mediate without violating and, above all, to facilitate an awareness that the literature we call Native American is indeed an "other" literature that nonetheless—in keeping with trickster's ubiquitous and uncontainable presence—participates profoundly in the discourse we call American and World literature.

Through an Amber Glass

Chief Doom and the Native American Novel Today

◆

Novels by Native American writers have a relatively short history, but a history not significantly shorter than that of the American novel itself. If we can date the first American novels to the late 1700s and early 1800s, with authors such as Hugh Henry Brackenridge and Charles Brockden Brown, it is not a great leap to John Rollin Ridge's *Joaquin Murietta* in 1854, the first novel we know of today that was written by a Native American. Since 1854, the so-called Native American novel has come a very long way, like its canonical cousins in the American mainstream having to traverse the quagmire of romanticism, the minefields of realism and naturalism, and the maze of modernism to arrive relatively healthy if a bit fragmented in the labyrinth of the postmodern age. Like all travelers, the Native American novel has picked up the scars and scuff marks of its travels. Naturally enough, what I am calling the Native American novel has quite a lot in common with its non-Native relatives in the same genre. We are discussing novels, after all. The big question after almost a century and a half, however, is where has the Native American novel arrived? Has it discovered America? How has it evolved? Can it be accurately called a part of the American canon as we move into the next millennium?

As I have suggested above, Ridge in 1854 and Mourning Dove, with *Cogewea* in 1927, were forced to disguise or embed their disturbing and even brilliantly subversive "Indian" texts within the parameters of the western romance, appropriating vehicles with the audacity of highwaymen (or highwaypersons). It is crucial, however, that in admiring the subtle subversiveness of these authors we remember that they could appropriate their vehicles only because the western romance was in the literary air (becoming a little shopworn by 1927, admittedly, but still current). In the same vein, Native American writers such as John Joseph Mathews and D'Arcy McNickle in the 1930s took on much of the hard-surfaced fatalism of the Hemingway noir era of modernist naturalism. It was inevitable that they would do so, given the period in which they learned their craft, for no writer exists or creates in a vacuum, regardless of what ethnic group or marginal culture he or she inhabits. The Pulitzer Prize–winning Kiowa author N. Scott Momaday, for example, wrote an unmistakably late modernist text in *House Made of Dawn*, a work that bears all the trademarks of the first fifty years of American literature in the twentieth century. Even the protagonist's search for identity and a coherent center mirrors the typical modernist hero's quest for a truth that will take the place of the lost God of the previous century, with the crucial difference being the Indian protagonist's ability to recover the center that inevitably evades the modernist hero of Euramerican texts. Following the same line of argument, it should surprise no one that the 1980s and '90s fictions of Gerald Vizenor bear the burdens and experimental challenges of the postmodern period's reaction against the certainties of modernism.

Though I have discussed Momaday's *House Made of Dawn* at some length elsewhere,[1] I want to use that breakthrough novel for Native American writers as a beginning point for a discussion of where we are today. When Momaday received his Pulitzer in 1969, a member of the Pulitzer jury declared that "an award to its author might be considered as a recognition of 'the arrival on the American literary scene of a matured, sophisticated literary artist from the original Americans" (Schubnell, 93). It is almost universally recognized today that *House Made of Dawn* was a seminal work for contemporary Native American writers, a novel that in the most sanguine interpretation seemed to show that the U.S. publishing world was at last ready for fiction that both rejected the too familiar clichés of Indian representation in American literature and was written out of a different consciousness and with a different effect and purpose. Certainly such a pat on the head from the privileged center seemed like manna from publishing heaven for artists struggling to make their voices heard from the distant margins. As I have suggested elsewhere, however, the Pulitzer jury's words beg for closer scrutiny, for in the wording of this laudatory statement we can easily find signs of the manifold and seemingly inexorable forces operating to determine and contain Native American art. In short, I believe we must examine very carefully what the event of a Pulitzer Prize for *House Made of Dawn* means for Native American writers both before and after this signal moment.

The unconsciously authoritative nature of the Pulitzer juror's discourse actually does an extraordinary job of defining the obstacles faced by Momaday and all artists who exist beyond the privileged center of American culture. The juror's statement most particularly illuminates the kind of double bind that faces the American Indian writer who must demonstrate a dexterity with the "master's tools" while simultaneously bearing and baring sufficient traces of subservient savagery to provide a kind of "ethnostalgia," or literary tourism, for the white reader. And if he or she is skillful, determined, dexterous, and cunning enough, the same author may succeed in embedding within the convolutions of such mimicry a significant artistic creation for Native American peoples, cultures, and readers. Most often, however, such success is limited and such voices are heard outside of those works allowed to play upon the stage of the American literary scene.

Let us begin with a consideration of what it means for this juror to call N. Scott Momaday "a matured, sophisticated literary artist from the original Americans." Putting aside for now the temptation to see "original" as "ab/original," let us ask ourselves what, in such a context, "matured" could possibly mean?[2] I will suggest that it means—in this jury's view—that an indigenous artist has finally evolved, or become acculturated, to a point at which he can successfully imitate the "grown-up" discourse of the dominant culture. And "sophisticated"—how can we read that signifier other than as an index to the author's ability to mimic the overt complexities and intellectual sleights-of-hand of those writers already accepted as "sophisticated" mainstream artists? Together, maturity and sophistication seem to create that peculiar alloy called a "literary artist." "Mature" and "sophisticated," I would suggest, participate in what Mikhail Bakhtin calls authoritative discourse, that discourse which arrives with its political authority intact, indissolubly fused to the utterance (342). And I would further suggest that in 1969 what the Pulitzer jury meant by this flattery was that at last a writer recognizable as "an [ab]original American" by the unmistakable indices of authentic "Indianness" within his work had learned, despite the primitivism signifying that essential Indianness, how to manipulate the techniques and tropes of high modernism: the discontinuous narrative popularized by Joyce, Faulkner, Stein, and uncountable others; the deracinated protagonist at the center stage of all modernism; the intertextuality and interreferentiality made a requirement for serious writers after T. S. Eliot, Joyce, and Pound; plentiful stream of consciousness; and, finally, heavily ironized Christian symbolism. Momaday did it all, and did it well.

In 1969 a novel that did not bear these signposts of privileged discouse could never have been called either mature or sophisticated, just as a work that did not bear indices of aboriginality could not have been then, as it could not be today, a recognizably "Indian" novel. In the first novel of this Kiowa writer with a Ph.D. from Stanford, however, the Pulitzer jury would have no trouble locating ubiquitous intertextual echoes of Faulkner, Lawrence, Hemingway, Dickinson, and other noted precursors. This, a sophisticated modernist-schooled reader would think, is what serious writers do, from the "jug jug" of Fitzgerald's motorcycle in *The Great Gatsby* (cf. *The Waste Land*), to Faulkner's heavy allusions to Saint Francis in *The Sound and the Fury*, not to mention the literary anthologies that inform the works of Eliot, Joyce, Pound, and others ad tedium. In Momaday's protagonist, Abel, the same reader could locate the familiar alienated, rootless, lost-generation shadow of Jake Barns, Quentin Compson, Jay Gatsby, and so on. And in Momaday's moderately difficult discontinuous, nonlinear narrative, the reader would find a comfortably familiar modernist pattern. Thus, *House Made of Dawn* approached in these ways what the critic Charles Newman a few years ago termed "presold" fiction: it contained unmistakable signifiers of both predetermined critical success and marketability (Newman, 113). Clearly it wasn't for naught that N. Scott Momaday worked with the formalist poet Yvor Winters and completed his doctoral studies in American literature at Stanford. In *House Made of Dawn* we find the first, and perhaps the only, almost perfectly crafted modernist American Indian novel.

The next logical question, of course, is what might this jury have meant by "the American literary scene"? The answer is quite simple: the literary scene is the established canon of literary works already stamped with the emblem of greatness—those works that, as Barbara Hernstein Smith has explained, reinforce the values of the dominant culture ("Contingencies of Value," 6) while, we might add, supporting a very privileged kind of restricted discourse that in turn reinforces the privileged positions of the hierophantic academic interpreters who mediate between canon and commoner. To this special group we should add those emerging works that look enough like their distinguished predecessors to qualify for admission to the club. Essentially the "literary scene" is the stage upon which mostly white, mostly male literature performs, with occasional admissions of "other" works either because—despite bearing the burden of marginal experiences—they look enough like the canon (c.f. Ralph Ellison's *Invisible Man*, with its extreme intertextuality, deracinated protagonist, and so forth) or because they provide a touch of exoticized color to the periphery of the canon (Richard Wright's *Native Son* comes to mind). The Pulitzer jury found in Momaday's fine novel enough of what it was accustomed to finding in a canonical work so that it could accept *House Made of Dawn* into the privileged realm of serious literature that it chose to call "the American literary scene." At the same time, with its fairly detailed depiction of Pueblo culture and daily life, the novel provides the kind of literary tourism usually found in works by non-Native authors such as Oliver LaFarge or, perhaps, in the distinctly nonsophisticated (in Pulitzer jury terms) "performance" writings of someone like the mixedblood Mohawk artist Pauline Johnson, who before the turn of the century was self-consciously parodying the "absolute fake" with her Indian princess costume and stage acts.

Anyone with knowledge of and an intellectual or emotional stake in Native American literature preceding Momaday must wonder why a Native American novel did not arrive on the "literary scene" prior to 1969. If Euramerican writers could achieve maturity and sophistication at least a couple of centuries earlier, why did it take so long for an "original" writer—even a 50 percent ab/original such as the half-Kiowa Momaday—to mature and find sophistication? Given the jury's statement, such Native American predecessors of Momaday as novelists John Rollin Ridge, Mourning Dove, John Milton Oskison, John Joseph Mathews, and D'Arcy McNickle—all of whose books are today kept in print by university presses, despite the complexity, subtlety, power, and craft of their art, were neither "mature" nor "sophisticated," and certainly none ever arrived on the "American literary scene."

The reasons for exile to the liminal hinterlands of American literature are undoubtedly many and varied, and it must be confessed that among the works of these authors one seldom finds the literary polish of a Momaday, a Leslie Silko, or a James Welch of today. However, I would argue that even more than any lack of artistic polish or merit it is the distinct "otherness" of these works that kept them out of the "literary scene" for so long. They are novels of a different order of maturity, representing a sophistication and complexity not easily accessible to even the most conventionally educated white reader. Within these novels one does not find the kind of modernist scaffolding that allows a non-Native reader to scale the difficult terrain of alien story and discourse. A brief look at the truly subtle sophistication and maturity of *House Made of Dawn*—a sophistication and maturity that underlies and actually subsumes the obvious modernist techniques of intertextuality, interreferentiality, and so forth—may, in fact, shed light on what is genuinely original and valuable and almost universally overlooked in Momaday's predecessors.

House Made of Dawn is indeed everything the Pulitzer jury declared it to be. However, the true sophistication of Momaday's novel is of an order beyond the scope of the Pulitzer jury that recognized its merits. It is a sophistication evidenced in the novel's very first word, "*Dypaloh*," a storyteller's invocation from Jemez Pueblo oral tradition signaling the beginning of a story, and in the word that ends the novel: "*Qtsedaba*," another storyteller's conventional utterance signifying the completion of the story.[3] Encountering the first word of Momaday's work, the reader is forced to acknowledge that he or she is confronted with another language, another epistemology, another way of knowing. To enter the novel is to cross a threshold into another cultural realm and to submit to being something other than the privileged center of the text. Such has always been the experience for minority or marginalized readers in America reading the texts assigned in school or published in New York, but it is very likely a new experience for members of the dominant Euramerican culture. Between these beginning and ending invocations, Momaday structures his novel not according to the paradigms of classical and Christian mythology per Joyce, Eliot, Faulkner, and all the icons of modernism, but rather in accordance with Pueblo and Navajo mythology. Just as Eliot recognized that, in *Ulysses*, Joyce (and Eliot, himself, of course, in *The Waste Land*) was incorporating mythological structure to organize the chaos and futility of modern existence, Momaday is constructing his novel upon the mythic paradigms of inherited culture. The impulse is the same. However, Momaday's mythology is foreign to the great majority of his readers, and rather than shoring intractable fragments against our collective spiritual and moral ruin, in the modernist sense, Momaday is disclosing a moral universe that remains whole and comprehensible for the Native characters about whom he writes. Things may seem to fall apart for Momaday's protagonist, but in the end the falcon hears the falconer, to paraphrase William Butler Yeats, and the center easily holds.

It is important to recognize that in *House Made of Dawn* Momaday actively and brilliantly engages in dialogue with and in effect subverts those measures of maturity and sophistication recognized and required by a Pulitzer jury. It is at the same time important to note, however, that *House Made of Dawn* would very likely never have been published in New York at all had it not provided enough of the unmistakable signs of privileged and presold modernist discourse to be recognized by a jury from that same arena, a jury that could and undoubtedly did overlook the true brilliance of the achievement.

The magnitude of Momaday's appropriation and subversion of modernist paradigms is impressive. First, the mythological structure so essential to the major works of modernism—a structure mined from Sir James Frazer and the Christian tradition—has metamorphosed into the Navajo Night Chant and a rich weaving of Navajo and Pueblo oral tradition. Second, the alienated protagonist, a Christ-like antihero in so much twentieth-century American fiction, has become an alienated Indian seemingly trapped between cultures and doomed to a kind of schizophrenic inarticulateness. However, whereas the modernist hero lies solipsistically upon his floor like J. Alfred Prufrock or wanders like so many others in a wasteland between the lost God of the nineteenth century and the psychic dissolution of the modern world, looking for fragments to shore against spiritual ruin, Momaday's protagonist moves in an archetypal circular journey from community into chaos and back to community. For Momaday's Abel, the center remains intact (if at times out of focus), and Abel succeeds in completing the questing hero's journey in the pattern of the Stricken Twins and other Native American culture heroes.[4] For Momaday, as for other Native American writers, the story does not end with a castrated idiot (Faulkner's Benjy) bawling in meaningless circles, or a Jake Barnes cynically muttering that it is pretty to think there could have been meaning, or a Nick Carraway hopelessly rubbing foul words off a doorstep. We could go on in this way, but Momaday's novel has been rather fully dissected elsewhere, and perhaps a final note is sufficient.[5] Whereas Momaday's modernist predecessors and even contemporaries constructed discontinuous narratives in futile attempts to escape the tyranny of linearity while simultaneously illuminating the "more real" realism of the unconscious, Momaday's nonlinear, spatially ordered narrative, with its seven-part structure and cyclical patterning, works in contrast to illuminate the cyclical contemporaneity of the Indian world and oral tradition.

What is fascinating in thus examining Momaday's novel in the context of the Pulitzer jury's statement is the fact that Momaday is able to pull it off so successfully. He ingeniously gives the conventional Euramerican reader a novel that is instantaneously recognizable as a "sophisticated" literary work while at the same time he entirely appropriates that sophistication to make it bear the burden of an Indian world utterly alien to the same jurors who awarded him a Pulitzer Prize.

All of the above leads to the overwhelming question of what happens to the work of art that fails to offer such familar Euramerican signifiers of "sophistication" and literary "maturity"? What happens to the work that adheres more closely and narrowly to Native American storytelling traditions and eschews the surface complexity of modernism or the surface self-referentiality of postmodernism? The answer is that such a work may take a dozen years and partial subsidy by the author and editor before it is published, as did Mourning Dove's *Cogewea, the Half-Blood*, and that it may then promptly vanish from sight or may simply find no mainstream publisher at all. *Cogewea* is, in fact, a very telling example, for in that novel—nearly half a century before Momaday wrote *House Made of Dawn*—Mourning Dove effected her own subtle appropriation and subversion of Euramerican literature. *Cogewea*'s subtitle, *A Depiction of the Great Montana Cattle Range*, indicates the direction Mourning Dove's appropriationist move would take, for, as I argued earlier, *Cogewea* is indeed a western romance, a novel that bears all the requisite hallmarks of that very popular genre: a western ranch setting; a cast of rough-and-ready cowboys; a beautiful young woman who will conveniently become the necessary damsel in distress; a dastardly "easterner" who comes to plunder Eden; and a strong-and-silent, quick-triggered cowboy hero ready to save the hapless female. Clearly the author knows the genre and just as clearly she knows how to subvert it.

Mourning Dove's subversion takes a variety of forms, all of which add up to the fact that she has hijacked a genre in which Indians are reserved for marginal, binary roles as bloodthirsty or noble savages, and she has turned that genre into a vehicle for a very "Indian" story. Just as Momaday deftly derailed the quintessential modernist novel, Mourning Dove does the same to the western romance. To begin with, the mythic paradigm of the novel is not the typical western story with its errant Grail knight (beginning, of course, with Cooper's Natty Bumppo), but rather the oral tradition of Mourning Dove's Okanogan Indian ancestors. In addition, Mourning Dove's helpless rancher's daughter (in this case rancher's sister-in-law), while she may be tied to a tree (instead of railroad tracks) in the end, turns out to be a pretty tough character who can ride and shoot with the best cowboys and who uses language as a shrewd political weapon. And she turns out to be a "half-blood." The novel's cowboys in turn prove to be a carnivalesque collection of mixed-bloods, and the hero, bearing all the required marks of a Gary Cooper or John Wayne, is— inconceivably—an Indian. Simply put, the novel's best cowboy and western hero is an Indian.

Cogewea is instructive because it did not win a literary award and did not make its appearance upon the "literary scene." While it must be confessed that the confused editing of the novel and the often less-than-polished prose are unavoidable obstacles to literary acclaim for *Cogewea*, I would suggest that a greater reason for this novel's very belated discovery lies in the fact that it did not give Euramerican readers what they expected or desired. It is neither a noble-savage tableau of Vanishing Americans a lá Cooper, La Farge, et al, nor a recognizable "American" novel. It is unmistakably an American Indian text, and as such cannot earn the labels of sophisticated or mature despite the acute, even brilliant, satire and subversion, the self-reflexivity, that permeate the work.

Without reploughing the textual grounds of novels by Mathews and McNickle, it may be sufficient to say that neither of these Native American authors "arrived" upon the American literary scene because both wrote fiction that bore the burden of Native sophistication and maturity but failed to cloak that art within the recognizable signifiers of canonical literature. Despite the fact that, long before the West discovered Bakhtin, McNickle was writing explicitly about "discourse" and, throughout his fiction, was foregrounding the political linguistic struggles that take place within dialogically agitated space, neither Mathews nor McNickle wrote enough like a candidate for the Euramerican canon. Both, however, wrote with a sophisticated awareness of Native American oral traditions, cultures, and histories—and wove this awareness deeply into the fabric of their fiction.

All of this should help somewhat to shed light upon contemporary literature by Native American authors as well as all writing by marginalized or "minority" artists. We can learn a great deal by paying attention to what is published and praised by the metropolitan center in the United States—what is allowed to arrive upon the American literary scene. Listen, for example, to the words of the late Chicano author Arturo Islas, whose novel *The Rain God* has become something of a classic on college campuses and among Chicano readers:

> I've waited eight years to see it [*The Rain God*] in print. . . . My experiences with the New York publishing establishment, which decides what the rest of the country reads, have been heartbreaking. I know, I know, I'm not alone; but my experience is unique in that my background is unique and has been all but ignored by the establishment. Is there anyone in New York interested in good writing from a point of view that has not been given the exposure it deserves? Does the writer from a "minority" point of view always have to be bitter and screaming that the establishment (i.e., New York and the East Coast) ought to be torn down in order for justice to be served? Or, at the other extreme, does a writer from my point of view have to kowtow to the reactionaries within the establishment. . . ? New York trade publishers do not recognize that there is an audience for good work written from within Mexican American culture.

Of the two "Chicano" works published by New York during the period of Islas's struggle to see his work in print, Islas pointed out:

> One was written by a "scholarship boy" who speaks against bilingual and affirmative action programs and who has a very hard time bringing his heritage together with his Anglo-American education. And the other work, it turns out, is by a rich Communist-American who was blacklisted in the thirties and who, when he sits at his typewriter, becomes a young Chicano East Los Angeles gang member named Danny Santiago. It is enough to make angels weep.[6]

Although New York has recently discovered Sandra Cisneros and has found what it apparently believes to be a gold mine in the works of Louise Erdrich and Sherman Alexie, examples similar to Islas's are easy to find among so-called "minority writers." Rudolfo Anaya's *Bless Me, Ultima*, an unquestioned classic of Chicano literature, was published and kept in print for years not by New York but by a small western publisher. Subsequently, Anaya's work was published by the University of New Mexico Press before he was—only recently—discovered by New York. Jeanne Wakatsuki Houston and James D. Houston's *Farewell to Manzanar*, a powerful and beautifully written account of Japanese American internment during World War II, could not even find an agent in New York and was finally accepted sans agent by a San Francisco publisher. The book, the authors were told by one prominent New York agent, was "too issue" oriented to be successful—the issue being, one suspects, that the subject of the book was oppressed Asian Americans and an ugly moment in the manifestation of American destiny. Since its publication in 1973, the book has gone through more than thirty printings.[7]

The most vivid example among Native American authors of such marginalization is Chippewa novelist, poet, essayist, and playwright Gerald Vizenor. Vizenor, whose more than thirty published works challenge the privileged center more brilliantly and fiercely than the works of any other American author, found his extraordinary 1978 novel *Darkness in Saint Louis Bearheart* not only rejected but actually "lost" by the first three New York publishers to whom it was sent.[8] *Bearheart* was finally published by Truck Press, a small press in the Midwest. Since that time, every one of Vizenor's numerous novels, story collections, and nonfiction titles has been published by a university press. Vizenor stands virtually alone, in fact, among American Indian writers for the lengthy steadfastness of his refusal to "kowtow to the reactionaries within the establishment." While the handful of commercially successful Native American authors scrabble to give New York publishers exactly what they are expecting to see, Vizenor writes again and again against such commercially trite and culturally damning demands. As a consequence, his works continue to be published by noncommercial presses, with the result that one of the most demanding, challenging, and brilliant of American authors continues to be admired by scholars and celebrated abroad while being almost unknown among readers in the United States, including American Indian readers.

The logical direction of a discussion such as this would seem to be toward at least a cursory examination of what is published today. Momaday's *House Made of Dawn*, I would argue, was a Trojan-horse novel, an unmistakably modernist, though deeply metaphysical, novel in the mainstream tradition that nonetheless contained within its shell of modernist sophistication a thoroughly "Indian" story and discourse. Has Momaday's pioneering journey into the domestic garden of the "American literary scene" then opened the way for other serious Native American authors? Can we now dispense with the wooden shell of Euramerican "sophistication," write honestly and directly from an "other" position, and expect critical and commercial success? I think, as Vizenor's example indicates, the answer is a rather firm NO. If we examine the works by Native American authors that have found acclaim in New York, a pattern asserts itself. What we are seeing, not only in the myriad New Ageish nonfiction books mostly by non-Indian writers but also in novels by American Indian authors, is at times what I earlier called a kind of literary tourism. Again, Vizenor serves as a defining contrast. From *Darkness in Saint Louis Bearheart*, Vizenor's first novel, to *The Trickster of Liberty*, *The Heirs of Columbus*, and his most recent work, *Hotline Healers*, this Chippewa author's goal has been, in trickster fashion, to upset the reader in a healthful and positive manner. Just as the traditional Native American trickster's job is to trick us into self-knowledge, to outrage us into disequilibrium and confusion that lead to understanding, the "job" of Vizenor's writing is to cleanse us of the heavy sludge of cliché and stereotype that eventually kill spontaneity and truth in art. The role of Vizenor's works is to confront the non-Indian world with its greed, lust for Indianness, fatal violence, and self-deception and to expose the falseness of the hyperreal fake. At the same time, Vizenor carefully works to strip his Indian readers of the comforts of the same clichés and stereotypes: those people who would define themselves as "Indian" according to imposed, static Euramerican definitions will probably feel quite uncomfortable reading Vizenor's prose (indeed, many do). In fact, all of us will feel uncomfortable, guilty, and moved toward self-awareness. This is trickster's role. It is not, however, what commercial publishers seek, for this is a healthy, vital declaration of traditional Native American epistemology and is therefore unfamiliar terrain. Like Raven, Vizenor flaps down before us to mock, scorn, and laugh us into self-awareness. That is a life-giving posture.

If we have collectively learned anything over the past five hundred years, however, it is that the American Indian is not supposed to live and certainly not supposed to write back. The Indian, as we all know ad nauseum, is supposed to vanish, to die, culturally and literally. He/she is above all not supposed to be an impediment or disturbance. The Indian is valuable as a bit of color, as an invaluable link to the stolen landscape of America, as an index to the Euramerican's lost "mystical" self. One need not think very long about the age-old representations of Indians in our fiction and other media to recognize the truth of this. Rather recently, the immensely popular film *Dances With Wolves*, which I discuss further below, provided a brilliant example of this concept of doomed Indianness.

Given what I have argued thus far, what kind of fiction would commercial publishers search out for commercial success? Certainly not Vizenor, who upsets people a bit too much. In fact, what commercial publishing houses seek with fevered breath is the novel that provides very definite qualities. First, a novel should be immediately recognizable as "Indian," which means it must very visibly present signifiers conforming to publishers' and readers' expectations of what "Indian" is. Since Euramerica invented its own Indian to replace the indigenous inhabitant of the Americas, Euramerican readers are well primed to recognize that Indian when they see it. It is not absolutely necessary, but it helps if the author can be labeled on the book jacket by tribal affiliation and if a phenotypically "Indian"-looking photograph can be placed on the jacket. A photograph of a Greek in fringed buckskin and black braids might work nicely. I have in front of me at this moment, in fact, a recent (1996) novel titled *Crota*, whose author, named Owl Goingback on the title page, is identified on the jacket as "a member of the Choctaw tribe" but whose large and delightful dust-jacket photograph shows a handsome, very "Indian"-looking man holding a spear and wearing wrapped braids, bone choker, bone breastplate, and generally what appears to be a mixture of traditional Plains tribal attire. A traditional Choctaw *shapo*, the word for "hat" borrowed from the French *chapeau*, and a shotgun instead of spear probably would have seriously damaged the "Indian" quality of the photo and the commercial value of the book, though both might have been more tribally "real," given the Choctaw nation's very early contact with and quick assimilation of European dress and tools. I do not know a thing about this author whose work I discovered on a bookstore shelf just a few days ago, but I do know that my Choctaw grandmother would have had a fit about naming a child "Owl," an animal whose presence for Choctaw people signifies death and the possibility of sorcery. "Goingback" is also a nicely metaphoric name for a "traditional" Indian whose photograph seems bent on going way back to some kind of generic, "hyperreal" Indian. All of this may, of course, be "authentic" and nicely coincidental to the packaging and selling of a "real" Indian novel.

More important than these signifiers beyond "END," however, an Indian novel should contain universally acceptable and easily recognized signifiers of Indianness. An Indian gumshoe working his sleuth trade in an urban center (the protagonist of an exciting novel now in progress by Michael Roberts, an Indian acquaintance of mine whose brother is a "real" Indian cop) is not ideal for this kind of high-recognition factor. The preferred list of such signifiers would seem to include a reservation setting of one sort or another, but not just any reservation will do. A mixedblood inhabiting an urban landfill reservation (as in Vizenor's fiction) ranks low on the commercial survivability quotient. It is best if the reservation is both vague and intensely dysfunctional. In Louise Erdrich's very popular novels, the reservation seems to be little more than a place where people live in cheap federal housing while drinking, making complicated love, feuding with one another, building casinos, and dying self-destructive and often violent deaths. In Sherman Alexie's stories and novels the reservation is a vaguely defined place where people live in cheap federal housing while drinking, playing basketball, feuding with one another, and dying self-destructive and often violent deaths. In Susan Power's *The Grass Dancer*, a more full and positive representation of an Indian community, the reservation is a place where people live in a believable variety of housing while drinking, dancing, feuding with one another, and occasionally dying violent deaths. In Adrian Louis's *Skins*, the reservation is nothing more than a bad and very deadly joke.

Because poverty and hopelessness are such unavoidable realities of Indian existence, it is natural that poverty would be a part of such fiction. To ignore the painful would be to falsify the picture. It is also true that alcoholism is an enormous and even tragic problem in reservation communities, just as alcohol and drugs are incredibly destructive forces in virtually all poor urban communities. Poverty and an inability to imagine a future different from the intolerable present lead to despair, and despair leads to abuse of self and others as well as the natural desire for temporary escape. However, such portraits not only present just one side of Indian existence, but more unfortunately conform readily to Euramerican readers' expectations that American Indians are all doomed by firewater; white readers find their stereotypes comfortably reinforced by sensationalized alcoholism and cultural impotence. The professional victimage and romanticized self-destructiveness of Janet Campbell Hale's fiction and nonfiction certainly conform to these popular stereotypes. If one is to sell such a portrait to the Euramerican world responsible for the creation and sustaining of these conditions, however, it is crucial that non-Indian readers not feel too responsible or guilty. A little guilt is good, but too much turns off not just readers and reviewers but also publishers who accurately suspect low sales. A reviewer of my own 1996 novel, *Nightland*, illustrates this point nicely. First the writer complains that the book is too inaccessible: "Wolves, vultures, coyotes, and crows seem to surface in many scenes. They may have meaning in Native American folklore, but they are never explained in the book." "Folklore"? A Native American reader encountering Faulkner or Ken Kesey might similarly complain, one supposes, that Christ figures seem to surface rather frequently and that while they may have meaning in Judeo-Christian folklore, they are not adequately explained in *The*

Sound and the Fury or *One Flew Over the Cuckoo's Nest.* More to the point, however, the reviewer complains that "Owens also seems to throw some low blows to the white man who invades his country. . . . I was looking for action and thrills, not a lesson in morality" (Curan, 23). It should be noted that, being more than half "white man" myself, I must be throwing some low blows to the part of me who invaded "my" country. One should begin to suspect the complexity at work here.

Leslie Silko, author of the most aggressively disturbing and revolutionary Native American novel yet in *Almanac of the Dead*, addressed the issue of self-neutralizing portraits—the kind of writing that allows white readers to avoid excessively distressing guilt—when she reviewed Louise Erdrich's *The Beet Queen*. The world of Erdrich's novel, Silko protested, "is an oddly rarified place in which the individual's own psyche, not racism or poverty, accounts for all conflict and tension. In this pristine world all misery, suffering and loss are self-generated, just as conservative Republicans have been telling us for years." Silko labels Erdrich's novel "an eloquent example of the political climate in America in 1986" ("Here's an Odd Artifact," 10). Although in my 1992 study, *Other Destinies*, I disagreed to some extent with Silko, emphasizing instead Erdrich's portrayal of the internalized colonialism and racism that destroy Native people and communities, Silko nevertheless raises a very important issue here.

Marlon Sherman, a Lakota writer and lawyer who was born and grew up on the Pine Ridge reservation, provides a more harshly critical analysis of Adrian C. Louis's novel *Skins*, set at Pine Ridge, beginning with the fact that, as discussed above, an author had better know his subject. Louis, for example, writes in the novel that the Lakota boys have trouble with an ex-priest's story: "They could never figure out why his name was Williams, because he'd told them his parents were Greek. They figured all Greek names should sound like Aliki, Plato, or souvlaki" (132). In response, Sherman explains that "Lakota rez boys would never have laughed at a Greek for having a name like Williams, not because we were polite, but because we had no idea what a Greek name should sound like. In my experience, no mid-60s high school student had the slightest idea who Plato was, and certainly none of us had ever heard of souvlaki, much less tasted it."[9] Given such a statement by a Lakota who grew up precisely where Louis sets his novel, it is surprising to see Sherman Alexie declare, "when I read a poem about rez life written by Adrian C. Louis, I know that he lives on a rez and can trust that he has seen what he's talking about."[10] Does living on a "rez" make whatever one says entirely trustworthy? If so, anthropologists might make reliable Indian novelists. Sherman goes on to point out that Louis gets the date of Custer's demise wrong by a decade in his novel and aims a still more damning criticism at the book:

> What's more, Louis exploits alcoholism and other severe social problems on Pine Ridge, just so he can get a few laughs. A non-Oglala critic might say he uses graveside humor as a way of contrasting fuzzy ideals with the icepick realities of reservation life, but I just found myself offended at his liberal use of Oglalas as the butt of every joke, the subject of every caricature. It was like Amos 'n Andy Visit the Rez.
>
> True, Sherman Alexie uses humor to show the difficulties of living on a reservation, but his sharp humor is softened by a real humanity, a deep caring for the people about whom he writes. Adrian Louis, by contrast, does no more than tell outhouse-wall one-liners about drunks and sex addicts. He occasionally descends into bathos, which he seems to see as the true depth of emotion underlying the Lakota version of stoicism. He doesn't have Alexie's talent, nor, it seems, his love for the people.[11]

Gloria Bird, echoing Marlon Sherman's criticism of Louis but apparently not quite agreeing about the depth of Alexie's compassion for his Indian subjects, brings an even more critical eye to bear in a review of Sherman Alexie's best-selling first novel, *Reservation Blues*, labeling the work "an exaggerated version of reservation life, one that perpetuates many of the stereotypes of native peoples and presents problems for native and non-native readers alike." Bird argues that not only are alcoholism and drinking "sensationalized" in the book, but that "Stereotyping native peoples does not supply a native readership with soluble ways of undermining stereotypes, but becomes a part of the problem, and returns an image of a generic Indian back to the original producers of that image." Perhaps Bird's most perceptive criticism of this novel is that it "omits the core of native community, and exists solely in the marginal realm of its characters who are all misfits: social and cultural anomalies. It is a partial portrait of a community wherein there is no evidence of Spokane culture or traditions, or anything uniquely Spokane" (47, 49, 51).

The Lakota writer and critic Elizabeth Cook-Lynn has published a similar if idiosyncratically skewed analysis of both Louis and Alexie, arguing that

> Several new works in fiction that catalogue the deficit model of Indian reservation life, such as *Skins* by Adrian Louis . . . and *Reservation Blues* by Sherman Alexie . . . have been published in this decade. These are significant because they reflect little or no defense of treaty-protected reservation land bases as homelands to the indigenes, nor do they suggest a responsibility of art as an ethical endeavor or the artist as responsible social critic, a marked departure from the early renaissance works of such luminaries as N. Scott Momaday and Leslie Marmon Silko.

Cook-Lynn, while seeming to base the largest portion of her analysis of Indian writing on whether that writing reflects what she very vaguely terms "tribal realism," cites Bird's statement that in Alexie's work "Native cultures are used like props," and that "Sprinkled like bait are sage-smudging, stickgame, sweet grass enough to titillate the curiosity of non-Indian readers" (68). I would be quite a hypocrite if I did not point out that Cook-Lynn also targets just about every other Indian writer in this same essay, including not only Erdrich but also "the works of writers who call themselves mixed-bloods," a list that begins with the names of Gerald Vizenor and Louis Owens (66–67).

Putting aside for now Cook-Lynn's troubled attitude toward "mixed-bloods," a subject to be addressed in another chapter of this volume, I will add that virtually the same critique Cook-Lynn aims at *Reservation Blues* might be made of Alexie's extremely popular *The Lone Range and Tonto Fistfight in Heaven*, though in this story collection the compassion Marlon Sherman alluded to is more evident, the exploitation less so, and the art far more impressive. Portions of my own very enthusiastic review of this collection, always identified not with me but with *The Boston Globe* for which it was written, keep turning up on Alexie's dust jackets, as in this quote from the jacket for *Indian Killer*: "Again and again, Alexie's prose startles and dazzles with unexpected, impossible-to-anticipate moves. . . . Sherman Alexie has become quite clearly an important new voice in American literature." This review has been quoted on the jackets of *The Lone Ranger* and *Reservation Blues* as well, with the most lengthy blurb on each jacket, in fact, taken from the review. I must confess to feeling somewhat slighted when Leslie Silko's much briefer blurb on the jacket of *Indian Killer* (just below my own words on the same jacket) is cited as "Leslie Marmon Silko, *The Nation*." Humbled, I can only accept the fact that while my words are deemed worthy, my name apparently has little market value.

Obviously, blurb credit or no blurb credit, I found Alexie's prose in *The Lone Ranger* original and in many ways brilliant and extraordinary. Nonetheless, I also find myself in strong agreement with Bird's and Cook-Lynn's critiques, and would expand those critiques to include several of the more commercially and popularly successful Native American novels. Furthermore, I would argue that self-destructive, self-deprecatory humor provides an essential matrix for this fiction because such humor deflects any "lesson in morality" from the non-Native reader and allows authors to maintain an aggressive posture regarding an essential "authentic" Indianness while simultaneously giving the commercial market and reader exactly what they want and expect in the form of stereotype and cliché: what Vizenor terms the "absolute fake."

Why would a non-Indian, predominantly white Euramerican audience want such fiction? To begin with, such novels depict Indians who are nonthreatening to a white readership. It took five hundred years to sweep Indians off the main playing board of American expansionism, to mold Indians into something of "ethnostaligic" value that was not also obstructionist to the manifest dreams of America. The last thing a mainstream readership wants today is a body of writing that presents Indians as threatening and disturbing in any way, that is, Indians as vital and able to assert control over their own destinies and, in so doing, assert a degree of control over white American destiny as well. That does not mean that the reader should not feel sorry for the Indian. Feeling sorry, as I noted above, is good, for it means that the object of our pity is at least relatively impotent and nonthreatening. A fiction that shows Indian communities in dysfunctional disarray, fragmented and turned inward in a frenzy of alcoholism and mutual self-destruction—whether the community be Pine Ridge or a Spokane reservation—is both entertaining and comfortable to the non-Native reader. Such fiction tells the reader that the Indian is a helpless, romantic victim still in the process of vanishing just as he is supposed to do.

Alexie's subtly named John Smith, the utterly lost and suicidal protagonist of *Indian Killer*, fills this role perfectly. He is a noble prototype of the Indian warrior, but because he was adopted at birth by white parents, he has absolutely no cultural foundation, no identity. He is not tragic, but romantically pathetic. His suicide is telegraphed from the first moments we meet him, and all attempts by the author to make him intimidating are as limp as steamed frybread. The same can be said of the disenfranchised protestor of the novel, Marie Polatkin, and the probable "Killer Indian" himself, who survives the novel. Each of these characters appears menacing to whites in some ways, including the killer with his sensationally nightmarish violence, but there is absolutely nothing new or very interesting about this representation because it is so deadeningly familiar. When the Puritan minister Jonathan Edwards, in "Sinners in the Hands of an Angry God," was terrifying his congregation near the beginning of the eighteenth century with the image of the bloody "arrows of death" that fly unseen from the dark forest, he was invoking precisely the same lurid vision of the vengeful savage that Alexie constructs. The effect on Edwards's audience was merely an extreme form of the general terror of unbridled "Indianness" with which the colonizer has been delightfully frightening himself for centuries, the same dark "pow wows" of Hawthorne's foreboding forest.

In *Indian Killer* and other works, Sherman Alexie, a perhaps unwitting product of the dominant culture he abjures in his writing, is telling horror stories to titillate white readers and also presenting readers with a darkly comical, pathetic, self-destructive "lost genera-tion" Indian. Alexie's killer Indian is the psychologically savaged savage, another version of Injun Joe from Twain's *Tom Sawyer* or Blue Duck from Larry McMurtry's *Lonesome Dove*. The reader can both shed a tear and shiver a little, but at the same time feel secure while shaking his head in disbelief and humorous disgust. Too bad the Indians are living such hard lives and destroying themselves, but they are colorful and entertaining at least—if a tad scary in Alexie's latest gothic getup—and of course our metanarrative always told us they would end up this way.

Alexie's *The Lone Range and Tonto Fistfight in Heaven*, its sequel, *Reservation Blues*, and *Indian Killer* are good illustrations of a kind of presold, commodified Indian fiction, at least partly because Alexie has such an indisputably large degree of talent. A fine poet and prose writer at the level of image, phrase, and anecdote, Alexie presents his reader with sometimes dazzlingly written scenes of Indians who drink themselves to death, beat one another senseless, and survive for the moment with brutal, self-destructive humor. As Gloria Bird has pointed out, there is no community represented in *Reservation Blues* except the community of imploding and vanishing Indians; the same is true for other Alexie fictions. The mystical center in *The Lone Ranger* and *Reservation Blues*, or one might say the traditional and sacred center, would seem to be a cartoonish character called Big Mama who appears in both books and who lives somewhere outside the vague community on a mountain that is a kind of Never-Never Land. She communicates with her Indian relations via a very cute, miniature tom-tom pager. Characters and culture in these works represent vague, decaying fragments incapable of being shored against anyone's ruin.

In his second novel, *Indian Killer* (1996), Alexie moves still farther away from the surface brilliance of *The Lone Ranger* into a flat-footed prose that preaches didactically at the reader while foregrounding, yet again, Indians who repetitiously protest the exploitation and appropriation of their cultures while exhibiting almost no traces at all of the cultures supposedly being appropriated. Epitomizing this is the primary female character, Marie Polatkin, who organizes protest after protest but almost never returns to her own reservation community (or does so secretly by night) and shows no signs of being a product of any coherent community, Indian or otherwise. All Marie knows how to do is to protest the existence of white people. She exists only in her absent Indianness—like Belladonna Darwin Winter-Catcher in Vizenor's *Bearheart*—the breathing example of Euramerica's long determination to define Indian by absence. In this work, Alexie simply tells the reader what he wants the reader to hear, with some attention to a who-done-it plot but very little attempt to construct artful literature. Rather than resonating with the richness of traditional oral storytelling found in such a work as *The Lone Ranger*, the novel reads like a prosaic university case study, with the prose seldom if ever rising above the too-obvious level of basic information. In an April 1997 Internet exchange, Alexie complains, "Well, what would a twelve year old rez kid do with Vizenor's transgressive lit?" and confesses, "I don't know what's going on in Vizenor's work most of the time." Finally, in the same "chat-line" conversation, Alexie says, "And if a work of Nat Lit is unusable by a 12 year [sic] Indian kid living on the rez, then what's the purpose?"12 Perhaps *Indian Killer* represents Alexie's attempt to write literature "usable" by a twelve-year-old rez kid. But what kind of model, one must ask, does such a novel provide, even if such an adolescent could slog his or her way through it?

With *The Lone Ranger*, *Reservation Blues*, and *Indian Killer*, it has become obvious that Alexie's fiction, while at times exposing the same dazzling surface Silko found in Erdrich's best writing, too often simply reinforces all of the stereotypes desired by white readers: his bleakly absurd and aimless Indians are imploding in a passion of self-destructiveness and self-loathing; there is no family or community center toward which his characters, like Momaday's Abel in *House Made of Dawn*, Welch's unnamed narrator in *Winter in the Blood*, Silko's Tayo in *Ceremony*, or Thomas King's Will in *Medicine River* might turn for coherence; and in the process of self-destruction the Indians provide Euramerican readers with pleasurable moments of dark humor or the titillation of bloodthirsty savagery. Above all, the non-Indian reader of Alexie's work is allowed to come away with a sense—as

Silko said about Erdrich's fiction—that no one is really to blame but the Indians, no matter how loudly the author shouts his anger.

Alexie himself seems to coyly, even guiltily, confess his own culpability as author when, in a brief story from *The Lone Ranger* titled "Amusements," he describes two young Indians putting a drunken Indian friend—"Dirty Joe"—on a roller coaster as public spectacle. "Twenty or thirty white faces, open mouths grown large and deafening, wide eyes turned toward me and Sadie," the narrator confesses. "They were jury and judge for the twentieth-century fancydance of these court jesters who would pour Thunderbird wine into the Holy Grail" (567). Court jesters indeed, the two young people are enacting in miniature precisely what Alexie has done with his work thus far. The wide eyes and open mouths describe the titillated reader rather well. As a result, the reader gets an entertaining roller-coaster tour of a vague place called Indian Country, along with a good example of Indian self-loathing, and goes home guiltless and tickled pink (not quite red) by the Indian shenanigans. (After all, "they" put the Indian on the amusement park ride, not "we.") When Alexie poses aggressively in his writing and public appearances as a "real" Indian writer—in contrast to "unreal" Indian writers such as the shallow character of Jack Wilson in *Indian Killer*—he is being accurate, for the "real" Indian is the one created by the Euramerican culture that defined the authoritative utterance "Indian" and the construction thus signified. The average white novel buyer can easily recognize a real Indian, of course, and Alexie gives the reader both sides of the static coin Gerald Vizenor condemns: the noble savage and the bloodthirsty savage, both of whom are doomed with a big and static "D". In summary, one must say that it is a shrewd posture for an author who wishes to have an essentialist cake and sell it, too, even if he does not perhaps understand what he is doing.

Writing of the earliest publications by Native American authors, David Murray has stated: "Anything that was published [by Indians] at least until the point of widespread Indian literacy, was likely to reflect the tastes of a white audience, and conform to a large extent to what at least some of them thought it was appropriate for an Indian to write. Indian writers are mainly going to materialise, therefore, only when what they say meets a white need" (*Forked Tongues*, 57). I would argue that anything published by Indians that meets with widespread popular and commercial success today must still conform to Murray's definition. If a writer is a brilliant tactician, like Momaday in *House Made of Dawn*, for example, the text may "reflect the tastes of a white audience" or Pulitzer jury while simultaneously reflecting a deeply indigenous world view. But even such a subtle and aesthetically impressive accomplishment is not likely to achieve bestsellerdom.

Gerald Vizenor and Sherman Alexie are at opposite ends of the spectrum of contemporary Indian writing. Vizenor shuns the Trojan horse that allowed N. Scott Momaday to cleverly subvert modernism; instead, as what might be termed in Vizenorese a poststructuralist postindian, Vizenor comes out directly in his trickster discourse and attacks all hypocrisies from a very traditionally Indian point of view— as trickster—appropriating poststructuralist discourse in the process. Alexie, operating securely within the tragic, causal parameters of modernism, constructs a different kind of Trojan horse in the form of "Indian anger," posing militantly while giving the white audience what it already knows and desires and, as Gloria Bird astutely observed, offering Indian readers plenty of anger but no ground upon which to make a cultural stand.

To put this critique into the critical/historical perspective I began to establish at the beginning of this chapter, I will add that I believe the most popularly and commercially successful Native American works thus far are marked by a dominant shared characteristic: They are the direct heirs of the modernist tradition of naturalistic despair, of which the Indian is the quintessential illustration, as we see clearly in Faulkner and Hemingway (Willa Cather would be another good choice). My favorite example of this iconography of the Vanishing American in American modernism is Faulkner's "Chief Doom," or "l'Homme," whom Faulkner called "a man of wit and imagination" and who (being a man of foresight, we assume) anglicised his own name to "Doom." Faulkner himself never seemed able to decide if Ikkemotubbe, the original of "Doom," was Chickasaw or Choctaw. Hemingway's doomed Indians, for their part, drink uncontrollably, are sexually "loose," are close to nature (as guides for white men), and cut their throats as Indian babies are born in a nicely neutralizing metaphor.[13]

What we find in the modern versions of "Chief Doom" are caricatures inherited from the centuries-old tradition of the doomed, tragic savage. These "new" Indian novels, by "authentic" Indian authors, articulate in sometimes extraordinarly well-disguised form the familiar stereotype of the Vanishing American, the crucial difference being that white people no longer have to shoot or hang the Native, who is quite willing to do the job him- or herself. Most crucially, they are human beings incapable of asserting any control over their lives, infantalized and cirrhotic, waiting to exit stage west. What do Euramerican readers want to see in works by American Indian authors? They want what they have always wanted, from Fenimore Cooper to the present: Indians who are romantic, unthreatening, and self-destructive. Indians who are enacting, in one guise or another, the process of vanishing. Borrowing from William Faulkner, that epic poet of inexorable, tragic history, I'll call this the "Chief Doom" school of literature. It seems we cannot escape it, even when it is manifested as a form of inner-colonization.

"Grinning Aboriginal Demons"

Gerald Vizenor's *Bearheart* and the End of Tragedy

◆

The Anishinaabe writer Gerald Vizenor will have none of Chief Doom, the tragic mixedblood, or the pathos of self-destructive, culturally impotent tribal peoples; nor will he accept the gothic inheritance that figures as what an Indian person might call "ghost sickness"—that haunting presence reminding Euramerica of a lost innocence and a displaced and doomed (ghostly) race. Mixedbloods, on the contrary, in Vizenor's writing become vital signifiers of what he calls "survivance," tropes that "loosen the seams in the shrouds of identities." The mixedblood, Vizenor declares, "is a new metaphor . . . a transitive contradancer between communal tribal cultures and those material and urban pretensions that counter conservative traditions" ("Crows Written on the Poplars," 101).

In his first novel, *Darkness in Saint Louis Bearheart* (1978), Vizenor contradances across the gothic landscape of postindustrial America with a band of mixedblood pilgrim clowns on a quest for both liberation from artifact and a self-forged identity as a "new metaphor." In this postapocalyptic rejection of modernist despair, Vizenor inverts the inherited paradigms of the American gothic, substituting what Vizenor himself calls a "postindian" perspective for that of the feared and fearful American Adam so vividly elucidated by D. H. Lawrence, Leslie Fiedler, Richard Slotkin, et al. For Vizenor's Indians, the haunted landcape of America is not the "New World wilderness" with its terrifying disintegrative potential that transfixes the Natty

Bumppo of the Euramerican soul. For these characters the whispers of "Doom! Doom! Doom!" that Lawrence found "in the dark trees of America" emanate from the ruined machinery of Western civilization, and that particular doom signifies new life. The gothic disturbance that assaults cultural identity and coherence arises not out of the pure "otherness" of wilderness in Vizenor's writing, as it does in the American canon, but rather out of the immanently present landscape of a ravaged postindustrial world. Vizenor's Native Americans find themselves in a position paradoxically similar to that of present-day Romans: they inhabit a world of ruins that testify to past greatness. It is deeply ironic, however, that for American Indians the existing monuments to an ideal past consist of mountains, rivers, and trees—topographical tropes of a seemingly lost coherence and identity-conferring order.

Even more ironic is the fact that the American Indian finds him/herself in a never-ending struggle to escape from imprisonment as static artifact within the discourse of the American myth—a struggle Vizenor has defined as the "word wars." The evolving myth of Euramerica—depending even from colonial beginnings upon guilt and fear as the essential flip side of platonic self-realization (the eighteenth-century genius Jonathan Edwards brilliantly exploited this awareness in his most famous sermon, "Sinners in the Hands of An Angry God")—demanded the presence of the Indian in the dark heart of the continent as the mirroring "other." Melville illuminates this point superbly in the final scene of *Moby-Dick* with his doomed native, Tashtego (described as "the sunken head of the Indian at the mainmast"):

A sky-hawk that tauntingly had followed the main-truck downwards from its natural home among the stars, pecking at the flag, and incommoding Tashtego there; this bird now chanced to intercept its broad fluttering wing between the hammer and the wood; and simultaneously feeling that etherial thrill, *the submerged savage beneath, in his death-grasp*, kept his hammer frozen there; so the bird of heaven, with archangelic shrieks, and his imperial beak thrust upwards, and his whole captive form folding in the flag of Ahab, went down with the ship, which, like Satan, would not sink to hell till she had dragged a living part of heaven along with her, and helmeted herself with it.

Thus the "submerged savage" takes the doomed bird of heaven down into the center of the great naturalistic vortex, an index to the heart of ultimate darkness in the colonial experience. And as Melville so splendidly recognized, without the Indian as a static referent, the threat to the white psyche would remain unacceptably disembodied and amorphous, internalized and unsignified.

"Some upsetting is necessary," Vizenor has warned, and in *Bearheart*, as his pilgrims move across the devastated surface of an America whose machinery has broken down, Vizenor undertakes this upsetting in an act of deconstruction, freeing "postindian" identity from the "shroud" of the American metanarrative, inverting the gothic landscape, liberating language from what he calls "terminal creeds." *Bearheart*, in fact, effectively scuttles the currency of the tragic mixedblood in American literature. A wild parody of Chaucer and the entire westering metanarrative of American history outlined in Turner's famous essay, Vizenor's novel draws deeply upon Anishinaabe trickster tales to let loose upon corrupt America a horde of shape-shifting mixedblood clowns on a quest for liberation from artifact and a search for identity as "new metaphor." Inhabiting that space of infinite chance falling between signifier and signified, Vizenor's trickster mixedbloods refuse definition and thus all borders.

In an interview, Vizenor has described his desire to deconstruct the artifact of static "Indianness":

what I'm pursuing in much of my writing is the idea of the invented Indian. The inventions have become disguises. Much of the power we have is universal, generative in life itself and specific to our consciousness here. . . . There's another idea that I have worked into the stories, about terminal creeds. I worked that into the novel *Bearheart*. It occurs, obviously, in written literature and in totalitarian systems. . . . This occurs in invented Indians because we're invented and we're invented from traditional static standards and we are stuck in coins and words like artifacts. So we take up a belief and settle with it, stuck, static. (Bowers and Silet, 45–47)

In *Bearheart*, as his pilgrims trek across ravaged America, deconstructing all border signs as they wander, Vizenor accomplishes an impressive range of satirical upsetting.

Though I have discussed this seminal work at length elsewhere, this complex novel bears some brief recapitulation, for it stands in vivid contrast to certain of the works discussed above.[1] Vizenor's novel-within-a-novel that tells the story of the mixedblood pilgrims is authored by a character named Bearheart, a mixedblood trickster employed in BIA offices under attack by American Indian Movement radicals. "When we are not victims to the white man then we become victims to ourselves," Bearheart declares, in a statement aptly describing integral elements of the fiction of Erdrich, Alexie, Louis, and others.

"In trickster narratives," Vizenor has written, "the listeners and readers imagine their liberation; the trickster is a sign, and the world is 'deconstructed' in a discourse."[2] All of Vizenor's work represents such a liberation, a brilliant attempt to free us from romantic entrapments—especially victimage—and to liberate the imagination. The principal targets of his writing are the signs "Indian" and "mixedblood," with their predetermined and well-worn paths between signifier and signified. Vizenor's aim is to free the play between these two elements, to liberate "Indianness" in all its manifestations. Like the trickster of traditional Native American stories, Vizenor's mixedbloods militantly resist definition. For Vizenor, who insists upon conflating trickster/mixedblood, the role of trickster is to dismember all constructions that impose definitions and limit possibilities, to ensure that signifier and signified participate in a process of "continually breaking apart and re-attaching in new combinations" (Harvey, 49). In his essay, "Trickster Discourse," Vizenor quotes Jacques Lacan, who warns us not to "cling to the illusion that the signifier answers to the function of representing the signified, or better, that the signifier has to answer for its existence in the name of any signifier whatever."[3] At the same time, however, trickster shows by inversion—negative example—the necessity for humanity to control and order our world.

Just as Mourning Dove, in *Cogewea*, clearly identified with her codeswitching, mixedblood protagonist, Vizenor identifies with trickster, the figure that mediates between oppositions, and in the words of Warwick Wadlington, "embodies two antithetical, nonrational experiences of man with the natural world, his society, and his own psyche." Citing Wadlington, Vizenor stresses the duality of trickster's role as on the one hand "a force of treacherous disorder that outrages and disrupts, and on the other hand, an unanticipated, usually unintentional benevolence in which trickery is at the expense of inimical forces and for the benefit of mankind."[4]

Out of his determined resistance to the terminal definitions of "Indianness" imposed upon indigenous Americans for five hundred years and his insistence upon what he calls "trickster discourse," Vizenor has almost single-handedly, and in the face of astonishing ignorance on the part of literate, critical America, moved toward a theoretics of Native American writing, which he terms "trickster hermeneutics." "The tragic tribal tales," he argues in *Manifest Manners* (1994), "are simulations for an audience familiar with manifest manners and the literature of dominance. Decidedly, the stories that turn the tribes tragic are not their own stories." In the same text, Vizenor declares:

> The sources of natural reason and tribal consciousness are doubt and wonder, not nostalgia or liberal melancholy for the lost wilderness; comic not tragic. . . .Trickster hermeneutics is the interpretation of simulations in the literature of survivance, the ironies of descent and racialism, transmutation, third gender, and themes of transformation in oral tribal stories and written literature. . . . Tricksters are the translation of creation. (15)

Bearheart charts a new course for American Indian fiction and American literature as a whole.[5] If Momaday's *House Made of Dawn* is the nearly perfect simulacrum of a modernist novel, Vizenor's *Bearheart*, published only ten years after *House Made of Dawn*, is the first and still the most noteworthy postmodern Native American novel. At the same time, however, it is a narrative thoroughly in the tradition of Native American trickster tales, insisting as it does upon values of community versus individuality, upon syncretic and dynamic values versus the cultural suicide inherent in stasis, upon the most delicate of harmonies between human beings and the world we inhabit, and upon humanity's ultimate responsibility for that world. The primary trickster and fictional author of this novel-within-a-novel is old Bearheart, the mixedblood shaman ensconced in the BIA offices being ransacked by American Indian Movement radicals as the book begins.[6] Bearheart, who as a child achieved his vision of the bear while imprisoned in a BIA school closet, has written the book we will read. He directs a female AIM radical with her chicken feathers and plastic beads to the novel locked in a file cabinet, the "book about tribal futures, futures without oil and governments to blame for personal failures." To her question, "What is the book about?" Bearheart answers first, "Sex and violence," before adding, "Travels through terminal creeds and social deeds escaping from evil into the fourth world where bears speak the secret languages of saints" (xii–xiv), certainly not a blurb to encourage major New York publishers.

"Terminal creeds" in *Bearheart* are beliefs that seek to fix, to impose static definitions upon the world. Such attempts are destructive, suicidal, even when the definitions appear to arise out of revered tradition. Third Proude Cedarfair expresses Vizenor's message when he says very early in the novel, "Beliefs and traditions are not greater than the love of living" (11), a declaration repeated near the end of the novel in Fourth Proude's statement that "The power of the human spirit is carried in the heart not in histories and materials" (214).

While the authorial voice explains that Rosina, Proude's wife, "did not see herself in the abstract as a series of changing ideologies" (35), most of the pilgrims in this narrative, to varying degrees, do indeed suffer from the illness of terminal creeds. Bishop Omax Parasimo is "obsessed with the romantic and spiritual power of tribal people" (71), a believer in the Hollywood or New Age version of Indianness. Matchi Makwa, another pilgrim, chants, "Our women were poisoned part white," leading Fourth Proude to explain, "Matchi Makwa was taken with evil word sorcerers" (55).

Belladonna Darwin-Winter Catcher, the most obvious victim of terminal creeds in Vizenor's novel, attempts to define herself as "Indian," and can only do so, of course, by resorting to the "absolute fake" that is the "Indian" invented by Euramerica. Belladonna does not heed the warning Proude offers when he says, "We become the terminal creeds we speak" (143). Belladonna attempts to become the "hyperreal" simulacrum, which is the absence, as Vizenor explains, of the "tribal real." There is no life, no change, no future in such a static pose. When the pilgrims come to Orion, a walled town inhabited by the descendents of famous hunters and western bucking-horse breeders, Belladonna is asked to define "tribal values." She replies with a string of well-worn clichés most readers will recognize, stating, "We are tribal and that means that we are children of dreams and visions . . . Our bodies are connected to mother earth and our minds are part of the clouds . . . Our voices are the living breath of the wilderness." A hunter replies, "My father and grandfathers three generations back were hunters. . . . They said the same things about the hunt that you said is tribal . . . Are you telling me that what you are saying is exclusive to your mixedblood race?" Belladonna snaps, "Yes!" adding, "I am different than a whiteman because of my values and my blood is different . . . I would not be white." She continues, contradicting much of what we have witnessed thus far in the novel: "Tribal people seldom touch each other. . . . We do not invade the personal bodies of others and we do not stare at people when we are talking . . . Indians have more magic in their lives than whitepeople" (190–91).

A hunter responds: "Tell me about this Indian word you use, tell me which Indians are you talking about, or are you talking for all Indians" (191). Finally, the hunter asks the question that cuts through the dark heart of the novel and all of the novels we call "Native American": "What does Indian mean?" Not understanding that to attempt to answer is to fail the test, Belladonna replies with more clichéd phrases, and the hunter says flatly, "Indians are an invention. . . . You tell me that the invention is different than the rest of the world when it was the rest of the world that invented the Indian. . . . Are you speaking as an invention?" (191). The hunters and breeders applaud Belladonna's pose and then give the invention her "just desserts": a cookie sprinkled with a time-release alkaloid poison. "Your mixedblood friend is a terminal believer and a victim of her own narcissism," a breeder says to the pilgrims (194). That the poison is a "time-release" is finely ironic, since the goal of the invention of "Indianness" has been to freeze the indigenous inhabitants of America within timelessness, outside of history. Time, that is life, destroys the unchanging "authentic" Indian.

At the What Cheer Trailer Ruins, the pilgrims encounter additional victims of terminal creeds, the Evil Gambler's mixedblood horde: "The three mixedbloods, dressed in diverse combinations of tribal vestments and martial uniforms, bangles and ideological power patches and armbands. . . . Deep furrows of ignorance and intolerance stretched across their unwashed foreheads" (99). In an experience common not merely to Native Americans but to all marginalized peoples in the nation, the three killers feel themselves, with some accuracy, to be the victims of white America. In a familiar pattern, however, the oppressed become the oppressors. Vizenor and his pilgrims will have no part of self-pity and abdication of personal responsibility and use withering satire to dismantle what the novel calls, "Breathing plastic artifacts from reservation main street" and "classic hobbycraft mannikins dressed in throwaway pantribal vestments, promotional hierograms of cultural suicide" (100).

From the Trailer Ruins, the pilgrims travel westward on foot, encountering hordes of deformed stragglers on the broken highways. These cripples and monsters are, in the words of one pilgrim, "Simple cases of poisoned genes" ravaged by the horrors of the modern world. The authorial voice in this very ecologically conscious novel describes the national suicide: "First the fish died, the oceans turned sour, and then birds dropped in flight over cities, but it was not until thousands of children were born in the distorted shapes of evil animals that the government cautioned the chemical manufacturers. Millions of people had lost parts of their bodies to malignant neoplasms from cosmetics and chemical poisons in the air and food" (142). Insisting blindly on identifying the cripples as romantic, tragic signifiers, Little Big Mouse is attacked and torn to pieces by a mob of technology's victims.

Following the canonization of Saint Plumero, a ceremony making Bigfoot a "double saint," the pilgrims arrive at Bioavaricious, Kansas, and the Bioavaricious Regional Word Hospital, where terminal creeds—language whose meaning is fixed, language without creative play—are the goal of the hospital staff. In an attempt to rectify what is perceived as a national linguistic breakdown, the scientists at the word hospital are using a "dianoetic chromatic encoder" to "code and then reassemble the unit values of meaning in a spoken sentence" (163). We are told that with "regenerated bioelectrical energies and electromagnetic fields, conversations were stimulated and modulated for predetermined values. Certain words and ideas were valued and reinforced with bioelectric stimulation" (164). This attempt to create an impossibly pure "readerly" prose stands in sharp contrast to the oral tradition defined in a description of life among *Bearheart's* displaced just a few pages earlier:

> Oral traditions were honored. Families welcomed the good tellers of stories, the wandering historians of follies and tragedies. Readers and writers were seldom praised but the travelling raconteurs were one form of the new shamans on the interstates. Facts and the need for facts had died with newspapers and politics. Nonfacts were more believable. The listeners traveled with the tellers through the same frames of time and place. The telling was in the listening. . . . Myths became the center of meaning again. (158)

In oral traditions people define themselves and their place in an imagined universe, a definition necessarily dynamic and requiring constantly changing stories. The listeners recreate the story in the act of hearing and responding. As Vizenor himself has written elsewhere, "Creation myths are not time bound, the creation takes place in the telling, in present-tense metaphors" (*Earthdivers*, xii). Predetermined values represent stasis and thus cultural suicide. Critic Roland Barthes says simply, "the meaning of a work (or of a text) cannot be created by the work alone. . . " (Barthes, *Critical Essays*, xi).

Two of the pilgrims, dazzled by the word hospital, remain at Bioavaricious while the others continue their journey toward New Mexico (the very name, like so many others on the American map, suggestive of the myth of an older world made new). As they move westward, the pilgrims and sacred clowns meet fewer deformed victims of cultural genocide until finally they encounter the modern, ancient pueblos of the Southwest and a people living as they have always lived. At Jemez Pueblo, the Walatowa Pueblo of N. Scott Momaday's *House Made of Dawn*, the pilgrims encounter two sacred clowns who, with their traditional wooden phalluses, outclown even Saint Plumero himself. The clowns direct Proude and the others toward Chaco Canyon—home of the "old ones"—where, finally, Proude and Inawa Biwide soar through the vision window into the fourth world as bears at the winter solstice.

Central to *Bearheart* is the identification by the author's author, Vizenor, with trickster, the figure that mediates between oppositions. In the figure of trickster, all dialectics are resolved through a rejection of resolution or closure, including that dialectic between light and dark, past and present, civilization and wilderness, empiricism and intuition, coherence and psychic disintigration that is at the core of the American gothic. Harsh laughter is the matrix out of which Vizenor's fiction arises, the kind of laughter Mikhail Bakhtin finds at the roots of the modern novel. "As a distanced image a subject cannot be comical," Bakhtin writes; "to be made comical, it must be brought close" (23). The Indian in the American imagination is such a distanced image, one weighted with epic, and thus tragic, significance, a creature of the absolute past. This is the hero who, according to Bakhtin, "by his very nature, must perish" (36). The Indian's unwilling role in the drama played out along America's receding frontier and upon center stage in the drama of America's mythmaking is inexorably epic and tragic. Once the Indian is free to imagine his own destiny or plot—and, incredibly, to empower himself through laughter at others as well as himself—he escapes from the gothic dialectic that demands nothing less than his doom (and gloom). Without "Chief Doom" (or "Injun Joe," et al) that mirroring "other" of Indianness would disappear, running off like Ken Kesey's "Chief Broom" (Chief Doom's un-evil Twin?) toward a revitalized and disastrously unthreatening wilderness and leaving the gothic imagination half-formed in America. Writing of the novel, Bakhtin continues:

Everything that makes us laugh is close at hand, all comical creativity works in a zone of maximal proximity. Laughter has the remarkable power of making an object come up close, of drawing it into a zone of crude contact where one can finger it familiarly on all sides, turn it upside down, inside out, peer at it from above and below, break open its external shell, look into its center, doubt it, take it apart, dismember it, lay it bare and expose it, examine it freely and experiment with it. Laughter demolishes fear and piety before an object, before a world, making of it an object of familiar contact and thus clearing the ground for an absolutely free investigation of it. (23)

In Bakhtin's words, we find a precise definition of the humor and method of the Native American trickster, s/he who brings the world close and directs this "comical operation of dismemberment" (24), laying bare the hypocrisies, false fears, and pieties and clearing the ground "for an absolutely free investigation" of worldy fact. This is not the kind of self-deprecating, self-destructively bleak humor found in fiction by such writers as Alexie or Louis, however, for the static referent at the heart of books such as *Reservation Blues* or *Skins* is the self-destructive, doomed savage. Fear and piety are not demolished before this static "object" or doomed Native world; rather the distance is assured by keeping the reader voyeuristically outside of the pathos and inexorability of the Indians' doom. The Indian world is made familiar only insofar as it gives back to the reader the preconceived stereotype constructed by Euramerica, and that world is the world of the "absolute fake" invented Indian.

Bakhtin's explanation of the effects of these parodic forms in ancient art applies well to Vizenor's fiction: "These parodic-travestying forms . . . liberated the object from the power of language in which it had become entangled as if in a net; they destroyed the homogenizing power of myth over language; they freed consciousness from the power of the direct word, destroyed the thick walls that had imprisoned consciousness within its own discourse, within its own language" (60).

The liberation of language and consciousness is Vizenor's aim, particularly the liberation of the signifier "Indian" from the entropic and peculiarly gothic myth surrounding it. Vizenor's method resembles Bakhtin's definition of Minippean satire:

The familiarizing role of laughter is here considerably more powerful, sharper and coarser. The liberty to crudely degrade, to turn inside out the lofty aspects of the world and world views, might sometimes seem shocking. But to this exclusive and comic familiarity must be added an intense spirit of inquiry and utopian fantasy. In Minippean satire the unfettered and fantastic plots and situations all serve one goal—to put to the test and to expose ideas and idealogues. . . . Minippean satire is dialogic, full of parodies and travesties, multi-styled, and does not fear elements of bilingualism. (26)

Vizenor's "parodia sacra" is often shocking, his plots "unfettered and fantastic" and designed to serve the one goal Bakhtin defines: to test and expose ideas and idealogues. This "one goal" is largely missing from the one-dimensional black humor of some contemporary Native American novels, as is the "intense spirit of inquiry and utopian fantasy." The humor of victimage—of Alexie's "Dirty Joe" on the roller coaster—participates not in dialogic but in the monologue of dominance that puts no idea or idealogue to the test and appears unaware of the utopian implications of trickster discourse.

In achieving his "transitive" balancing act, Vizenor frees the American Indian from America's narrative of tribal doom. He "demolishes fear and piety" before the American myth so deadly to contemporary Native American identity and destroys the walls that imprison the consciousness—Indian and Euramerican alike—"within its own discourse." The "grinning, unappeased aboriginal demons" of D. H. Lawrence's American gothic metamorphose into powerful Native tricksters as Vizenor mocks the American myth with its sacrosanct westering journey into psychic and literal wilderness.

What must be most strongly emphasized is Vizenor's mockery of those, non-Native and Native American alike, who would recreate the static artifact and incarcerate once more the "object"—Indian—within "the power of language in which it ha[s] become entangled as if in a net"; unlike Vizenor, the writers who manipulate the new Vanishing American (the "absolute fake" that signals the "absence of the real") through blackly humorous and culturally empty representations of dysfunctional, self-destructive, vaguely defined communities and individuals are reestablishing what Bakhtin calls "the homogenizing power of myth over language." Such exploiters of Indian stereotypes, while giving the publishing/reading world what is expected, reimprison "consciousness" within the power of the direct word, reconstructing "the thick walls that [have] imprisoned consciousness within its own discourse, within its own language: the discourse and language of Euramerican "Indianness."

2

Filming the Territory

◆

8

The Invention of John Wayne

◆

I grew up distrusting and even disliking John Wayne. Even before I learned that the "Duke" began life as a midwestern boy named Marion Michael Morrison, I suspected that he was not real. For one thing, he seemed too big and too inescapable, always there during my childhood, spurring his horse across all of our lives, looming large in doorways and blocking the light. Sure, there were others such as Tex Ritter, Hoot Gibson, and Tom Mix; there were the Sons of the Pioneers and still more. But compared to John Wayne the rest were unimposing and rather likable heroes, resembling a bunch of friendly but ineffectual uncles. John Wayne was bigger and more dangerous than all of them, and from the beginning he seemed both mean—the kind of uncle who might backhand you after a few drinks—and unconvincing (maybe ill tempered because he himself suspected that he was not real).

I was conscious of being Indian—part Choctaw on my father's side and part Cherokee on my mother's. I was not sure exactly what it meant to be "part" something, especially in California where we had come to live, but I knew I was in some inexorable way "Indian" just as I knew I was a hick from Mississippi who said "Yes, Ma'am" and Yes, Sir" to teachers and was therefore an appropriate object of ridicule for the kids in school. It did not take long to recognize that Indians inhabited a troubled and troubling space in John Wayne movies. It was not only that Indians—fullbloods like Geronimo or mixedbloods like me—were simply moving targets in his films, as they were in most westerns. In nearly all the films I saw in theaters or on television, the Indians' role was to ride wildly in circles on painted ponies while sturdy white men crouched behind covered wagons and shot the Indians off their horses, one by one, to protect white women and children. Sometimes the Indians got to ride in slow single file along a distant mesa or ridgetop just out of rifle range, silhouetted against the horizon while tom-toms beat in the background. In John Wayne movies, actually, Indians were sometimes treated pretty well, with at least a passing nod to their humanity. There was, nonetheless, an ever-present sense in the "Duke's" films that the Indian did not count and was just a colorful residue of the past, with no stake in the world John Wayne was helping to construct. In fact, after I became an adult and looked more closely at John Wayne's movies, I discovered that as his career developed the Indian faded, so that one of his final movies would be *The Cowboys*—"cowboys-and-Indians" with the cows and boys but no Indians.

As an eight-year-old, however, just inside from playing cowboys and Indians with my ten-year-old brother—who always got to be the cowboy—I listened to young Breck Coleman, John Wayne's character in *The Big Trail* (a 1930 film ancient even in my childhood) explain, "You see, the Indians was my friends. They taught me all I know about the woods. They taught me how to follow a trail. . . . And they taught me how to make the best bow and arrows too." I instinctively knew Breck Coleman was lying. If the young white man had stopped short of the last line, I might have bought the whole thing, but I did not believe Indians would ever have taught that wimpy guy how to make "the best bow and arrows too," or that he even would have been capable of learning. It sounded like the kind of thing I would have said if I was making the same story up on the spot: "And they taught me how to make the best bows and arrows, too." Ha. When I found out John Wayne's real name was Marion, that cut it. I knew then that he had made up everything, the whole kit and caboodle from beginning to end.

I was right about John Wayne. The truth is that he was indeed the great American cowboy hero and Indian fighter, throwing his stalking shadow across the continent and beyond. But it is even more true that he made everything up, reinventing himself during an incredible career in the same way that America has for five hundred years invented and reinvented itself out of its inconsistent and fevered imagination. In the course of more than 150 films, with the Indian as mirroring "other," Marion Morrison grew into the giant figure America demanded, molding himself to match the nation's pathological craving for an archetypal hero fitted to the great, violent myth of the American West. When he died in 1979, the whole world knew clearly that a hero was gone.

Not merely from a Native American point of view but from the perspective of any thinking human being, however, the essential truth about the American hero is his falseness. The giant is a hollow shadow cast by an insecure and alienated population of colonists who have never come to terms with the land they invaded or the people they attempted to both exterminate and emulate. That false and empty shadow is illuminated brilliantly in the shapeshifting that allowed a young Iowa boy named Marion to journey into the mythical American West and become something grand and new and strangely pure while the Indian watched with bemusement and perhaps not a little horror.

As many writers and thinkers have understood, the West the "Duke" rode through was, and continues to be, the greatest dream of all. It is the place where, like F. Scott Fitzgerald's Gatsby, the white man sloughs off old names and histories, sheds whatever flaws he may bear, and makes himself anew. This phenomenal process began, of course, with the Pilgrims and Puritans, who looked westward from the Atlantic shore and saw the Promised Land of something they called the New World. In this untainted New World the European could begin again, unencumbered by anything as old as yesterday. And if the Old World threatened to catch up with him, he could continue westward, ahead of history. He could reimagine himself, leave Marion Morrison behind, and become John Wayne, the "Duke." In the West, no one asked questions and history ended with each breath. In the West, Californians could hunt down the indigenous inhabitants like vermin, slaughter fifty thousand in just two decades in the mid-1800s, enslave their children, steal all of their land, and then forget every bloody thing they had done, their souls washed clean by dreams of El Dorado and Hollywood. In the West, the invader, soaked in blood and lies, could return to the womb of self and be reborn fresh and clean and more deadly than ever.

The true hero of the American West is beyond mundane law because he is beyond its reach—beyond civilization—and he operates not within the laws of man but within those of a manifest God. His great novel *Huckleberry Finn*, Mark Twain once explained, was about a struggle between "a sound heart and a deformed conscience," a struggle won by the heart. However, at the end of that novel Huck knows he can live true to his heart only by escaping from civilization. He declares his intent to "light out for the Territory ahead of the rest." The "Territory" is Indian Territory, the realm beyond civilized consciousness and conscience. In an important sense, the entire American West was "Indian Territory," where men (seldom women) lived according to the heart, not the social conscience. And the heart proved too often to be a sad and brutal measure of humanity. In the West, which began, of course, a few feet beyond the first invader's footfall on the Atlantic Coast, any atrocity was tolerated and ultimately erased from history. In the West, a California newspaper could editorialize: "Now that the general hostilities against the Indians have commenced we hope that the Government will render such aid as will enable the citizens of the north to carry on a war of extermination until the last Redskin of these tribes has been killed." In the West, California's first American governor could declare that "a war of extermination will continue to be waged between the races, until the Indian race becomes extinct" (McGovern, 68, 65).

Regardless of the horrific results, to live true to what Twain called the "sound heart"—and to impose the rules of that heart on a lawless place—requires that the hero approach, in all innocence, a state of divinity. Such a man was Natty Bumppo, the Deerslayer and Leatherstocking of James Fenimore Cooper's nineteenth-century romance novels, and such a man was John Wayne, the direct descendent of Natty. Natty himself, of course, was descended from Lancelot of the Arthurian romances, the flower of knight errantry in fruitless quest for the Holy Grail. Maidens stayed more or less the same, but the dragons became bloodthirsty Indians for the flower of American knighthood. For the American cowboy-quester cum Fisher King, the grail became the American dream of endless youth and unlimited potential, freedom from the constraints of civilization. That so many western heroes are called "Kid"—Billy the Kid, the Comanche Kid, the Ringo Kid, and so forth—testifies to America's desire to hold to a self-willed innocence associated with a preadult state. That these "Kids" are one and all a terribly violent bunch is pretty good evidence that Americans both desire this deadly innocence and recognize its dangers.

To see the pattern of this American myth in John Wayne, one need only examine a handful of the actor's great westerns. A fine example is *Stagecoach* (1939). Set in Monument Valley—one of the unmistakable signifiers of "Indian Country" in westerns and a favorite prop of director John Ford—*Stagecoach* is the story of the Ringo Kid's quest for vengeance against the killer of his father and brother.

Civilization itself is represented in *Stagecoach* by, among other elements, both the proper wife who has come to rugged Arizona to join her husband and the corrupt banker who mouths such oddly contemporary sounding platitudes as "America for Americans" and "What's good for the banks is good for the country." Though the wilderness is obviously a place of cleansing and purification, Ford's version of civilization is inexorable; the time of wild Apaches and rugged individualists such as Ringo is ending. In the second scene of the film, we see a citizens' committee ejecting undesirable elements, a drunken doctor and a prostitute, from their raw Arizona town. Unacceptable to the social conscience of the town, both characters will turn out to have sound hearts, and one, the prostitute Dallas, will be given the chance to reclaim her innocence and start anew with John Wayne, the Ringo Kid.

Ringo has escaped from prison to pursue his murderous quest, but he is quickly arrested by a sympathetic sheriff. However, as the quintessential American hero, Ringo cannot be contained by mundane law. A radical innocent, even projecting a nonsexual aura in his courtship of the demure ex-prostitute, Ringo is freed by the sheriff to execute his personal justice by shooting his family's killers. Like the American hero he is, Ringo is godlike in his freedom and willingness to deal out justice. That his quest ends in "Lordsburg" underscores this aspect of his character. In the end, having cleansed the earth through violence, Ringo is set free by the sheriff to begin a new life with Dallas on Ringo's ranch somewhere "across the border." The couple departs from Lordsburg with the rejuvenated doctor's benediction: "Well, they're saved from the blessings of civilization." The American hero is always saved from civilization, always moving across the border, always lighting out for the territory ahead of the rest. The Indians, meanwhile, fade into the landscape with which they are associated, indices of the place called America with no role in "civilization" and no place across the border.

In *Stagecoach*, John Wayne was a young man playing a young man's role. He embodied the possibility of starting over, of sloughing off the corrupt past (for Ringo, prison) and reclaiming innocence. In keeping with American history and the American metanarrative, the process of reclamation is intensely violent. The ambiguity that might logically spring from this paradox is not apparent in the character of Ringo, however. He begins the film as an innocent and, despite a few killings, seems unchanged in the end. In that early film, the Apaches (played almost exclusively by Navajo actors) are for the most part an offstage menace, symbolizing the undercurrent of violence always threatening to rise up and overwhelm the uncivil West. When for an instant the camera focuses on Geronimo (actor Chief White Horse), on a bluff looking down at the moving stagecoach, however, the face reflects an introspective dignity and strength.

It was Ford's classic, *The Searchers*, that most fully illuminated John Wayne's violently ambiguous relationship with the Native inhabitants of America. The movie opens with a song by Stan Jones that asks questions the film will not answer: "What makes a man to wander? What makes a man to roam? What makes a man leave bed and board and turn his back on home?" The song's refrain is "Ride away." Thus the film's title song evokes the American icon of the individual isolationist, the self-orphaned outcast who leaves community, family, and history behind. That icon appears in the opening scene as a lone rider framed against the familiar backdrop of director John Ford's beloved Monument Valley. Ethan Edwards, whose name is suggestive of both Calvinist minister Jonathan Edwards and Hawthorne's misanthropic Ethan Brand, is returning to his brother's home from fighting for the Confederacy in the Civil War. With a mysterious three-year gap in his history and saddlebags full of freshly minted gold, Ethan returns a bitter misanthrope. When, moments after Ethan's arrival, a second rider appears, it is young Martin, an orphan saved as a child by none other than Ethan Edwards, whose first words to the young man are, "Fella could mistake you for a halfbreed," muttered like a threat. Though Martin is quick to explain (a bit too thoroughly) that he is only one-eighth Cherokee, throughout the film he remains the "breed" and a target of contempt for Ethan.

The gist of the film's plot involves Ethan and Martin's seven-year search for Ethan's niece, who has been taken captive by Comanches after the massacre of her family by the same Indians. Martin correctly suspects that his "Uncle" Ethan intends to kill the young woman as soon as he finds her because she has been defiled by "living with a buck," as Ethan puts it. In the end, Ethan does not kill his niece, thanks most likely to Martin's intervention, but relents and says to her, "Lets go home, Debbie." The film ends where it began, in Monument Valley, with John Wayne walking away into the landscape from which he originally appeared.

Much has been written about *The Searchers*, and I do not intend to review that mountain of scholarship here. What is most intriguing about this midcareer film for John Wayne, however, is the intense ambiguity of his character's regard for and attitude toward Indians. On the one hand, following Alan LeMay's novel, Ford casts Wayne as an extraordinarily bitter Indian hater as well as a general misanthrope. On the other hand, the signifiers of Indian identity in Wayne's character are unmistakable. To begin with, though he hates the Comanche and apparently all Indians with vehemence, Ethan Edwards appears to speak a good deal of Comanche. He also knows and even respects what is supposed to be Comanche belief, as is evident when he shoots out the eyes of an Indian corpse so that, as he explains, the Indian's spirit cannot enter the "spirit land." Finally, the character of

Ethan Edwards curiously parallels that of the Comanche war chief, Scar, who has kidnapped Ethan's niece. Of similar age and stature, both men are acting out of what seems immeasurable bitterness, striking at the enemy because of past suffering. If the Comanche named Scar bears the mark of his naming on his face, Wayne's character bares his scar in every word and action of the film. And in a fine moment of doubling, Edwards tells Scar that he speaks pretty good English, asking if someone taught him, only to have Scar, moments later, comment on Edwards's good command of Comanche and ask if someone taught him.[1]

Embedded in John Wayne's role is America's five-hundred-year-long desire to become Indian, that unconscious but oft-articulated yearning to empty the space called Indian and reoccupy it. Only thus, America instinctively feels, can it ever achieve a direct and intimate relationship with the place it has stolen. Like Huck, Ethan Edwards has lit out for the Territory; however, Edwards, fresh from a fratricidal war, bears the scars of deformed conscience upon his unsound heart. Whereas Martin, with his one-eighth Cherokee blood, can be Indian and retain a sound heart, the message seems to be that the purely white Ethan's identification with the enemy—somewhere back in the history erased from the film—has twisted him irreparably. One cannot destroy the enemy in order to replace him without suffering in the process.

The Searchers is Wayne's most profound role in what it has to say about America's eroticized hatred of the indigenous peoples of America. In Ethan Edwards's pathological fear of miscegenation we see a perverse representation of the erotics of desire that have driven white and Indian relations since John Smith invented his fantasy about a girl named Pocahontas. In this regard, *The Searchers*, as I shall suggest later, is a much more honest and penetrating film than Kevin Costner's 1990s reply, *Dances With Wolves*.

It is a long journey from *The Searchers* to Wayne's 1972 film, *The Cowboys*. In *The Cowboys*, John Wayne is no longer young, or even middle-aged. Deeply scarred by life, Wayne's character of Will Anderson seems at first glance to refute the crucial aspect of the American myth that insists upon a Fountain of Youth, an eternal belief in new beginnings and endless possibility. That there can be no new beginning, no regeneration for Will, is suggested in his two long-dead sons, whose graves he visits. "They went bad on me," Will says, before adding, "Or I went bad on them." It is the future, the quintessence of the American Dream, that seems to have "gone bad" on Will Anderson, just as life itself had gone bad on the solitary Ethan Edwards nearly two decades earlier. At sixty years of age, Will must now summon all the will he has to get a herd of 1,500 cattle to a market four hundred miles away simply to ensure that his wife will be provided for after he is dead. The American Dream has given way to social security.

When Will discovers that every adult male in his area has run off in search of El Dorado, the dream of easy gold, Will is forced to hire a gaggle of boys to move the herd. The boys, only one of whom is over fifteen years old, represent extreme innocence. None has even seen a black man before, and they are quick to declare that the black man, Nightlinger, is "the same as us, except for that color," a similarity Nightlinger angrily rejects. The boys are Will's chance to live beyond himself, to symbolically start anew. As Nightlinger, the trail drive's suggestively named black cook, says to Will, "You got another chance." When Will replies, "They're not mine," Nightlinger adds, "They could be."

In the end, the boys are indeed Will's. After he is shot in a very brutal scene, Will gasps to Nightlinger, "Summer's over," a nice allusion to the coming fall—a time of harvest, of death for the cowboy Fisher King—and to the inevitable fall from innocence awaiting the boys. However, Will's last words are addressed to the boys: "Every man wants his children to be better'n he was. You are." Clearly, they are symbolically children of this iconic American hero, and in being so they allow Will to defy death, to live on. Perhaps, the film implies, the boys can grow beyond the scarred old man, beyond the history represented by the Ringo Kid and Ethan Edwards, even beyond the extraordinary brutality that is the American story. Perhaps in the boys Will can truly start over, springing from his own Platonic conception of himself, as an F. Scott Fitzgerald narrator might put it.

The boys, however, prove themselves his heirs by coming of age as they kill Will's murderers, who are led by the purely evil Asa Watts (brilliantly played by Bruce Dern). In a highly symbolic motif, the boys begin to kill the villains one by one. As each bad guy dies, one of the boys puts on the bad guy's clothing and temporarily assumes the villain's place with the stolen cattle herd. The message is clear: the boys are becoming like the American hero, Will Anderson—and like earlier John Wayne characters—by going outside the law and executing their own justice. However, in so doing, as the appropriated clothing suggests, they also partake of the evil of those they kill, just as Ethan Edwards looked into the mirroring hatred of the Comanche named Scar. If the boys become like Will, they also become like their evil adversaries. Killing as initiation rite is further underscored in the film's climactic scene as the camera closes in on each of the boys in succession killing one of the rustlers. In the lethal children, the film underscores the nature of the western hero. He is a cow*boy*, a *kid* like all his namesakes in western lore. The western hero is not supposed to grow up, just as the West and America itself are not supposed to grow old. When that happens it seems, as Will says, that something has gone bad.

At the end of *The Cowboys*, Nightlinger and the boys search for Will's grave in order to place a marker there. But the grave has been erased by rain—suggestive of regeneration and new beginning—and the stone must be left randomly on the wide prairie. Thus, just as Ethan Edwards walked away into the Monument Valley setting that in *Stagecoach* had absorbed shadowy Indians, Will has become a part of the American landscape, nourishing the common soil. Nightlinger (whose name alone may suggest the lingering stain of the dark night of slavery) provides a eulogy that underscores this point: "This may seem like a lonesome place to leave him. But he's not alone. Because many of his kind rest here with him. The prairie was like a mother to Mr. Anderson." Will Anderson, the cowboy hero, was born of America. Symbolically, he is also the father of us all. And very significantly, he has died in a land seemingly emptied of all traces of Indians. Ethan Edwards seems to have done his work well in this late film, and the invading colonizer has erased the original inhabitant only to face the consequences of his brutal history.

Native Americans were from the beginning the fly in the New World ointment for invading Europeans. How could the true American hero, the new-made man, maintain his giant stride across the continent when he kept tripping over communities of people who had already inhabited that so-called New World for tens of thousands of years? For American Indians, the New World was a very old world. Furthermore, to Indians the very idea of the American hero could only be absurd. While the hero must operate alone, ahead of the rest, for the Indian the community was and is essential to both physical and psychological survival. To be isolated, like all those wandering cowboy heroes, was to have no identity and to perish. To be alone, outside the tribe, was not to be heroic but to have been, in Indian terms, "thrown away." Finally, how could the American hero maintain the aura of innocence necessary in this new Eden when he had to drive the Indians from their ancestral homes and murder countless thousands in the process? It was an ugly, unconscionable business, troubling even to an American society bent on cultural and physical genocide for Indians.

In the movies of John Wayne—the actor who not only endorsed the witch-hunts of McCarthyism but also in a *Playboy Magazine* interview justified the extermination of Indians—America found the answer to such an uncomfortable dilemma. That answer, of course, is to assume that the Native American is on the verge of extinction, the uncomfortable business of genocide practically over and forgotten. The ugly facts of extermination become merely an unfortunate part of the past that, in the American tradition, can be forgotten as once again we reinvent ourselves as a kinder, gentler nation. As an added benefit, on the brink of extinction the Indian is seen as no longer either a real threat to the European invader or significant enough to stake a convincing claim to the continent.

Once it is assumed that the Indian neither threatens white civilization nor possesses a meaningful claim to property, America is finally able to look at the indigenous American sympathetically. The Indian then becomes a historical artifact of distinct value. The role of the white man at that stage is to learn as much as possible from the Indian—that is, to become as much as possible *like* the Indian without *being* the Indian—before the race of Native Americans disappears with the setting sun. It is at this point of cowboys-and-Indians history that John Wayne enters the picture. At that moment in history when full appropriation of everything Indian, including not only land but every cultural vestige that may be of value to the white world, seems justifiably inevitable, the Indian can finally be pitied, protected, and emulated safely. In the John Wayne canon, *The Searchers* stands out as the turning point, the film that honestly faced the consequences of American history. Subsequently, the Indian in Wayne films dances with disappearance.

In the '90s, Kevin Costner's *Dances With Wolves* illustrated this convergence very clearly, as Costner's protagonist goes into Indian Country, desperate to see the frontier "before it's gone," strips himself bare, and appropriates all that he can of the Indian. He then returns to the white world bearing the recovered white female. The Indian, Costner's audience understands by the end of *Dances With Wolves*, is a doomed artifact, and the audience is invited to shed a crocodile tear for a lost people and lost time. However, that which is valuable and retrievable in Sioux culture has been absorbed and thus salvaged by Costner's character to make the white world a better place; even the symbolic threat of miscegenation so troubling to Ethan Edwards has been removed, as the protagonist returns bearing the recovered white woman.

Among contemporary films, *Dances With Wolves* illustrates this pattern of thought most clearly, but it is a pattern obvious in the films of John Marion Michael Morrison Wayne. A crucial difference between Costner's character of Dunbar in *Dances With Wolves* and the John Wayne hero, however, is that at the end of his film Dunbar returns to civilization. It is evident that he has never really deserted that other world. For the Wayne hero, on the other hand, there can be no place outside of "Indian Country"—even when Indian Country has become devoid of Indians. The Wayne hero, too, is an artifact so damaged by his brutal task that he cannot go home again. It was this discovery that provided the greatest roles for an aging John Wayne, in such films as *True Grit* (1969) and *The Shootist* (1976).

As Rooster Cogburn in *True Grit*, Wayne is a man out of time and place, once again beyond civilized law, dealing out violent justice according to his own values. To find room where his kind of hero can operate, Rooster must leave civilization and, like Ethan Edwards, go into "Indian Territory," where, as Mark Twain suggested, the "sound heart" can overrule the "deformed conscience." In the civilized world, Rooster complains about "pettifogging lawyers" and serves a "writ" on a rat by shooting the animal. In essence, John Wayne is playing the same role he played in *Stagecoach* almost half a century earlier. Having sloughed off the tormented soul of Ethan Edwards, he is once again charmingly innocent, offering not the faintest hint of sexual threat to the attractive young woman, Mattie Ross, whom he takes into the Territory. Mattie, who dresses in rather asexual clothing and constantly challenges the men in masculine terms, is called "Baby Sister" by Rooster. It is clear that it is not the hero but his environment that has changed. The marked difference between the two versions of the hero in *Stagecoach* and *True Grit* rises out of John Wayne's comically self-conscious parody in the role of Rooster. Civilization has engulfed him and age has shockingly tracked him down. It may be true that "Rooster" suggests the Second Coming or rebirth of Christ and the Fisher King, and "Baby Sister" may be a dark nod to Francis of Assisi's Little Sister Death who haunts Faulkner's Quentin Compson, but putting such portentousness aside, John Wayne camps his way through the role, a charming (though still lethal) drunk.

Like the archetypal hero he is, Rooster has no family, living his liminal existence with an old Chinese man, a distinct icon of otherness whom he introduces as his father, and a cat he calls his nephew. Rooster's encounter with a mixedblood Indian policeman in the Territory (to all appearances the only Indian left in the Territory) is marked by mutual respect and familiarity; they seem to recognize that as marginal figures they are much alike. In the film's final scene, Mattie Ross, whom he has aided in avenging her father's murder, tells him, "You're getting too old and too fat to be jumping over fences," and our last view is of Rooster defying time by jumping his horse over a distant fence. Just like the Ringo Kid, he is heading across a border into a place where he can live beyond civilization. However, where he is really headed is suggested in Mattie's invitation to him to be buried in her family's plot. Only beyond this world, which he must traverse alone, can the American hero find a family, and as *The Cowboys* showed, that family is the earth itself.

The Shootist (1976) was John Wayne's last film. In it he plays John Bernard Books, a legendary gunman dying of cancer. A reprise of his life's roles, the film pays tribute to John Wayne the actor, giving him the opportunity to close out his career with the enormous, tragic dignity befitting the great American hero that he was. After a ritualistic cleansing, Books goes forth to die by violence on his birthday in a manner he himself has predetermined. That his name is Books tells us volumes about the John Wayne hero: as his name announces, he is the product of white America's collective self-imagining, an animated text that tells the story of this country. Most incredible in all of this is that Marion Morrison did, in fact, give himself over to the Euramerican imagination to be reshaped, reborn into a fictive hero with his off-screen self formed entirely by the camera's view. In the end, Marion Morrison was John Wayne through and through—a most strange kind of self-sacrifice.

From a Native American perspective, the John Wayne figure is unsurpassingly strange and disturbing. He is a renegade, an orphan without family or community, a throwaway who in seeking to bond with the very earth destroys all possibility of belonging to anything at all. In every inch of his large frame, he embodies the contradictory and immeasurably destructive essence of the American self, that pathological destructiveness which for an incredible five hundred years Native America has most astonishingly survived. My childish suspicions about Breck Coleman were correct: the Indians never taught him a thing.

Apocalypse at the Two-Socks Hop

Dancing with the Vanishing American

◆

Imagine a solitary wolf alone on the Great Plains in 1863, silhouetted by the tallgrass prairie like a vast, empty sea. Now imagine that he is alone because his pack has been exterminated during a time when the unthinking response of humans was to kill every wolf encountered, the anticarnivore instinct that would lead to the eradication of even the last gray wolf in Yellowstone National Park and every other park in the lower forty-eight states by 1930 (Coates, 241). This particular solitary prairie wolf, however, is about to be named Two Socks, and he is on the verge of bonding with an equally isolated white man named Lieutenant John Dunbar in Kevin Costner's *Dances With Wolves*.

It is worth our time to inquire into the nature of this filmic friendship of wolf and man. The immediate question that leaps to mind is "why?" Why would a wolf be hanging around a frontier outpost like Fort Sedgewick in Costner's movie and in the Michael Blake novel upon which the film is based? The primitive fort is the very recent home of a group of pathological killers in the uniforms of the U.S. Army, men so depraved that they have slaughtered whole piles of animals and left them to rot both on land and in their only source of drinking water. Men so insanely depraved that, according to Blake and Costner, they have left whole carcasses to rot even though they were "starving," the same kind of men who will gleefully kill Two Socks later in the movie, just before Costner's Lakota friends put the finishing touches upon the wolf killers themselves. (The soldiers kill the wolf earlier in the novel version of the story.) In fact, Costner is sensible enough to make Dunbar's first reaction upon seeing the wolf that of instinctively raising his rifle, before the Christ-like soldier's innocent heart asserts itself.

The answer, of course, is that only in a cartoonish Hollywood film or a badly written, romantic novel would a wolf come seeking suicidal companionship in such a way.[1] So the next logical question is, why do Blake and Costner construct such a ridiculous plot contrivance in a movie both author and director touted for its supposed "authenticity"? My guess is that Two Socks is an essential metaphor for the submission of natural America to the "white god"—as Blake repeatedly calls Lieutenant Dunbar—who has come to stake his colonial claim to the territory. In this role, Two Socks effectively foreshadows the submission of the Lakotas to the same white god, and together wolf and Indian serve to authorize the rightful role of the European invader in asserting his dominion over the continent and its occupants. In the end, the lone wolf will be dead and the solitary band of Lakotas will be facing certain cultural if not physical extermination, according to Blake's novel and Costner's film, and the "white god" will return to civilization, having established his natural supremacy and subsumed the powers of the natural world, including Indians, into his greater self. Dunbar's destiny to do so is made manifest in the beginning of the movie when he spreads his arms like a Christ ready to die for this New World.

Dances With Wolves is, from beginning to end, the perfect, exquisite reenactment of the whole colonial enterprise in America, and it is the most insidious vehicle yet for this familiar message because it comes beautifully disguised as its opposite: a revisionist, politically correct western, a vehicle one critic has seen as a "pointed reply, one suspects, to John Ford's 1956 classic *The Searchers*, often ranked as the greatest of westerns."[2] In his introduction to a book about the film, Costner declared emotionally, "It will forever by my love letter to the past," and explained that novelist and screenwriter Blake had "created a story that embraced a culture that has traditionally been misrepresented, both historically and cinematically." To his credit, Costner also writes, *"Dances With Wolves* is first and foremost a movie, and should be seen as one. . . . It wasn't made to manipulate your feelings, to reinvent the past, or to set the historical record straight. It's a romantic look at a terrible time in our history, when expansion in the name of progress brought us very little and, in fact, cost us deeply" (Landau, viii, vii).

Even some of the Native Americans involved in the project voiced unmistakable approval. The Lakota actor Floyd Red Crow Westerman, who played Chief Ten Bears, said, "I think this is an important film to show the world the reality of how it was then" (Landau, 117). Dorris Leader Charge, whose job it was to teach the Indian actors, as well as Costner and his female lead Mary McDonnell, to speak Lakota, and who had a small role in the film as Pretty Shield, said, "I was scared about doing this movie at the beginning, but it's been a good experience. It portrays us as we really are. They've gotten it right this time" (Landau, 53). Other Lakota viewers, not on the Hollywood payroll, had different reactions, however, as a reviewer identified as Shoots the Ghost indicates when he writes: *"Dances With Wolves* is a marvelous piece of propaganda, a pacifier shoved into Indian mouths, a balm to soothe White guilt. It exemplifies the strengths of the American Myth of the Frontier in which white males dominate their surroundings, and Indians and women are present only as props, as means to an end." The same writer, whose Euramerican name is Marlon Sherman and who is an Oglala Lakota born on the Pine Ridge reservation, adds: "I left the theater emotionally exhausted. People were crowding in on all sides, prodding cheerfully: How did you like it? What did you think? Explain that scene where . . ., as if it should be such an easy thing to pick my heart up off the ground. If we were at their mother's funeral, would I ask them to describe for me how they were feeling?" (Shoots the Ghost, 231).

Dances With Wolves may be "first and foremost a movie," but when we are dealing with a media invention such as the "Indian," we would be wise to pay attention to such a movie. Costner's "love letter to the past" is precisely that: a cinemagraphically powerful, lyrically moving, heart-string pulling love letter to an absolutely fake American past that Euramericans invented as a sanitized, romantic version of the ugly realities of colonization and genocide. Costner's film buys it all, repackages it, and makes more palatable the age-old clichés and unwavering metanarrative.

As anyone familiar with contemporary Native Americans, literature by Native Americans, or the more reliable aspects of American history should know, the so-called American Indian is a European invention that has little or nothing to do with the indigenous people who lived on this continent by the millions before 1492 and who live here still. The impulse behind the invention of this space called "Indian" is the colonizer's intense fear of what Heidegger termed "not-at-homeness," the inexorable deracination that comes with colonial displacement. The goal is rather simply to become the Indian and thereby achieve an intimate relationship with the place one inhabits, as Lieutenant Dunbar does. Just as Mark Twain's Huckleberry Finn finds peace only in a tipi on a raft in the center of his dark, maternal river to nowhere, and just as he can only plan to light out for Indian Territory at the end of his novel, the eternally orphaned American is forever seeking the home Huck could not find and still lighting out for the Territory. As we all know, Territory, like Frontier, means "Indian."

Now to become the Indian "other" requires first of all that one define the other as clearly as possible in opposition to oneself. I will call that defined space "Indian Territory," since Indian Territory is probably the best-known and most unavoidable metaphor for the definition and containment of the Native American. While Frontier, as writers such as Mary Louise Pratt, James Clifton, myself, and others have suggested in various publications, is an unstable, multidirectional, hybridized zone of contact—an inherently indefinable space— Territory, on the other hand, can be easily defined, surveyed, and boundaried. Once the boundaries, or borders, are established, of course, that demarcated space can be systematically emptied and reoccupied. While it is impossible to occupy the ever-shifting and infinitely permeable space of Frontier, the occupation of Territory is easily accomplished, as the Oklahoma "Sooners" quickly proved in their theft of Indian lands.

The actual living, surviving indigenous inhabitants of North America, the Native Americans or First Peoples, represent a kind of omnipresent, amorphous Frontier in which more than five hundred different cultures are incessantly involved in resistance, appropriation, assimilation, and dialogue with the dominant colonial culture. Such an infinitely unstable, dialogic space simply cannot be defined, much less occupied, and this has been the case since the first Europeans touched toes to the so-called New World and began to steal corn. In order to find a seemingly indigenous cultural space to occupy, the invader had to imagine and construct that space. Thus we have the constructed "Indian," from the original Pocahontas and Uncas to today's figurations.

This process of invention, definition, displacement, and reoccupation acts out a strange, perverse dialectic of erotic desire and destruction. The Euramerican, under the inspiration of Lord Jeffrey Amherst and others, passes out smallpox-infected blankets to Indians and generally engages in one of the most savage wars of extermination the world has ever seen—from New England to the Pacific Ocean—and then, once the Native space has been secured, reinvents both a cartoon Pocahontas with extraordinary breasts to illuminate the erotics of deadly desire and a dying Hollywood Uncas to reassure himself that the Vanishing American is still vanishing.

Indigenous Americans, or American Indians as post-Columbian Euramericans like to say, have a long and unhappy history in Hollywood films. Indians in movies have always had two roles: bloodthirsty savage or noble companion. In both of these roles, the one unchanging obligation of the Indian is to die by the movie's end. These three expectations—savagism, nobility, and death (with none of the three mutually exclusive)—delineate neatly the role of the indigenous Native in the Euramerican imagination, and they are expectations founded upon a metanarrative that insists upon the mythic and tragic "otherness" of Native Americans. Above all, the media have always been careful not to portray the Indian as a living, viable inhabitant of contemporary America.

Film director Stephen Feraca underscored America's nonhuman conception of Indians when he stated in 1964: "Now those movie Indians wearing all those feathers can't come out as human beings. They're not expected to come out as human beings because I think the

American people do not regard them as wholly human. We must remember that many, many American children believe that feathers grow out of Indian heads."[3] Thirty years after Feraca's telling comment, as we approach the end of the twentieth century, multiculturalism has become a controversial buzzword in U.S. academies and national politics, a new cliché replacing the old cliché of the melting pot. A current interest in the multiplicity of cultures supposedly woven into the fabric of North America is commonly thought to have engendered a social self-consciousness and an ostensibly more sensitive awareness of the representation and exploitation of minority cultures in this country. This despite a national reemerging fear of the "other" in the form of devious aliens sneaking across our borders to do cheaply the work we do not like to do.

Part and parcel of this new consciousness, perhaps stimulated by our collective sense that a new millennium is upon us and we're in big spiritual and ecological trouble, is a renewed fascination with the American Indian, a fascination manifested most clearly in the "New Age" movement's widespread attempts to appropriate Native American ceremonies and cultural practices. Given this new sensitivity—for better or worse—it might be reasonable to hope that the Native in American film-making and in the American imagination might finally emerge as recognizably "human." And in fact, Kevin Costner's enormously popular *Dances With Wolves*, released in 1990, impressed many viewers as doing just that. Philip Zaleski, writing for *Parabola*, notes a kind of reverse racism in the film ("all the whites here are drunk, filthy, brutal, or crazy") but declares nonetheless, "Let there be no doubt: *Dances with Wolves* marks a dramatic shift in Hollywood's treatment of Native Americans" (92, 93). A writer for *Rolling Stone* gushes about Costner's being "inducted into the Lakota Sioux the day of his film's Washington, D.C. premier," and notes that Costner "proves he isn't as low-key as he looks by tackling racial injustice in an epic of power and sweep" (Schruers, 55–56).

At a quick glance, *Dances With Wolves* would indeed seem to be a great leap forward as far as American Indian representation in Hollywood films is concerned. To begin with, Costner cast talented Indian actors in significant roles: Graham Greene, Rodney Grant, Floyd

Westerman, and Wes Studi among others. In an essay for *Commentary*, an astoundingly bitter attack on Native Americans that the author tries to pass off as a review of the Costner film, Richard Grenier expresses his shock at the success of such casting, declaring, "Most surprisingly, performances by the movie's Indian actors are excellent" (Grenier, 47). Grenier, we can only assume, must have been remembering the less-than-impressive Indian performances of non-Indian actors such as the late Sal Mineo and the current Lou Diamond Phillips. The Indian characters played by Costner's very talented actors are shown as individuals with at least some depth, capable of humor as well as stoicism, cruelty as well as generosity, cowardice as well as bravery. In short, while deeply romanticized, they are nonetheless depicted not merely as the clichéd inventions of conventional western movies and novels, but as human beings. Costner took pains to ensure that the Indians in his movie speak not pidgin English as in most past films—a kind of speech that confirms a linguistic hierarchy—but genuine Lakota (although the pan-tribal male actors, as well as Costner himself, were apparently taught a feminine inflection of the language by mistake) (Bowden, 394). When Costner's character, army officer John Dunbar, encounters the Indians, he is the one who is marginalized and made to inhabit, temporarily at least, a linguistically liminal state as he listens to a privileged language he cannot comprehend. It is also worth noting that Costner went to great efforts to make the details of nineteenth-century Lakota life culturally and historically accurate, locating a herd of 3,500 buffalo for the great bison scenes, borrowing two pet buffalo from singer Neil Young, and consulting experts at every level. Costume designer Cathy Smith, described as a "19th-century Plains Indian expert," declared it to be "a landmark movie in terms of costuming . . . the first Indian film that's been done really like it was." And according to the film's production designer, Jeffrey Beecroft, "Just about every-thing was built . . . by people who reconstruct artifacts for the Smithsonian." The film crew even went so far as to use more than 10,000 gallons of paint to render the grass, trees, and cornstalks the proper colors for the Civil War battle scene (Landau, 82, 105, 106).

Despite all of these efforts, a few reviewers could not resist the fun of quibbling with historical and cultural inaccuracies and just plain lack of verisimilitude in the film. Take the Pawnees, for example, who are depicted rather unflatteringly in Michael Blake's novel as "the most terrible of all the tribes" who "saw with unsophisticated but ruthlessly efficient eyes" and who killed with "psychotic precision" (Blake, 21), and who are shown similarly in the film. In fact, not only were the Pawnees not pressing the Sioux "hard" in 1863, as the novel and film tell us, but, as Native American historian Edward Castillo has pointed out, the Pawnees themselves were at that time in dire circumstances because of a combination of the purposeful introduction of smallpox by traders along the Santa Fe Trail and the disproportionate military power of their traditional enemy, the Lakotas. Like all Hollywood productions, Costner's film needs "bad" Indians as well as good ones, so Blake and Costner conveniently paint up some psychopathic Pawnee warriors. Caught up in the excitement of the Pawnees' dastardly and fatally unsuccessful attack on the peaceful village of Costner's Lakotas, the film viewer is not likely to remember that at that precise moment the best warriors of Ten Bear's Lakota band are off on a similar mission of vengeance against the Pawnees (a subtle point to Costner's credit in the film).

The fact that in Blake's novel the good Indians are Comanches while in the film they are Lakotas caused a few more problems not remedied during the geographical and cultural transfer. The Lakotas, for example, were never likely to have fought the Spanish and Texans as Costner's Ten Bears declares, although the Comanches did indeed tangle with those particular Indian haters. The historical Ten Bears himself was, in fact, a Comanche chief, not a Lakota, just as the real Kicking Bird was a principal chief and not a shaman, of the Kiowas, not the Lakotas. Castillo points out, furthermore, that "no US Army winter campaign was undertaken on the Plains until November 1868" and that that was by the famous Custer himself (15, 17).

Let me put my own two cents' worth in here by adding the cranky note that the novel and film script both tell us that the stream and watering hole at the abandoned Fort Sedgewick "were full of an assortment of rotting carcasses killed by the starving men for food." Blake's novel even adds the whole rotting carcass of an antelope to this scene of wasteful carnage (Landau, 22; Blake, 26). While the obvious politically correct message is that unlike the Indian the white man is a savage destroyer and polluter, this scene just does not work for a couple of very simple reasons. First: Why would starving men leave heaps of whole slaughtered animals lying around to rot? Would starving men not be inclined to eat the animals they shot? And second: Would any even half-sane group of men throw rotting carcasses into their only water source? As a metaphor for the fate of the planet this may work; as part of a film supposedly striving for authenticity it is just plain silly. Equally silly is the fact, as Castillo points out, that the Indians seem to wear their very best Sunday finery at all times, a most impractical habit.

Admittedly, *Dances With Wolves* marked an important breakthrough in the American film industry's conception and representation of Native Americans, and Kevin Costner deserves some credit for his achievements. Just as clearly, however, and partly for all of the reasons mentioned above, from an American Indian point of view *Dances With Wolves* is one of the most insidious moments yet in the history of American film. It represents, in fact, the apex in America's adroit, very self-conscious institutionalizing of the colonization of Native America. It is a movie that casts a vivid spotlight on Euramerican culture and history, providing an index to the power of the colonial metanarrative that informs the self-concept of contemporary America. If any of us thought the centuries-long desire to exterminate the indigenous American and subsume "Indianness" into the Euramerican self had disappeared, *Dances With Wolves* should serve to dispel that illusion.

Costner's film tells the story of young Lieutenant Dunbar, a hero of the U.S. Civil War who has left that war to journey—with an unmistakable nod to Joseph Conrad's *Heart of Darkness*—into the dark heart of savage America. Like Huck Finn, he has lit out for the Territory ahead of the rest. The morally unsullied Dunbar has won his right to head west by defying death before the amazingly inept marksmen of the Confederate army with his arms outstretched in Christ-like fashion, a cruciform image that resonates with America's millennial self-concept. Released from the conflict of the Civil War, Dunbar declares it his goal to see the western frontier "before it is gone."

Dunbar's quest takes him first into contact with a U.S. Army commander driven unmistakably mad by the Kafkaesque nature of his assignment and then beyond these military limits of "civilization" to an abandoned army outpost on the Great Plains of the central United States. At the empty outpost Dunbar finds a horrifying wasteland of preindustrial litter, which he immediately sets about to clean up. His final act of cleansing is to remove his clothes and immerse himself in a nearby pond, moments before his initial encounter with an Indian. A mythic Christ/Grail Knight figure, in the words of Michael Blake's novel, a "white god," Dunbar as the representative American attempts to redeem both self and landscape preparatory to finding and claiming a uniquely American grail.[4] The voluptuous landscape surrounding the outpost is vastly empty. It is depicted as an unpopulated New World Paradise (an Eden, where wolves lie down—or dance—with men) ready for inhabitation, just as the continent was viewed from the beginning by the colonial powers. However, from that same beginning the indigenous Americans—Indians—proved to be a significant impediment to such aesthetic appropriation, an impediment hinted at portentiously in this film by the presence of the military outpost. If Costner's film is to resolve the troubling paradox of the colonial chosen people inhabiting an already densely inhabited space, the Indian must be dealt with and, logically, erased. But because this is the 1990 version of a kinder, gentler America, the savages cannot simply be given infected blankets or forced to ride in circles around a wagon train while being knocked off like ducks in a county-fair shooting gallery. The kinder, gentler version of erasure takes a lot more time and care to accomplish.

This first outpost-frontier scene in *Dances With Wolves* is worthy of some attention, for it represents a seminal moment in American film fantasies about the Indian, and it tells us much about contemporary America. Once he has cleaned up the white man's mess, Costner, as Dunbar, rises stark-naked from his baptismal pond to confront the impressively dressed and very startled figure of Kicking Bird, a Lakota warrior and holy man played by the Canadian American Indian actor Graham Greene. Millions of people around the world had a good laugh over this scene. On the surface Costner appears to be playing subtly with comic inversion: The very proper "civilized" Indian goes out sight-seeing and meets the naked white savage. Close beneath this comic veneer, however, lies a more interesting reading, for this scene illuminates the crucial Euramerican fantasy of being inseminated with Indianness, of absorbing and appropriating everything of value in the indigenous world as a prelude to eradicating and replacing the actual Native.

Having stripped off the garments of civilized Europe, Dunbar exposes himself like a newborn to the potency of the American landscape represented by Kicking Bird. The image, however, is perversely layered, for within the naked "Adamic" innocence of the quintessentially American Dunbar is an unmistakable, highly phallic threat to the timorous (and oddly feminized) Indian played by Graham Greene. It is, in fact, the very nakedness of Dunbar that frightens the Indian warrior, as well it should, for Dunbar will soon be clothed in Kicking Bird's Indianness. Like a psychic vampire, the Costner character will from this moment on in the film become more and more "Indian" until, in the final absurdity, he is a better Indian than the Indians themselves. As the Indians grow more weak and vulnerable to the advancing edge of Euramerican civilization, Dunbar becomes stronger. When Dunbar has absorbed everything possible from the fragile Lakota band, the Indians become disposable. It is time then to erase and replace the Indian—the ultimate fantasy of the colonizer come true. The Indian in this fantasy enacts the role of the doomed nonelect for the New Adam in the Garden. The vanishing American is the millenarian figure who serves as a scapegoat so that the earth can be cleansed for the new man, the reborn European. Thus America can symbolically be the postapocalyptic earth, cleansed by the removal of the scapegoat. Costner's movie, with its "real" Indian actors and its "real" Indian language and props, sugarcoats the age-old fantasies of colonial America, repeating all of the deadliest clichés with devastating earnestness.

If Costner's character is a sort of colonial Christ/Grail Knight figure, the arrival in the film of Graham Greene's character, Kicking Bird, makes it clear what the Grail is for the Euramerican suffering from Heidegger's *Unheimlichkeit*, or "not-at-homeness," that torments the colonizer: It is nothing less than the indigenous relationship with place, with the invaded and stolen earth, that the colonizer desires. If that pure, original relationship represented by the Indian can somehow be claimed, the American imagination believes, then the morally tainted invader may be reborn from the womb of landscape in all innocence, springing from his own Platonic conception of himself as the great American child-man like James Fenimore Cooper's Natty Bumppo, the self-imagined Walt Whitman, F. Scott Fitzgerald's Gatsby, or any of the numerous film characters played by John Wayne.

The myth of the frontier, as U.S. historian Frederick Jackson Turner explained correctly a century ago, deeply informs America's sense of collective self and mission. In his desperation to see the frontier before it is gone, Dunbar is anticipating Turner's grand proclamation in 1893 that the American frontier had ceased to exist as of 1890, a date that, according to Turner, "marks the closing of a great historic movement." The American frontier, Turner wrote with a fine air of factuality, represented "the meeting point between savagery and civilization." "This perennial rebirth," he declared, "this fluidity of American life, this expansion westward with its new opportunities, its continuous touch with the simplicity of primitive society, furnish the forces dominating American character" (662). Essential to this "perennial rebirth" was the "touch with the simplicity of primitive society," or the *Indianization* of the European. "The frontier is the line of most rapid and effective Americanization," Turner stated. "The wilderness masters the colonist. . . . It strips off his garments of civilization and arrays him in the hunting shirt and the moccasin. It puts him in the log cabin of the Cherokee and Iroquois and runs an Indian palisade around him. . . . he shouts the war cry and takes the scalp in orthodox Indian fashion. . . . he fits himself into the Indian clearings and follows the Indian trails. . . . here is a new product that is American" (662–63).

Turner's words not only describe pretty accurately Dunbar's transformation in *Dances With Wolves*, but they underscore the contradictory and deadly nature of Euramerica's attitude toward and conception of the so-called Indian. On the one hand the European invader has demonstrated an extraordinary determination to exterminate the

Indian through every means possible, including genocidal warfare, uncountable massacres of women and children, the deliberate spread of deadly diseases, and the calculated destruction of Native cultures.[5] On the other hand, from the beginning of the colonial enterprise, the European invader has simultaneously demonstrated (and continues to demonstrate) a perverse and almost grotesquely paradoxical yearning to be Indian, to inhabit not merely the continent but the original inhabitant as well. Ultimately, the dark heart of this desire is to kill and replace the Indian.

When Costner's John Dunbar confronts Graham Greene's Kicking Bird with the phallic power of his white nakedness, *Dances With Wolves* acts out very effectively (if unconsciously) the erotic nature of Euroamerica's desire to simultaneously possess and destroy the Indian. And Costner's film follows out the logic of this desire perfectly, as most who saw the film will surely remember. The audience's first view of the Lakota village in the film, seen at epic distance through the eyes of the Costner character, shows us a small, fragile-looking encampment in a very beautiful and Edenic setting.[6] The subliminal message in the view is that this band of Lakotas, and synecdochically all Indians, are merely a delicate remnant of the original inhabitants of this New World garden. They are the tenuous remains of the frontier Dunbar wants to see and touch "before it is gone." In quick order, as Turner declared in 1893, the "wilderness masters the colonist," and Dunbar—the inherently superior white man—rapidly adapts to his environment so effectively that he will not only form an instinctual bond with a wild wolf, but most incredibly will be able to show the poor, ignorant Indians where to find a herd of buffalo. One might suppose that the Indians, having survived for thousands of years within this environment, and being at that moment in Costner's film somewhat hungry and worried about the absent buffalo, would have been aware of the arrival of a herd so large that it shook the earth, but it seems that Dunbar, the white colonizer, has already grown beyond them. If the relationship between Plains Indians and buffalo is a signifier of Native authenticity, then clearly the Costner character is more authentically "Indian" than the Indians in this scene as he leads the Lakotas to the herd.

Subsequently, Dunbar is the key to the Lakotas' ability to defeat their archenemy, the dastardly Pawnees, even though there is no indication that the Lakota warriors to whom Dunbar gives rifles have ever fired a rifle before. Finally, as the U.S. cavalry is closing in on Kicking Bird's retreating band of Indians, Dunbar rescues a convenient white woman (Mary MacDonnell, in the role of Stands With a Fist), who has been adopted by the Lakotas and with whom he has naturally fallen in love, and together the white couple head eastward. Costner and MacDonnell represent the primal couple—the American Adam and Eve—fully inseminated with Indianness and returning from a soon-to-be-emptied and thus accessible Garden to civilization.[7] It is the ultimate colonial fantasy realized.

Our final view of the Indians in the film shows them disappearing into a snowstorm as the inexorable U.S. Army approaches. The audience is left with an uncomfortable feeling that the Indians are vanishing under a literal and metaphorical blanket of whiteness as their doom closes in, but for non-Indian viewers the discomfort is minor because the white hero, who is riding eastward, has absorbed everything valuable in the Indian world. He is now the greater American, the "new product" that has fused the values of old and new worlds, and the actual Indians are of no more importance. As the film ends, a trailer scrolls across the screen to tell us authoritatively of the historical defeat and reservation impoundment of the Indians.

Thus the film has fulfilled all our expectations. The Indian of Costner's film is romantic—both noble and savage—just as everyone has long known; and most crucially the Indian is doomed to vanish, just as the American metanarrative has always insisted. In 1859, just four years before Dunbar goes in search of the frontier, Horace Greeley wrote of the Indians, "These people must die out—there is no help for them. God has given this earth to those who will subdue and cultivate it, and it is vain to struggle against His righteous decree" (Welch, *Killing Custer*, 47). With all its beautiful trimmings, *Dances With Wolves* nicely reiterates Greeley's message and presents the same old story, a narrative whose purpose is simply to erase Indians from the national consciousness as actual, living people. The real Indians all disappeared long ago, the fantasy insists. It is sad, but that is just one of the inevitabilities of history. Believing this, the conqueror is free to shed a crocodile tear for the people he has exterminated and romanticize them as an invaluable aspect of his—colonial—past.

Dances With Wolves depicts in marvelously complete fashion the crux of America's relationship with the indigenous peoples of this continent. American colonists began their mission into the American wilderness believing firmly that God was on their side, that they were the new chosen people, modeling their errand upon that of the Old Testament, and declaring themselves to be the new Israelites or the Army of Christ. The thickly populated American continent, home to hundreds of distinct and thriving Native cultures, was transformed in the colonial imagination into an empty Garden to be reclaimed. The westward movement was a quest for youth and reclaimed innocence, the ultimate goal being to reenter the garden/womb and be reborn. Unfortunately, however, there were indigenous populations in the way, and it became more and more difficult to reconcile the ruthless slaughter and removal of these peoples with the imagined quest for innocence.

For five centuries the invader has imagined that the "Indian" was vanishing. In poems, plays, novels, and films the noble savage and murdering savage alike were depicted as being at trail's end, wistfully in the twilight of existence. Given the incredible efforts expended to destroy the Indian, the Euramerican imagination should not be faulted for believing that the Vanishing American would be an inevitable result. The fact that out of an estimated six million indigenous inhabitants of what would become the continental United States, only 237,000 remained by 1900 attests to the effectiveness of this war of extermination. It is, in fact, truly incredible that today more than five hundred American Indian nations still exist in the United States. And by refusing to vanish, American Indians throw a monkey wrench into the American metanarrative. The dilemma for white America today is what to do with these uncomfortable phantoms, who not only refuse to go away but now want to open gambling casinos and effect a strikingly efficient transfer of wealth.

Perhaps the most effective means of denying American Indian people a contemporary identity and existence is to insist upon an authoritative definition of "Indian" that has remained fixed for centuries. No other utterance in the English language comes with as much authority indissolubly fused to it as the word "Indian." Not just America but most of the world knows precisely what a "real" Indian is supposed to be. Real Indians wear leather and feathers; they are stoic, mystical, dark skinned, and intuitively attached to Mother Earth. An Indian person can walk into any place in the Western world wearing what his or her great-great-great-great-grandparent might have worn—especially if that person is from a Plains tribe—and be immediately recognized as a "real" Indian. Conversely, if that same Indian were to enter the same room with short hair, wearing a coat and tie or evening dress, the chances are very good that no one would recognize him or her as "real"— especially if that Indian person happened to be relatively fair skinned. "Real" Indians inhabit a never-never land in the world's imagination. Living descendants of the original Americans, unless they impersonate that original "other," have no place in the world. No other people are expected to dress and live as their ancestors did five hundred years ago. Imagine the reaction if a Frenchman walked into a social gathering dressed as his ancestor had dressed half a millennium earlier. Would he or she be recognized as a "real" Frenchman, or might laughter be the result?

Because of the ongoing artifactualization of Indian identity, contemporary Native American people face a fascinating dilemma. In order to be seen and to have their voices heard, indigenous Americans must pose as "Indians."[8] Leaders of the militant American Indian Movement discovered this strange fact in the 1970s and used it very effectively, often beginning their careers wearing short hair and business suits but quickly learning to pose in braids and feathers, a strategic response to the expectations of white America. Such Indians, according to Chippewa writer Gerald Vizenor, were (and are) "simulated leaders in the cities who wore bone, beads, and leather, and strained to be the representations of traditional tribal cultures. . . . [T]he absence of the tribal real," Vizenor writes, "*became the real* in the public media" (*Manifest Manners*, 149, emphasis added). Indian leaders, artists, and public figures today are universally aware that to be taken seriously as "real" Indians, and listened to, they must pose as the (unreal) absent original "other." As a mixedblood writer of Choctaw, Cherokee, and European descent, I would be wise, for example, to darken my skin, buy a braided wig, and wear a traditional Plains Indian costume whenever I give a speech or read in public from my work; such a pose would make me more authentically "Indian" in the eyes of the non-Indian world (and even in the eyes of many Indians) and would surely sell a lot more books.

The five-centuries-long, deliberate effort to eradicate the original inhabitants of America and fully appropriate that colonized space is still going on today. The Indian is still supposed to be the Vanishing American, and his representation in the American media remains unequivocally that. As long as Native Americans who are very much alive today do not look, live, and talk like the anachronistic inventions portrayed in novels and movies, they remain invisible and politically powerless. If they caricature their ancestors by dressing and acting as they are shown to do in film and fiction, they become instantly recognizable as cultural artifacts of significance, but only insofar as they serve to inseminate the dominant culture with an original value. In discussing his film, Costner touched upon this dilemma, saying, "Casting the Native Americans was a challenge. We hired actors from all over the U.S. and Canada, and many tribes other than the Sioux participated (though 250 Sioux from the South Dakota Reservations worked as extras). One criterion was that we had to have people with an authentic period look, and a lot of urban Indians had cut their hair, or didn't have the right look" (Landau, xi). Costner even confessed to having doubts about casting the fullblood actor Graham Greene because he looked too much the professional actor and too little the "Indian." In the millennial drama of the American enterprise, the Indian plays an epic and tragic role, just as all colonized peoples must within the ideal drama of the colonizer.

The United States likes to pretend that the colonial era in North America is long over, that the colonies threw out the colonial oppressor and became a new nation. Native Americans, however, are fully aware that the colonial powers did not leave; they simply changed their names from British (or French, or Spanish) and became

"Americans." And the erasure of the indigenous people, who stubbornly remain an obstacle to the total appropriation of the continent, continues to be the usually unspoken goal of Euramerica. Media representations of Indians as romantic, noble, savage artifacts who inhabit an unchanging past are important weapons in this war of eradication. As long as the world is encouraged to imagine that "real" Indians exist only in the past, it will be easier to ignore the presence of actual Indian people living today in reservation communities where health care and education are abominable, unemployment is commonly as high as 80 percent, and the teenage suicide rate is at least ten times what it is for white Americans. Only in a society that refused to see its indigenous peoples as living human beings could Indians continue to be exploited as mascots for athletic teams such as the Washington Redskins or Cleveland Indians. Indians—like Vikings and Forty-Niners—are not supposed to inhabit the contemporary world.

Writing about the Palestinian struggle for recognition and self-determination, Edward Said has confessed that "it is very, very hard to espouse, for five decades, a continually losing cause" (*The Politics of Dispossession*, xvii). American Indians, who like Palestinians have had to struggle just to have a voice and be acknowledged as "real," have espoused what has seemed to be a losing cause for five centuries. In the face of such history, it is truly remarkable that American Indian people exist at all today; and it is more incredible that in 1994 there were more than three hundred published Indian writers whose collective project is resistance to and the destruction of that colonial American metanarrative that has long been and is still determined to make them invisible. The American Indian, looking back at this brutal history, might well echo Kurtz's final words in *Heart of Darkness*: "The horror! The horror!" But unlike Kurtz, we are not dead, and unlike the native people in Conrad's novel, we do not need a Marlow or a Costner to tell our story.

While the space labeled "Indian" may have been effectively defined and boundaried, and once defined, occupied, the indigenous Americans who are not "Indian," but Lakota or Choctaw or Yurok or Oneida, are still here. Lieutenant Dunbar would be surprised to return and discover that not only is Kevin Costner building a casino-resort in the sacred Black Hills of his adopted tribe, the Lakota, but the Lakota themselves are still there and, though having a tough time of it, still refusing to vanish.

3

Autobiographical Reflections, Or Mixed Blood and Mixed Messages

◆

Blood Trails

Missing Grandmothers and Making Worlds

◆

Oklahoma

The word "Oklahoma" resonates deeply through my childhood. This state with a Choctaw name meaning the land of red people was the "Nation" in stories told by my mother, aunt, uncle, and grandmother, a place of great pain and beauty often remembered in the same utterance. In very old photographs only recently discovered by my family, our ancestors—Indian, white, and mixed—pose rigidly or even elegantly in front of painted backdrops, or stand as tense families before log and stone cabins in the "Territory," or write on the back of a picture postcard of main-street Muldrow, Oklahoma, in 1913: "I her the train so bee good tell I see you."[1] One ancient photo in our family's collection shows an extraordinary man and woman standing in a flat-bottom skiff in front of a "riverboat" consisting of a one-window, crude wooden box on an even more crudely built raft. Atop the house-box are a tilting tin chimney and perhaps a dozen animal skins—mostly coons—stretched to dry and looking like the strangest kind of sails. Lying along the roof's edge are the freshly killed bodies of a very large bobcat and coon. The man wears a fur hat and proudly holds his rifle, while the woman wears undoubtedly her finest apparel and looks suspiciously toward the camera with cocked head. In my mother's cramped handwriting on the back are the words, "Boat mother lived on as child." Painted on the wood of the

Postcard of Muldrow, Oklahoma, addressed to Mother's great-grandmother from Great Uncle August Edward Bailey, "I her the train so Bee good tell I see you," April 17, 1913.

raft cabin in large letters is "BLESED. SUN. SHINE. 1917," with all the Ss backwards and "Shine" misspelled and repainted. Around the boat and couple appears to be a desolate landscape out of the dark heart of America, probably one of the many denuded steamboat landings along southern rivers.

We know the couple in this amazing picture are not our grandmother's parents, but no one alive in the family knows who they are. Family stories tell us that our grandmother's mixedblood father, John Bailey, had only a brief part in his daughter's life, and her supposedly fullblood Cherokee mother is said to have died in childbirth. This couple living in "Blesed . Sun . Shine" on a very distant, watery margin of America may have been merely temporary caretakers of a stray child, or perhaps they are unaccounted-for relatives or family friends who briefly took a young child in. This is one of many things we do not know. We do know, however, that our grandmother would have been six years old in 1917, only six or seven years away from motherhood herself, and that she had been at least partly raised by her grandmother, identified variously as Bettie Storms, Bettie Luther, and Bettie Bailey. Faded photos with even more faded scribbling on the back tell us much of this: Our grandmother as a beribboned toddler standing between her handsome young father's knees in a picture of the Cherokee mixedblood Bailey family—the only visual record we have of our great-grandfather. Ten of them pose in front of a blanket nailed against a log cabin, among them the always stern Great-Great-Grandmother Bettie and the much-photographed Aunt Nora. Missing from the photo are the family's father and grandfather, just as fathers and grandfathers seem to be missing in almost all photos on the mixedblood Indian sides of both my mother's and father's families. Another picture shows our grandmother as a very young child standing beside her own grandmother, who sits with a bible open in her lap. On the other side of the grandmother is Aunt Nora. With a very prominent headband and black hair parted severely in the middle, our young, serious-looking grandmother appears to have been made up "Indian style" for the photo. Most strangely, we have photos of our mother's mother, grandmother, grandfather, aunt, and other relatives—in fact, there are several pictures of the photogenic Aunt Nora—but nowhere, as far as we can be certain, is there a picture of our grandmother's mother; nor is her name recorded anywhere that we are aware of. It is as if Miriam Nora Bailey had no mother, a legacy of maternal absence she would pass on to her own children.

Though she apparently lived on the Trinity River in Texas at the time the photo of the "boat" was taken, my grandmother was born in Muldrow, Oklahoma, of a Cherokee mother and a Cherokee and Irish father, and my mother's family grew up in and around Sequoyah County. In Oklahoma my Uncle Bob, a deeply scarred and smooth-tongued trickster who spent more than half of his short life in prison, learned to set snares and build box traps for rabbits and squirrels, skills he later taught me and my brother during his brief but frequent visits. More than once we watched Uncle Bob walk away in handcuffs. And more than once we were reminded that the famous Bonnie Parker, of Bonnie and Clyde notoriety, was a family relation whom my mother had met as a child and remembered as a very nice person.

Coon hunters on the river. Photograph inscribed on back by my mother:
"Boat mother lived on as child, Trinity River." We do not know who these
people were: relatives, neighbors, caretakers for an abandoned child perhaps?

My maternal grandmother, Miriam Nora Bailey, in 1921, three years before she would herself be a mother.

In Oklahoma one night at a country dance—a moment and a place I imagine in stark light and shadow, the whirring of insects around kerosene lanterns, the shuffling and musty smells of patient horses standing amidst rattletrap cars, and the shouting of children backed by barn music—my own mother, uncle, and aunt were given away by their mother. Given away easily, in the told story, each to a different country farming family who could use another pair of small hands or even an infant who might grow into useful labor. Since hearing that story when I was myself a child, I have imagined it from a thousand

The mixedblood Cherokee Bailey family in front of their log home near Muldrow, Oklahoma, 1913. My maternal grandmother standing between the knees of her father, John Bailey.

perspectives, misremembered and retold it inaccurately, heard it again in its present form from my older sister, and felt the horror of it: my mother as a young child watching her toddler brother and infant sister taken into the dark with different strangers while she was carried off to labor on a farm where there were no children. Oklahoma in my childhood stories was a complicated, storied place of magic where one sought out lightning-struck trees, was visited in prophetic dreams by little people, and never had to go to school. And it was a place of unimaginable horror where three children, whose

My maternal grandmother, age six, on left, with her Irish grandmother, holding a bible, and her Cherokee-Irish aunt.

father had disappeared long before, watched their mother drive away into the night not to return for nearly seven years.[2]

My core subject in this book is writing by authors identified as mixedblood and the very meaning of the problematic word, "mixed-

One of my mother's great aunts, Oma, with unknown friend or husband.

blood," but since my family as well as the place called Oklahoma and its history figure so profoundly in my own work and my understanding of what the term "mixedblood" means, I will continue in this personal vein a bit longer. To get at that core requires some circumambience and patience, since to get at the concept of mixedblood, if one is of mixed bloods, requires negotiating personal as well as critical terrain.

Needless to say, my inherited memories of and feelings for Oklahoma are complex. In my own immediate experience, Oklahoma is primarily a place of transit, a long stretch of highway my family drove in our seemingly incessant journeys between my father's birthplace in Mississippi and our numerous homes in California. In that personal memory, Oklahoma is a place of dark green trees, red earth, sweating heat, canvas water bags, and stops beside the road to eat watermelons. On one side of Oklahoma lay the comforting dark-

Mother's often-photographed great aunt, Nora, on the Cherokee side.

ness of Mississippi and my Choctaw and Irish grandparents close to the Yazoo River; on the other side was a sweep of desert and then the brilliant light of California, a place where I never stopped being a stranger. In the kind of memory carried in stories and photographs, Oklahoma is a brown, black, and white place of awkwardly hewn log or piled-stone homes, desperate-looking families of differing complexions, and seemingly despoiled landscapes from which those families sought a living.

When I was invited to present the annual Oklahoma Lecture in the Humanities in Oklahoma City in February 1997, I thought that it might be nice to give other members of my family a chance to speak through me about what Oklahoma means to them, since my family came from Oklahoma. I wrote to my aunt, the only surviving member of my mother's family, the baby given away at that country dance, and asked if there might be anything she would like me to say to this place that holds such weight in family memory. I received a letter in reply from my uncle, writing for my aunt who is no longer able to write herself. Uncle Pete wrote, "Your Aunt Betty says that since she was really born just across the border in Texas, you can say anything you want about Oklahoma." A few days later I received a note from one of my cousins, saying, "I thought I'd write in case my dad's letter needed clarification or deciphering." My cousin added, "Mom was born in Texas and lived in Oklahoma from the age of one until about seven, which is when Grandmother came and got the kids. About the only thing she remembers is that they were very poor and she was mostly raised by people other than Grandmother." My cousin finishes with, "As for our grandmother: I was never close to her, but I feel she did the best she could under the circumstances. After all, she was only twelve or thirteen when your mother was born. Can you even imagine that?"

Being a person who imagines in order to write, I actually can imagine the life my cousin describes, and I have tried to write that imagining more than once. I imagine a plank-walled cabin like the ones I lived in in Misssissippi as a child, or perhaps one of the stone or log houses in old family photographs from the Territory, surrounded by ploughed ground and woods, a motherless and to all extents fatherless, uneducated, perhaps three-quarters Cherokee girl of twelve or thirteen already caught up in the terror of childbirth. I imagine the blank faces of people who must have been nearby, faces like those in the pictures. I like to think that her Aunt Nora was there, and perhaps her grandmother, too, but regardless of who might or might not have

Indian Territory neighbors of the Bailey family. Family portrait with stone house, names unknown.

been present, to an extent I cannot imagine, that child becoming a mother must have been alone, abandoned by her own parents through neglect or death, and the white father of her first child already absent (though he would turn up again many years later).

It is not my habit to write or talk in public about my family's everyday pathos or to quote various family members, for after all, each of us has a saga of our own to tell. However, I think this personal history has some bearing on the subject of mixedblood identity as it is articulated in literature. It has struck me that those historical and social forces that lead to the radical displacement and fragmentation that marked my grandmother's life from her first breath to her last, as well as the lives of her children—especially that empty place where all records of her Cherokee mother should be—are emblematic of the kinds of radically disruptive forces that have confronted and dismembered Indian peoples and communities for several centuries.

Many Indian people have been strong enough or fortunate enough to cling to family, community, clan, and tribe through this half millennium of deliberate, orchestrated, colonially and federally designed physical and cultural genocide. But a great many have not. Those mixed white-and-Indian families, or white-Indian-and-African American, with children sometimes resembling a Rainbow Coalition, assembled for somber photos in front of blanket-doored cabins, represent a crucial period in the histories of America and of mixedblood peoples in this country, a period that is often either unknown or misunderstood by Americans, Indian and non-Indian alike. Cherokees frequently bear the brunt of jokes throughout Indian Country because too many are blond and too many who identify as Cherokee have only the faintest and most clichéd ideas of Cherokee princess great-grandmothers. However, the Southeastern tribes did, in fact, have early and intense contact with Europeans, and a great many did, in fact, marry or cohabit with Europeans—especially Irishmen, Welshmen, Scotsmen, and Frenchmen. The results of these unions were those beautiful families, like the Timmons family in one of our photos, whose photographic portrait shows a near-blond child standing next to his very dark, earth-brown brother and the family arc continuing across mixedblood parents through boy and girl to a fine spectrum of hue and phenotype. These people were crossing and erasing borders and boundaries. Together these families embodied the "borderland" that is such a popular cultural studies topic today, and they did so unselfconsciously, purely, and out of human instinct and need. They

Timmons family portrait. Mixedblood Cherokee neighbors of the Baileys: a family rainbow.

were people simply surviving together—Indian and white—and they deserve to be honored rather than ridiculed despite the fact that they also stand as unwitting icons to both cultural atrophy for Indian people and the displacement of tribal nations from traditonal home-lands. It is as human beings who loved one another while crossing borders and erasing boundaries and, despite immeasurable odds, *surviving* that they deserve our recognition and utmost respect. These mixedbloods are the nineteenth- and early twentieth-century "post-indian warriors of survivance," to borrow the Anishinaabe writer Gerald Vizenor's term. Looking at them in those old photographs, I feel great pride—and that despite all the ordinary, painful human failings with which their stories are so undeniably riven.

Obviously, what I am describing is also a history of disjuncture and loss, but I do not think of it as the kind of "absence of the real" that Vizenor identifies as the false presence of simulated Indianness.

Church picnic day, Bailey family neighbors in Oklahoma, names unknown.

Rather, I see it as a microcosmic representation of the extraordinary disintegrative and assimilationist pressures American Indian people have confronted for many generations. I come from families of mixedbloods, Oklahoma Cherokee on my mother's side and Mississippi Choctaw on my father's. Anyone who has ever tried to mix disparate elements knows that it is very hard to achieve a pure blend. In the end, despite the long struggle for "survivance," there are often gaps and voids, dangerous pockets of emptiness that can burst unpredictably, but the process of mixing itself requires motion, the swirl of the blender, the whirl of contrary elements in the bucket or bowl. Mixedbloods, I am suggesting, are the products of motion, or what Vizenor, in *Fugitive Poses*, calls "transmotion."[3]

I will try to explain my lurid title for this chapter, a title which, in addition to having marquee value, actually does have meaning for me. Behind a title like "Blood Trails" lies, of course, the "Trail of Tears," a commonly recognized name for one of the brutal removals of Native people that created the foundations for the state of Oklahoma—a state that bears a Native American emblem and logo on its automobile license plates. It seems fitting that an Indian emblem and logo should be on automobile plates in a state that once made up much of so-called Indian Territory, for as I have just suggested, given the almost universal tribal attachment to place, or sacred geography, motion is paradoxically an image associated profoundly with Indian people. This notion of motion is a concept to which I will return soon.

To complete an explanation of the first part of my title, let me say that the phrase "blood trails" came to me as an amalgamation of imaginative concept and historical fact. The mixedblood Kiowa writer N. Scott Momaday, also from Oklahoma, has written of "memory in the blood," the kind of memory that allowed his grandmother to see perfectly in her mind's eye a place she knew only through her ancestors' stories of a long migration from the Northwest. Now "memory in the blood" is not some kind of racist concept as Arnold Krupat has suggested (*The Voice in the Margin*, 178). It is a trope, a figurative motion. Momaday, in fact, once told me that his own numerous personal peregrinations are, in his mind, an acting out of the migratory impulse deeply embedded in Kiowa culture (Owens, "N. Scott Momaday," 65).

In thinking of what I knew personally of Oklahoma, I realized that although I had passed through it numerous times during my family's many journeys between Mississippi and California, my knowledge of this place had come to me almost entirely through stories: my mother's, uncle's, aunt's, and grandmother's stories of growing up in what they insisted on calling the "Nation." It was only after years of hearing this as a child that I realized that "Nation" meant Cherokee Nation. And it was only when I was well into adulthood that I finally saw the old photographs taken in this "Nation."[4] This kind of knowledge sifted through generational storytelling is yet another sort of removal most American Indian people have experienced, another kind of trail that winds through generations and locations and finally leaves us sometimes in a kind of suspension. These are the blood trails that we follow back toward a sense of where we come from and who we are.

Furthermore, in pondering this concept of blood memory, I wondered how it is that we remember or hold to such tenuous connections, and why it is that we do so. What impulse drives us to recall, remember, and retell those stories the way my grandmother, mother, aunt, and uncle did way out in California to children who knew Oklahoma only as a place to pass through in 1940s and '50s vehicles with canvas water bags and a sufficient supply of mongrel dogs, and who knew any kind of traditional Cherokee homeland only as the vaguest of storybook places. For me, as for many of us, there are enormous gaps, voids that cannot be filled. These are the missing grandmothers, and grandfathers, too, and the results are mixed messages, messages that become stirred in the very blood of which N. Scott Momaday wrote.

In a recent issue of the *American Indian Quarterly* devoted to "Writing About (Writing About) American Indians," the Lakota author Elizabeth Cook-Lynn published an essay titled "American Indian Intellectualism and the New Indian Story." I will not recap the rather meandering thread of the essay's ruminations, but I want to address a particular point the author raises in a section she calls "The Urban Mixed-Blood Indian and American Writing." Since I do indeed identify as a writer of mixed heritage, and since I have gone on record in a book called *Other Destinies* as suggesting that the question of mixed and relational identity is at the heart of nearly every novel published by an Indian author, this seems like an issue that needs to be addressed.

"In American Indian scholarship and art, the works of writers who call themselves mixed-bloods abound," writes Professor Cook-Lynn. "Their main topic is the discussion of the connection between the present I and the past They, and the present pastness of We." Leading Cook-Lynn's list of what appears to be a kind of mixedblood hall of shame are the names Gerald Vizenor, Louis Owens, Wendy Rose, Maurice Kenny, Diane Glancy, Thomas King, Joseph Bruchac, Michael Dorris, and a few others she defines as "the major self-described mixed-blood voices of the decade" (66–67). The first thing I want to say is that back in 1981 when I was reviewing a great novel called *Darkness in Saint Louis Bearheart* for *Talking Leaf*, the Los Angeles-area Indian newspaper, I could never have imagined that one day I would find my name in print immediately following that of Gerald Vizenor, the author of that novel and to my mind one of the most innovative of not just American Indian authors but all authors today. I wish to thank Cook-Lynn for this distinction as well as the designations of "major" and "intellectual." I have certainly never claimed to be either of the two. But I also want to explore a little the statement Cook-Lynn makes about what she calls the "present I," the "past They," and the "present pastness of We." While being a lover of words and especially delighted by cleverly manipulated juxtapositions of alliterative words and phrases embedded within riddlelike constructions, I find myself questioning what I think this may mean, though I am far from certain of any meaning.

At least one thing I am certain of is that I cannot accept the title of "urban mixed-blood" bestowed upon me in this grouping by the distinguished Lakota writer. I have lived in an urban setting for only two of my forty-eight years, in the smog-throttled San Fernando Valley where I taught at California State University Northridge and cosponsored the Native American Students Association with the noted Native American scholar Beatrice Medicine. I also doubt that Professor Medicine would accept the title of "urban" Indian based on two years in that metropolitan nightmare. My urban experience was, in fact, so terrible that I decided to abandon academics, applied for admission to the M.S. program in forestry at Utah State University, and was admitted, though I did not ultimately enroll. My formative years were spent in a two-room cabin a stone's throw from the Yazoo River in Mississippi. Not only was our home not urban, it was not even sub- or ex- or anything remotely connected to urban. In fact, it was simply rural, as in boonies, since there was no town or paved road anywhere that I can recall, no electricity or plumbing, and few shoes. Kerosene lamps, wood stoves, an outhouse, and a rain barrel formed the basis of our "utilities." Following those early years, I grew up in rural parts of California, where my eight brothers and sisters and I could invariably pick up a gun and start hunting rabbits, quail, or deer a few steps out the back door. Currently I live in the Manzano Mountains of New Mexico at about seven thousand feet, where we have bears and mountain lions paying occasional visits and coyotes marking our doorstep nightly to enrage and embarrass our English Setter. In short, I firmly disclaim the "urban" label even if I embrace the identity of mixedblood. I do not mean to call people names, but I daresay that Cook-Lynn may be more urban than I. The question remains, however, as to what Cook-Lynn's "present I," "past They," and "present past We" may mean. Such a question may be fruitful.

It is a commonplace to say that in traditional American Indian cultures "I" has little place. Even the notorious nonurban mixedblood writer Louis Owens has written that "the concept of a single author for any given text, or of an individual who might conceive of herself or himself as the creative center and originating source of a story, or of the individual autobiography, would have made as little sense to pre-Columbian Native Americans as the notion of selling real estate" (*Other Destinies*, 9). However, let us begin with that present "I" nonetheless. After all, I cannot deny the fact that "I" am the Louis Owens whose name is on books, just as I cannot deny the fact that "I" am one of the principal subjects of those books sometimes disguised in varying levels of fiction.

A place to begin may be with the following question: If a writer happens to be of mixed ancestry and aware of and interested in one or both sides of that mixture, and if that writer seeks understanding through language for himself and his reader by the telling of stories, should the writer not write of that "mixedblood" subject that is the complex self? That is, should we not write of what grips and absorbs us? To do so, of course, is to write of those tensions, dynamics, and torsions of family, history, community, and nation that give rise to the hybrid self. What are our other options? Shall we blush at the fact of hybridization and write detective thrillers about Irish-American investigators in Chicago or Los Angeles, opting for the other side of the mix that will not be challenged by a Cook-Lynn or someone else? For after all, no one disputes the "authenticity" of white America, just as no one would question a mixedblood's right to fictionalize white America. Is it better to be a Martin Cruz Smith and write about intrigue aboard a Soviet nuclear submarine while also claiming our mixedblood heritage? Is it worse to change one's name to William Least Heat Moon in order to publish an entertaining travelogue like

Blue Highways? Or shall we distance ourselves from the mixedblood hall of shame by reimagining ourselves—despite those incriminating turn-of-the-century photographs of mixed ancestors—as fullbloods raised squarely within the traditions of a coherent Indian community, thereby writing what Cook-Lynn calls "tribal realism," whatever that vague phrase may mean, and thereby becoming exemplars of Vizenor's "absent other"?

Cook-Lynn also takes the loudly self-defined "real" Indian writers Adrian Louis and Sherman Alexie to task in her essay, as I have noted above, arguing that these two authors' works fail to "suggest a responsibility of art as an ethical endeavor or the artist as responsible social critic." And she criticizes both Russell Means, Vizenor's quintessential "postindian warrior of survivance," and Louise Erdrich, certainly the most commercially successful of all Indian authors. As I have already made clear in a previous chapter in this book, I would tend to agree with certain key principles of Cook-Lynn's criticisms of Alexie, Louis, and to a lesser degree Erdrich, but the fact remains that the answers to the questions raised are not simple ones, nor should they be. For nothing in the world today is more complex, difficult, disputed, divisive, or so highly charged with dynamic energies as the question of "Indianness."

Now what about Cook-Lynn's past "They?" I assume "They" are ancestors, the people who survived through extraordinary times to give us life. If "They" are who I assume they are, then I also assume they are not past. They are given life and voice through the Anishinaabe stories of Gerald Vizenor, the ancestral voices of N. Scott Momaday, James Welch's historical novel *Fools Crow*, the extraordinary poetry and prose of Luci Tapahonso, the Navajo and Laguna fiction of A. A. Carr, and the Trail of Tears Diane Glancy retraces in her novel *Pushing the Bear*. "They" exist always in the present, in the utterance of story. For me they are my mother and father, aunts and uncles, grandparents on both sides, great-grandparents whom I did not know, and all of the people who gave them breath and voice. "They" walk the Trail of Tears, abandon Mississippi homelands or stay in Mississippi and starve, scratch survival from removal lands, remember stories, and nurture or abandon their children. They suffer inconceivable hardships and survive. They come from Europe to new lives, find Indian wives and children who eventually richochet around America, bring souvenirs back from World War II or medals from Vietnam. They are mixedbloods on the loose who refuse to be clichéd past or stereotyped present. And those people who refuse to be "past" but insist on having voices in the present include not only indigenous American Indians but also the French and Irish traders who ended up deeply bound within the Choctaw and Cherokee communities and bore children who posed for itinerant photographers in front of Indian Territory cabins. After all, among the first and foremost Cherokee mixedbloods was John Ross, who was perhaps one-eighth Cherokee by blood quantum but led his nation's fight against Removal. Among other significant Cherokee mixedbloods were John Rollin Ridge, the first American Indian novelist and grandson of Major Ridge, and Elias Boudinot, the famed Cherokee journalist killed along with John Rollin Ridge's father and grandfather as a result of Removal politics, not to mention Sequoyah himself, an unquestioned genius who, one might say, invented Cherokee literacy.

Now what are we to make of Cook-Lynn's invocation of something called "the present pastness of We"? The author herself provides the following definition: "While there is in the writings of these intellectuals much lip service given to the condemnation of America's treatment of the First Nations there are few useful expressions of resistance and opposition to the colonial history at the core of Indian/ White relations. Instead, there is explicit and implicit accommodation to the colonialism of the West that has resulted in what may be observed as three intellectual characteristics in fiction, non-fiction, and poetry: an aesthetic that is pathetic or cynical, a tacit notion of the failure of tribal governments as Native institutions and of sovereignty as a concept, and an Indian identity which focuses on individualism rather than First Nation ideology" (p. 67).

Apparently this defender of "First Nation ideology" and "tribal realism" against the cynical individualism of mixedbloods has not read very closely or well the writings of Gerald Vizenor, the primary villain in her mixedblood lineup. In fact, though Cook-Lynn, along with many other readers, may have considerable difficulty penetrating the brillant razor-wire of Vizenor's "trickster discourse," no writer in America has so forcefully exposed the raw villainy, larceny, greed, hypocrisy, and cupidity of Euramerican colonial policy toward Native peoples. And no writer has more subtly and effectively demonstrated the ability of the tribal voice and tribal sovereignty to resist, outlast, and overturn all colonial burdens. No writer has, in fact, accomplished as effectively what Cook-Lynn describes as the "responsibility of art as an ethical endeavor or the artist as responsible social critic." A perceptive reader, one—unlike Cook-Lynn—who is willing and able to do the hard work that will take her or him behind the easy surface of cliché and stereotype found in other art, will find no cynicism in Vizenor's writing. If his writing must be labeled, we had better call it tribal utopianism, for in Vizenor's work one finds an undying insistence that Indian people—whatever we call ourselves—are capable of confronting painful truths about ourselves and others and have the abilities necessary to manage our own lives and to construct both a present and a future independent of the authoritative discourse of colonial America that has always sought to infantalize as well as disenfranchise Indians.

It must also be said that no other writer has so penetratingly punctured the pompous posturing of those who would wrap themselves in the mantle of indigenous ingenuousness as they claim to be "real Indians." Such a phrase as "tribal realism," as undefined and perhaps undefinable as that is, rings of what, in his first novel, *Bearheart*, Vizenor called a terminal creed: a static utterance that insists upon its own authority, taking part in no dialogue. Since, as Vizenor has explained again and again, the "real" Indian is a colonial invention, to be thus real, to engage in "tribal realism," is to conform to the invented stereotype. A Euramerican viewer could walk out of films such as *Last of the Mohicans* or *Pocahontas* and immediately recognize such a "real" Indian. Such posturing is indeed pathetic and even cynical if it is at the expense of the human capacity not only to endure but to survive, adapt, and triumph with a native voice intact. I would suggest, in fact, that what contemporary American Indian writers—among them the very writers Cook-Lynn names—are attempting, in an astonishingly wide variety of ways, is to make "We" very much part of the present tense and not an artifact of the past.

In her rather scathing indictment of nearly all contemporary Indian artists, herself and a very select few excluded, Professor Cook-Lynn focuses upon N. Scott Momaday and Leslie Silko as paragons of what she feels Indian artists should be and do. The failure of responsibility noted above, she writes, is "a marked departure from the early renaissance works of such luminaries as N. Scott Momaday and Leslie Marmon Silko" (68). Of Momaday, she writes that his first novel, *House Made of Dawn*, "is considered a classic because it is a work that explores traditional values, revealing truth and falsity about those values from a framework of *tribal realism*." Now what Cook-Lynn fails to note, or conveniently sidesteps, is the fact that in his famous novel Momaday, himself half-Kiowa and perhaps a thirty-second Cherokee if we are playing the blood-quantum game, is writing about Jemez Pueblo in New Mexico as an outsider while assuming insider privilege. He is also writing a novel that is replete, in fact bulging at the seams, with the easily recognizable techniques and tropes of modernist American literature. In short, Momaday borrowed a tribal culture other than his own as his subject, and he appropriated modernist fiction as his dominant paradigm. This is not to say that *House Made of Dawn* is not indeed a brilliant, subversive, and groundbreaking novel that effectively shows the coherence of a tribal community. It is to say, rather, that to ignore the truly extraordinary hybridization and heteroglossia that permeates and gives form to this Pulitzer Prize–winning novel is to miss the most essential truth of the work. The "tribal realism" of this Pueblo novel by a mixedblood Kiowa writer with a Ph.D. from Stanford University is a bit more complicated than Cook-Lynn would make it seem. A more perceptive critic would take note of the heteroglossia, dialogism, and hybridization that make this Pulitzer Prize winner truly extraordinary.

On the subject of mixed identity, Leslie Silko has written of her family: "We are mixed bloods—Laguna, Mexican, white. . . . All those languages, all those ways of living are combined, and we live somewhere on the fringes of all three."[5] *Ceremony* is a novel about mixedblood identity by a mixedblood novelist who has declared her writing to be about mixed and relational identity.

Cook-Lynn includes both of these authors in her list of "writers who do not situate themselves within the mixed-blood or mainstream spectrum" and admires both as writers "for whom books matter and intellectualism has meaning" (75). Apparently Cook-Lynn either has not read or has forgotten Silko's self-description quoted above and has not thought very carefully about Momaday. It is always much easier to make broad, general categorizations of convenience if we do not look at the cultural fine print; essentialist list makers usually take care not to look too closely, in fact. Needing two very well-known figureheads for a list of "tribally real" writers, Cook-Lynn appropriates these two mixedblood authors without very careful study.

Both Momaday's protagonist Abel in *House Made of Dawn* and Silko's Tayo in *Ceremony*, in fact, make circular journeys in the archetypal pattern of the culture hero, from community into the external, dangerous world and back to community, and both also fit the mainstream pattern of the individual American hero rather neatly. Though I have spoken of the modernist elements in Momaday's work at some length above, I will add here that if a reader does not have a working knowledge of canonical American literature, she or he may indeed fail to notice that the key figures in both Momaday's and Silko's novels are recognizable protagonist-types in the modernist pattern of the alienated, isolated outcast, though in the end both repudiate the linear directionality of the American hero by coming home again. The same circular directionality can be found in Thomas King's protagonist Will in the beautifully crafted novel *Medicine River*, in Vizenor's many tribal baronage tricksters, and so on. However, with all of that said, let me add that there are indeed countless thousands of Indian people in the positions of a Momaday, Silko, King, Vizenor, and so forth: people who do not live in reservation communities and who, if they are artists, may create art about urban or rural mixedblood experience at a distance from their tribal communities. Should the stories of such people, the products of colonial America's five hundred years of cultural wars against indigenous peoples, not be told because they do not fit the definition of what one Lakota critic thinks is tribally "real"?

Are their stories not ones that "matter" or have "meaning"? Contrary to what Cook-Lynn asserts, this is a powerful literature of resistance, a countervoice to the dominant discourse that would reduce Indians to artifactual commodities useful to tourist industries.

What is truly pathetic is the shell game in which writers posing as "real" Indians again and again give us new versions of the age-old Euramerican invention called the Vanishing American: Indians who inhabit dysfunctional and vaguely defined tribal communities, drink themselves to death, abuse self and other within a matrix of dark humor, and save the colonizer the trouble of genocide. This is literary tourism. I will not list the titles by contemporary Indian writers that illustrate such real cynicism and defeatism—I have done a bit of that in an earlier chapter in this book, and Cook-Lynn has done even more of it in her essay—but I will suggest again that these are the works most popular with commercial publishers and non-Indian readers, and I am sure we have all read more than one novel that fits the description.

The fiction of a Gerald Vizenor or a Thomas King, on the other hand, replete with the humor that has kept Indians alive for generations and the enduring power of story, directly counter such entropic tales. Cook-Lynn seems incapable of seeing this. While she argues that "Almost all of the current fiction being written by Indians is created within these aesthetics in contradistinction to the hopeful, life-affirming aesthetic of traditional stories, songs, and rituals," she would appear to have never truly read Vizenor, Glancy, King, Betty Bell, Linda Hogan, Aaron Carr—or many, many other Indian writers—with any understanding, for as a body this is a hopeful, life-affirming literature. It is a literature that, often invoking traditional stories, songs, and rituals with discretion, tells the stories of who we are today, not only yesterday, with humor and strength so that we may, as a people, continue to survive. There is no more life-affirming aesthetic arising from traditional culture than Vizenor's Anishinaabe fiction and poetry. In selecting Vizenor as her arch-villain in this awful new writing, Cook-Lynn illuminates a failure of understanding. In including Thomas King, she demonstrates a refusal or inability to acknowledge the crucial role of humor in the long survival of Native

American peoples. And in placing my name in this nefarious mix, she gives me great pleasure.

As writers, we tell stories, weaving what we have been told, what we have experienced and felt, and what we have read into a fabric of imagination, and I assume that most of us who have no fantasies of growing rich from words tell stories that are necessary for survival in one way or another, stories that we must tell and that come out of our larger selves.

In an old, cheap tin trunk in the house of one of my younger sisters is a collection of letters, photographs, silk scarves from the World War II Pacific; medals from Vietnam that my brother bitterly discarded but my mother saved; and postcards: all gathered and cherished over a lifetime by my mother and now, after her death, guarded by my sister. A couple of years ago my sister Judy and I finally worked up the courage or strength to go through that trunk, looking at the photographs of strangers to whom we are often related and carefully not reading the many letters even if we could not avoid the few words on postcards. Two things stand out in my memory of that sorting through mementos of a life so close to me. The first is that among all the pieces of paper were a score of postcards written many years ago by my grandmother to my mother, her eldest daughter, from widely scattered places across America. That wild, burdened, mixedblood Cherokee woman was caroming all over America in the 1940s, from coast to coast, Northeast to Southwest, sending picture postcards always saying "wish you were here." But my mother was never there and had seldom been there in her mother's life. I wonder what my grandmother was doing in all of those places. What force sent that tiny woman born with no mother and almost no father, no birth certificate or record of her existence, a mother herself before realizing her own childhood, bouncing all over America?

The second thing that stands out for me, and struck me powerfully at the time of viewing, is that so many of the old black-and-white photographs in that trunk were of our family seated upon or leaning upon or standing around automobiles. In photograph after photo-graph, my mother and father, aunt, uncle, or grandmother, my pudgy

Always there were automobiles. My mother, Ida Brown Owens, and me during a California visit.

baby self, my brothers and sisters and cousins, are sitting on the chrome bumper or shiny fender or hood of a thirty- or forty-something Chevy or Ford or Buick. Except for an occasional lone toddler, there is seldom only one person in a photograph. Almost always there are parents and children, or cousins with cousins. Always there is family associated with each automobile, and an almost tangible sense of pride in that association. Adult hands casually touch the chrome and caress the shining hood and shoulders lean confidently into sturdy metal, feet possessively lifted onto running boards. Only one house holds in my memories of those photographs—the cabin we lived in when I was little in Mississippi—but I remember what seems like scores of sleek, sloping-fendered, chrome-edged cars and an obvious desire to be associated with those vehicles.

Something is going on in my grandmother's instability and this strange, vehicular, photographic iconography, and I think it has to do with the past, present, and present past of Indianness that I discussed earlier. Part of it, certainly, is purely American, for motion is the real

My mother holding me, with my brother Gene, setting out for Mississippi in style.

American dream. To be on the road indefinitely, free of roots and responsibilities to family, community, or the earth itself, is the oldest and most destructive of all American metanarratives, exactly the damaging kind of individualism Cook-Lynn claimed to find in mixed-blood writing. Huckleberry Finn and Natty Bumppo and Ishmael are the quintessential Americans, for all three literary creations remain suspended in eternal, isolated motion for us through literature. Very interestingly, however, all three of these Euramerican literary icons are closely associated with indigenous Americans. For Huckleberry Finn it is Indian Territory, that realm of freedom he aims to light out for ahead of the rest at the end of his novel. For Natty Bumppo it is the Indian brother whose blood he absorbs as he moves westward, becoming ever more Indian while proclaiming the undying separateness of the races, a nineteenth-century *Dances With Wolves*. For Ishmael it is the tomahawk pipe and bed he shares with Queequeg as *Moby-Dick*

Me, surrendering with car, July 4, 1949.

opens, and not only the Indian's coffin he floats on amidst that vast, empty sea at the novel's close but also the novel's final scene, in which the Indian Tashtego nails the hawk of heaven to the acutely named *Pequod*'s sinking masthead.

It is not difficult to see why the American Dream is one of motion, for after all that is how every European colonist came to this continent and how every new generation succeeded in further displacing the indigenous inhabitants. Constant motion meant renewed freedom and gain at the cost of others. And, just as obviously, it must be a deep consciousness of both the injustice of murder and displacement as well as the impossibility of ever truly knowing the stolen land that has for five hundred years driven the obsession of Euro-America with everything Indian.

But something else is also going on in all of those postcards and photographs in my mother's trunk. It has to do with what I will call indigenous motion. Tribal people have deep bonds with the earth, with sacred places that bear the bones and stories that tell them who they are, where they came from, and how to live in the world they see around them. But of course almost all tribal people also have migration stories that say we came from someplace else before finding home. The very fact that tribal nations from the Southeast were so extraordinarily successful in making so-called Indian Territory a much beloved home after the horrors of Removal and before the horrors of the Civil War underscores the ability of indigenous Americans to move and in so doing to carry with them whole cultures within memory and story. Motion is genetically encoded in American Indian being. Look at a map of supposed and historical migrations of tribal people in the Americas, such as the long migration of the Kiowas of which N. Scott Momaday writes so beautifully in *The Way to Rainy Mountain*, or the tribal memory of Choctaw people moving toward Nanih Waiyah from the west, the Woodland tribes out onto the open prairies so that the westward-moving Lakota would eventually know the Black Hills as sacred, the Navajos and Apaches into the lands of the Pueblos and Hopis, and so on. Add the enforced displacement of Native peoples by colonial invaders: tribe after tribe pushed westward. On a map the arrowed lines of such movement give the impression of a vast cauldron stirred with a very big spoon. How in the world did tribal people survive all of that unless we know how to pick up and carry our selves, our histories, our stories, our self-knowledge?

My novels are stories of survival, not cynical or life-opposing reflections of the Euramerican construction called the Vanishing American. And in thinking about them spatially, I recognize that nearly all of the stories I tell move on an axis between Mississippi and California. Each one arises out of a place I know, out of the feelings and smells and sounds and tastes of specific landscapes: the rotting mud of my childhood along the Yazoo River and the rich odor that hung in the viney forest between our cabin and that river; the warm oat hills and oak canopies of the California Coast Range; the rain forests of the North Cascades, where I worked as a wilderness ranger; and the piñon/juniper forests and river canyons of New Mexico and Arizona, where I now live. Within those places, as a nonurban, nonintellectual mixedblood, I try to tell stories built around characters that I admit have a lot in common with myself. Most often they are mixedbloods with Choctaw and Cherokee and Irish and maybe Cajun roots, and they inhabit complex worlds in which the overwhelming questions are, Who am I? and How do I live in this place and time? And, of course, answers to such questions must be found in the voices of family and stories. However, what I try to do with my fiction is to show Indian people—mixedblood or fullblood, Choctaw-Cherokees or others—who face their confusing existences with strength and humor, repudiating the easy roles of victimage and tragedy. If motion is the matrix within which identity must be forged, then you get out the Brownie camera and take a picture of family on the fenders of a thirty-six Chevy. If loss of parents or grandparents or tribal community is the residue of difficult history, then you recreate community beginning with the nucleus of family and extending through memory and imagination and nation. The impulse is always to create, never to destroy, even if self-destruction is the most negotiable commodity in publishing.

In summary I will suggest that, contrary to what Cook-Lynn argues in her essay, the "present I" cannot exist without the "past They," and the past "They" can exist only in the memory of the present "I." The "pastness of We" for many people may be an unavoidable fact of five hundred years of determined cultural destruction and displacement, but the whole point of contemporary American Indian writing is to demonstrate that the long five-hundred-year project of erasure has failed: "We" are not past, and "I" can exist only within the knowledge of "They" who are "We." Some of us may be born and raised within a tribal community, be it Pine Ridge, South Dakota, or Philadelphia, Mississippi. If so, it becomes our responsibility to continue the stories of those communities, to write, therefore, of what we know. Others of us may be part of the more than 50 percent of American Indians displaced far from traditional cultural centers. Those stories, too, must be told. For stories are what we carry with us through time and across distance.

11

Motion of Fire and Form

◆

Mississippi

I do not know how to write autobiography, and memory is the most unreliable narrator, so perhaps I should begin by at least trying to get a few things straight: I was born in prison. I grew up in Mississippi and California. I have lived a great deal in the outdoors. I am not a real Indian. I have eight brothers and sisters. My mother walked barefoot across half of Texas. My father killed and ate another man's pig. The world is dangerously literal. Autobiography contains too many "I's." Were they to read what follows, and undoubtedly they will, my family would surely remember our life differently. But since nothing has been written down, I must put things together from the scraps of stories in my memory and imagination, beginning with Mississippi, where everything begins.

How to evoke that feeling of a Mississippi mud road, late at night forty years ago in the middle of nowhere on the way home from Granma and Grampa's house, which at one time had been a small church and still had a steeple and cotton fields that came sneaking up from the woods on all sides? The black bones of trees, what I now after a college education call deciduous, on both sides of the road because it must have been winter, and probably there was ice in the ruts and in the muddy stream beside the road and no moonlight at all that I can remember. The winter air frozen cold and thick as Karo syrup. A big car, probably a forty-something Chevy or Ford, one of those cars that make your parents say repeatedly, "Now don't you go to sleep back there," because of carbon monoxide that would maybe kill you if you went to sleep with any or all of your eight brothers and sisters piled on top of each other. The same kind of car we would drive back and forth to California, across all that desert, with canvas water bags hanging and dripping from every sharp projection of mirror, hood ornament, and door handle. Big and solid and perfectly crafted for pig killing on a dark Mississippi night.

Dinner had been possum, I think, a greasy, strong-flavored, stringy meat my grandparents loved, and probably hominy, since there was always hominy at their house, and corn bread because there was always corn bread. There is the odor of woodsmoke, kerosene, and rusty pump-water, and in my memory a too-long farewell in the car out in the bare, hard-packed dirt yard, my grampa's two bony blue-tick hounds lying in the lantern light of the porch. Then the sullen comfort of too many kids tangled and tired on the wide back seat—although we were not nine yet, but only five. The Yazoo River, with its brown, impenetrable water, was off there in the dark, and perhaps I remember being six years old and sensing its presence not far away through the woods, maybe remember imagining that I heard the alligators barking the way I sometimes did at night in our plank-walled shotgun shack with its tar-paper sides and tin roof while our father was out there across the river hunting coons and, I now strongly suspect, poaching alligators. Our cabin stood a couple hundred yards from the river, facing the same mud road we were driving, with a big pecan tree across the road before the river jungle began, the tree underneath which I truly believe I saw one black woman cut another black woman with her straight razor one afternoon so that the cut one bled and died later, and even at five years old I knew or heard some-one in the crowd of black people and Indians say it was "man trouble." Muscadines grew on vines in the thick woods by the river, and the river mud flaked in big cracks by the leaky rowboat I pushed off in so we almost drowned trying to get to the other side, which was where they said Indians lived. Large, hidden things lived in the

My father's paternal grandparents in their home near the Yazoo River, Mississippi. They say he was a fine Irish fiddler.

river—alligators, snapping turtles, water moccasins, catfish big enough to swallow a dog, needle-toothed gar—shadowy things just waiting for a foolish child. Across the river was a world I wondered about and dreamed about but never saw. Out of that world came the panther that followed my father back from hunting one night, crying, he said, like a woman in pain. On the roof of our cabin, the black cat walked furiously, screaming and terrifying us kids before it knocked the tin chimney off and leapt away into the night. Into that world my father disappeared when darkness came each evening.

Rainwater collected in a barrel on the front porch. At night there would be the acrid small of my father's carbide hunting lamp, and by daylight there would be coon skins nailed to the shed wall and dark men and women coming to take away the bodies of naked flesh. In the fields I dragged a child-size cotton bag and the black cotton pickers laughed as they filled it for me and then carried me back to the shade of the trailers when I grew sleepy. All around me were relatives.

Our Mississippi home along the Yazoo. Me with sister and two aunts, the light and dark of things. One night a panther walked upon the roof and screamed.

Born in prison because my father ran away from home when he was fifteen and lied to join the army during World War II and then went awol from the paratroopers just before he was about to be shipped out for some invasion. His sharecropper parents were alone in Mississippi, and both had pneumonia at the same time and needed help to stay alive and get the cotton picked. When the army would not give him emergency leave to help, he just left anyway and took care of them until they were better and then came back to turn himself in. So they threw him out of the paratroops and for punishment made him a policeman at the military prison in Lompoc, California, "the Valley of Flowers," where he was walking down the street one day and saw Ida Brown, dark eyed and beautiful Oklahoman with long black hair already at age twenty married and divorced twice and the mother of a boy and girl, waitressing in a cafe and said to his buddy, "Hey, that's an Indian girl" and claimed later

Me, riding a plow in front of the chicken house, with sister, Betty, and an aunt, in Mississippi, 1951.

that he also said, "And I'm going to marry her." So I was born in the military prison hospital to which my mother was brought because she had left what she and my grandmother Miriam Nora Bailey—a more-than-half-Cherokee woman who bore my mother at age thirteen and was descended from a Cherokee mother who disappeared and left her to be raised by a grandmother named Storms and a mostly absent mixedblood father named John Bailey, said in undoubtedly apocry-phal family myth to have been an "Indian Scout" who guided wagon trains—had left what she and my grandmother called the "Nation" in Oklahoma and come out to California to work in the shipyards during the war and somehow drifted to Lompoc, where her sister married into an Italian family from near Pisa, Italy (the grandmother of which never did learn to speak English) and was working in a Chinese-owned American-style cafe when a cocky, nineteen-year-old fellow named Hoey Owens, whose mother was a Choctaw-Cajun woman from the Choctaw Strip in Catahoula Parish, Louisiana, and whose father was a dirt-poor Irish sharecropper across the river in Mississippi, came walking by and decided to marry her.

Nobody saw the pig, but everybody heard it. In the headlights it was huge and dead, with its throat cut by the time we kids were out looking and shivering in the cold night, the black blood spurting and pooling in front of the radiator. And then it was in the trunk of the car and we were home and a pit was dug beneath the big walnut tree behind the cabin, and fire, and neighbors from other cabins in the woods who today, more than forty years later, form a dancing, strutting tableau of mostly angular shadows around the corpse of the pig hanging over the fire from a big branch. Perhaps I remember staring through the rusty screen door of the kitchen at the gyrating, laughing, pig-eating men and women and wandering through the mess of shadows made by fire and fired people. By morning the pig is gone, and today I know, somehow, that it belonged to the rich white man "up the road" and my father almost went to jail for it. And it is funny how a lot of years turn memories into that kind of thing, the way family stories when nothing is written down become the same kind of moonless dance and wild dream.

California, because that was where we settled more or less for good when I was about seven. In my immediate memory, I always leap to the belief that we moved first to the oak-and-pine Coast Range of the Santa Lucia Mountains miles up a dirt road behind the serious ranching town of Paso Robles, California. I remember that place with a feeling I can only define as love—remember the texture of the dry earth and rustle of prickly oak leaves, the heat of summer on wild oats and manzanita, the taste of a spring hillside when the world seemed startled with new grass. But it is not true that we moved there first. We had already made at least one failed moved to the state of my birth, initially to California's great Central Valley, where we lived in a small tent "city" on the outskirts of Delano, California, while my father got work in the fields nearby. I recall now that our A-frame tent had a wooden floor and contained the chocolate cake of my fifth birthday. We lived there a few months (or weeks?) until my father was promoted and we moved into a little house on the "ranch" where

My father, Hoey Louis Owens, age nineteen.

he worked. It was there that he made slingshots for my brother and me, rock-hard oak forks with red rubber bands from old tire inner tubes. From that point on, we would always seek out the red "real" rubber from World War II as the best slingshot material, seldom finding it again. It was also here that I lurked just inside the kitchen door listening to my father explain to my mother that he had been called a "goddamn Indian" and fired by the field foreman, my very first concrete awareness that to be Indian was a bad thing. Only later, after we had returned to Mississippi in our shambles of a car, did I learn that somewhere before or after that exchange he had punched the foreman. Still an amazingly powerful man today, at age sixty-eight, my father has only struck two people in my lifetime, as far as I know: the foreman who cursed him and my mother's brother, bad Uncle Bob.

During that wandering time in California, we camped farther down the Central Valley, near the potato sheds at Shafter where for a while we gleaned potatoes after the fields were harvested, and then we moved to Paso Robles, into the county "Housing Project" where our low-income apartment was surrounded by a paradise of mown grass and wild children. The Project is still there today, seeming unchanged after so many years. Driving south from San Francisco on U.S. 101, I glance to my right and see the dull brown buildings and recall those months as a very happy time. It was in the Project that a beautiful border collie appeared magically during one of our baseball games and remained with us for the next nine years—Rex, the wonder dog. Still there between the freeway and the Project are the train tracks, where my brother and I would lay wire in the path of the Southern Pacific so that the wire would be flattened to razor-sharp blades. With the unflattened part wrapped around a stick, these were lethal weapons capable of beheading flowers, lizards, or anything with a low survival rate in a kid's world.

And then we were abruptly gone from the Project and living in Mississippi on a place still known in family stories as the "Hog Ranch," a time that has coalesced into a single image of a gray winter day and a mule with his head down against a muddy barn. I assume there were also hogs, but hogs do not populate my memories there. Then just as abruptly we were headed back to California, a trip that remains vivid because of a flash flood that swept like a mirage across the desert somewhere in New Mexico or Arizona, cutting the highway and leaving us stranded for some time—one day, two days?

Nine of us moved into a small house with flaking white paint set deep in the Santa Lucia Mountains west of Paso Robles, so remote that a bear came onto our porch one night and mountain lions left tracks in the yard. That was a secure and private world, where my older brother, Gene, looked up at me from deep in the cave we were digging and said, "Look at these Indian things," and we sat together in the sun to study two lovely arrow points and a tiny white stone doll dug from six feet down in the shaley earth. Who were those Indians, I wondered, finding it impossible to imagine real Indians amidst all that light. Why had they set such things so carefully in the earth, and where were those people now? And then, just before my fifth-grade year, we moved ten miles away to the crumbling bank of the Salinas River, which was not a river at all but a lovely, wide sand-and-brush-and-cottonwood world filled with the rabbits and quail and doves and pigeons and deer we hunted.

California was a world as different from Mississippi as day from night, where a river was white sand rather than brown water and the hillsides were golden grain and shiny oaks rather than the black tangle of that Yazoo country. A world where my nine-year-old self sat dreaming on a remote wild-oat ridge not far from the ocean and foolishly believed for a long time that everything was visible, nothing hidden. Where I followed after my brother as we learned from our father and Uncle Bob how to catch fish by putting crushed unripe black walnuts in a sack and dropping that sack into a pool so that the fish rose stunned and could be scooped out; how to turn a hollow log into a box trap for rabbits, possums, and most often, pack rats; how to grapple with our hands for fish in stream and tide pool; and how to set deadfalls that never worked for small game. We graduated from slingshots to twenty-two, shotgun, and thirty-ought-six—hunting everything from squirrels to deer.

California was a world in which on a strange kind of absentminded automatic pilot I became the second after my brother (and today still only the second) in the history of our whole extended family to graduate from high school. And then, while my brother served three tours of duty in Vietnam, I drifted from high school to work in a can factory in Hayward, California, and then to a junior college and then, to my amazement and the astonishment of the few who paid attention, on to the University of California at Santa Barbara. So that now for more than twenty years I have lived in a world incalculably different from that of everyone else in my family. In troubled lives scattered across America, from Oregon to Arkansas, they see my name on books and shadows of themselves in the same books and they tell me with great tact how proud they are.

Not a real, essential Indian because I am not enrolled and did not grow up on a reservation. Because growing up in different times I naively thought that Indian was something we were, not something we did or had or were required to prove on demand. Listening to my mother's stories about Oklahoma, about brutally hard lives and dreams that cut across the fabric of every experience, I thought that was Indian. We were "part Indian" she said, and my Uncle Bob, out of jail temporarily and strutting in new hundred-dollar, unpaid-for cowboy boots, would be singing about "way down yonder on the Indian Nation" and boasting that only a Cherokee could be as handsome as he. No one but a Choctaw, I thought, could be as beautiful as my father's mother, or as great a hunter as my father, and though in California I was embarrassed by our poverty and bad grammar, I was nonetheless comfortable with who we were. The only other Indian I knew in California was my best friend and hunting-and-fishing companion, an Osage with blond hair and light eyes. He was enrolled and somewhat smug about that fact, though it meant little to me then.

Now I know better, and in life's midpassage I have learned to inhabit a hybrid, unpapered, Choctaw-Cherokee-Welsh-Irish-Cajun mixed space in between. I conceive of myself today not as an "Indian," but as a mixedblood, a person of complex roots and histories. Along with my parents and grandparents, brothers and sisters, I am the product of liminal space, the result of union between desperate individuals on the edges of dispossessed cultures and the marginalized spawn of invaders. A liminal existence and a tension in the blood and heart must be the inevitable result of such crossing. How could it be otherwise? But the tension can be a source of creative power—as such brilliant writers as Gerald Vizenor and Leslie Silko have taught me. This is an "other" territory which I, too, have claimed, like those early Choctaws who migrated westward across the Mississippi River, reversing the direction from which their ancestors had come carrying bones, to hunt and live and remain in Louisiana. I am descended from those people, *but I am not those people*, just as I bear the blood of the Trail of Tears and of an enormous Owens clan that reunites periodically somewhere in Kentucky or Tennessee, but I am not those people either. The descendant of mixedblood sharecroppers and the dispossessed of two continents, I believe I am the rightful heir of Choctaw and Cherokee storytellers and of Shakespeare and Yeats and Cervantes. Finally, everything converges and the center holds in the margins. This, if we are to go on.

My paternal grandmother, Mahala Jobe Owens, whose name I have not seen written down and no one in my family is certain of spelling correctly, is sixteen years old in a photograph. She is Choctaw and Cajun, my mother tells me (though parts of my father's family prefer to deny the Choctaw side even today), and her hair is thick and black and falls straight to the floor. Her white dress is buttoned at the neck and descends to her feet. She is extraordinarily beautiful, somber and dark eyed, slim and proud looking, or so I remember, for I have not seen the photograph in at least twenty years. Like so much in our family, it has been lost, is perhaps hidden and forgotten somewhere in a box or suitcase. The photo was taken in Louisiana, I think, probably in Catahoula Parish where she was born, and probably just before she left home to begin dancing on riverboats. When she ran away with a gambler on the Mississippi River, her father tracked them down in New Orleans with a gun and brought her back and forced her to marry the son of Welsh-Irish sharecroppers next door. Or so the family story goes. What I have learned only recently is that when she returned she already carried my Uncle Bill, the child of the gambler who would himself become a doomed gambler. The story says my grandfather, my father's father, was her punishment, as was a lifetime of sharecropping in Mississippi before my father borrowed money to move his parents to California, to live on a chicken ranch in a converted barn outside Paso Robles, California, when I was in third grade. All of this is picture and story without text.

I believe she never cut her hair. When I was young I would watch her take it down at night and brush it, and just as in the photograph it touched the floor when she stood, but now it was silver instead of black. And almost as soon as they were in California, it seems in my memory, she was killed in an automobile accident and Grampa moved back to Mississippi.

Until very recently, I had never seen photographs of my mother's mother, who finally drank herself to death when I was twenty. But I lived with her for a whole year once, and I remember her well. Just this year my older sister uncovered a trove of photographs of our mother's family from the beginning of this century. Among them were pictures of our grandmother as a child. This was the grandmother who was between twelve and thirteen years old when she bore my mother, the first of her three children. She is the one who, at five or six, looks so somberly out of a photograph beside her aunt and grandmother, with eyes already far too old for the little girl who bears them. It was she who, already husbandless, gave her children away to three different farming families who admired them at an Oklahoma country dance. The three were united at a single farm after an indeterminate time, and after several years of beatings and worse abuse, my mother dreamed of little people who foretold the farmer's death. Three days after the dream, the man died from a snakebite and my grandmother returned to claim her children. My grandmother who had been left by her own mother—through death, it is assumed— shortly after birth and who had been raised for at least a brief time by her grandmother in what she persisted in calling the "Nation" until her death. It was she who went through men by the score and whose postcards I discovered in my mother's papers after my mother died, each postcard from a different place in America—Boston, Albuquerque, Laramie, Seattle, San Diego, Tulsa, Little Rock, Las Vegas. Almost as though the Removal had buried a seed that drove her just as it would drive her only son, my smooth-talking Uncle Bob, from state to state and in and out of prison all his short, hard-drinking life until he was finally murdered in a Texas oil field—but not before he totaled my thirty-six Chevy.

There are pieces of story, tantalizing fragments. Such as my mother's account of walking barefoot across half of Texas all of one long frozen winter with her mother, little brother, and sister, living in the woods or abandoned barns, eating roots, stealing food from gardens and chicken houses, living for two luxurious weeks in an empty railcar. They were going back to Oklahoma, I know, but I never found out why they were walking or where they were really headed. In retrospect, I believe I could see the marks of that journey in my mother's face all the years I knew her.

Not long ago my mother's sister, Aunt Betty, wrote to ask if I could find out who she was. The only surviving member of her family, my aunt—like my mother, uncle, and grandparents—has no birth certificate but only stories growing more distant each year. Born at home, in different homes, none of them had the luxury of a recorded birth. For fifty years she has lived in an Italian-American world where her dark skin and hair fit perfectly, but now that she is old, she has begun to wonder, begun apparently to desire a record of her existence, unwilling to remain liminal and unwritten. She told me the names of her mother's father and mother, my great-grandparents, and I dutifully took the names to the National Archives. Sure enough he was there in the 1910 census for Oklahoma, in the Indian section, and there also on the Dawes Roll. John Bailey, a Cherokee mixedblood, with his parents, brothers, and sisters. But my aunt's fullblood grandmother's name was not anywhere on paper and remains, therefore, unreal, without essence.

My sister's son, a father himself now and in the army, writes from Germany to tell her he wants to enroll his own infant son. He is thinking of college scholarships, an admirably farsighted young man. My good friend from childhood keeps a copy of his enrollment card taped to the wall above his computer, where he is active on an Indian Internet line. I imagine a vast new tribe of Internet Indians.

For seven years I worked seasonally for the U.S. Forest Service, building trails, being a wilderness ranger, fighting fires on a hotshot crew. I watched Rookie cut his big toe off with a double-bit ax and be packed out by mule, saw Mick laid out in an emergency room with his right hand severed at the wrist from a fire-line accident, and watched my friend Joe fell a tree the wrong way in a hard wind so that he turned and sprawled full length on his running chain saw. I climbed glaciated peaks to radio in reports of frozen lakes far below, and wandered the high country of the North Cascades when it was under ten feet of hard-packed snow, alone above timberline for days and weeks at a time in the most beautiful place in the world. I stumbled across a surly wolverine when there were not supposed to be any in that country, and one morning I watched a mountain lion walk slowly across the zenith of a snowfield, outlined by the bluest sky I have ever seen. I fought fires in Washington, Arizona, and California, watching a project fire crown out in hundred-foot walls of flame that raced from ridge to ridge one night south of Winslow, Arizona, and dodging flaming yucca balls at midnight in a steep canyon outside of Tucson. I learned to drink great quantities of beer and climb granite faces as a sawyer on the Prescott Hotshots, which they told us was the only technical rock-climbing fire crew in America. I careened through burning mountains in helicopters driven mad by Vietnam vets, and I listened to a phone call telling me that two friends had been killed in such a helicopter after I had quit to return to school.

Seven years of that, and then in the fall of 1990, as a newly appointed full professor at the University of California Santa Cruz, I returned to the Northwest with my old journals, determined, twenty years after first seeing the Cascades, to retrace familiar routes with the vague idea of writing another book. The third day out, I found myself alone on the edge of a glacier and looking across a high route to the summit of Glacier Peak, a mountain called Dakobed by the Salishan people born there. The edge of the glacier was a steep ice field covered by a few inches of snow with a run-out ending thousands of feet down in a glacial river. On the other side of the first slope a series of crevasses began, their blue mouths opening to the black depths of the mountain. My ice ax firmly buried, I hesitated. The world was suddenly unfamiliar and very threatening, and I had decided to turn back and retrace my route down the rocks when I saw a shadow on the ice. Looking up, I watched a golden eagle banking off an updraft overhead. When I looked back at the glacier, I saw the tracks. A fresh, clear set of coyote prints began near where I stood and continued out onto the glacier. Hesitating no longer, I began to follow coyote, crossing the steep slope easily, remembering even that it is fun to slide down a glacier. Where coyote leapt across the narrow end of a crevasse, I leapt full pack and all. Where he strolled across an ice bridge, I did the same. Together our tracks emerged onto the rock crest on the other side of the glacier, and as I stood there in a tearing wind and looked out at what seemed a thousand miles of Cascade peaks, I imagined coyote doing the same. Why would he be on a mountain of ice and rock except for the pure pleasure of it? As I cut across a snowfield to finish the high route, the eagle circled endlessly. Alone, as I would continue to be for the next ten days, thousands of miles from the Yazoo and Salinas Rivers, I had never felt so at home in my life. Home had become a much bigger place, and the book I had imagined writing seemed unimportant.

Perhaps I began to write novels as a way of figuring things out for myself. I think my works are about the natural world and our relations with that world, with one another, and, most crucially, with ourselves. Though each of my novels begins and ends with place itself, the mysteries of mixed identity and conflicted stories, both the stories we tell ourselves and the stories others tell about us and to us, are what haunt my fiction. In a novel called *Wolfsong*, I wrote of a young Indian coming home to a valley in the North Cascades, wondering who and where he is meant to be. In that novel, set in the Glacier Peak Wilderness, the omniscient narrator says,

> Sometimes at night, when he lay in bed and tried to figure it out, he felt as if he were descended from some madman's dream. Indians rode spotted horses over golden plains. . . . They lived in the light of the sun, where nothing was hidden and earth rose up to sky. . . . They sat horseback against the infinite horizon. . . . Those were the Indians they studied in school.

In a second novel, called *The Sharpest Sight*, a work moving between Mississippi and California and drawing heavily upon my own family, I wrote of a young Choctaw-Cherokee-Irish mixedblood who must learn who he is and how to balance a world that has led his brother to madness and destroyed him, a world of stories in deadly conflict. I used my father's name, Hoey, and my grandfather's name, Luther, in that novel, and I created a powerful old Choctaw lady named Onatima whom I modeled upon what I remembered and imagined of my grandma. Onatima, too, ran away with a gambler on the great river. I also based a major character in that novel on my brother Gene, who had come back from three tours in Vietnam with such pain that he became one of the psychological casualties who disappeared into the Ozark Mountains of Arkansas. For me it had been as if he never came back from the war, and that is how and perhaps why I wrote the novel. Later, after emerging from long familial isolation, he would jokingly say to our sister, "Gee, first he put me in a mental hospital and then he killed me. What's he going to do to me next?" Because I wanted to explore mixed and relational identity—the liminal landscape of the mixedblood—more fully, I also included in *The Sharpest Sight* a young mestizo named Mundo Morales who discovers in his own blood an inextricable web of inherited identities.

In a third novel, *Bone Game*, published in 1994, I reentered the life of Cole McCurtain from *The Sharpest Sight* and the lives of his family in order to examine imprints of evil left upon the American landscape by the European invaders' destructive violence. In that novel I delved further into my grandma's story—Onatima's story—imagining the feelings that must have driven her to flee with her gambler and the pain of returning home to marriage. In this third novel Cole McCurtain, twenty years after going home to Mississippi in *The Sharpest Sight*, is still uncertain as to who he is. Maybe the message is that certainty is not a condition mixedbloods can know.

In 1996 I published a fourth novel, *Nightland*, a work written for my mother, who had died five years before, and about whom I have never been able to write. She was a person of compassion so great it could only have come from long and difficult struggle. This novel was also written for and dedicated to my Aunt Betty, the last surviving member of my mother's family, who had telephoned to ask if I would help her find out who she was. I realized then with some guilt that I had written about the Choctaw side of my inheritance, my father's side, but not about my mother's Cherokee roots. By traditional values, of course, I would be identified matrilineally as Cherokee although I had not grown up among any Cherokee people other than my own family. Thus I wrote *Nightland*, a novel set in New Mexico but woven out of the specific fabric of Cherokee mythology and history.

Every work is a different gamble and exploration. Every work teaches me a great deal. As a university professor, I watch students bring me their stories, even their novels, and I marvel again and again at the force that drives us to so make and remake the world. I imagine a world crowded with stories that jostle one another and war for space, a world in which pigs are killed and eaten by dancing shadows and a young boy imagines that he watches and then carries that imagining with him for forty years. Stories that carry us from the muddy waters of the Yazoo River to a tent in California and a glacial world of sheerest blue and frozen light. What is this thing that so compels us to thus organize and articulate the world? It is all in the way family stories when nothing is written down become the same kind of moonless dance I recall from that Mississippi night so long ago, the motion of fire and form.

12

Water Witch

♦

California

For a while when I was very young, my father was a water witch. He took us with him sometimes, my older brother and me, and we walked those burned-up central California ranches, wherever there was a low spot that a crop-and-cattle desperate rancher could associate with a dream of wetness. The dusty windmills with their tin blades like pale flowers would be turning tiredly or just creaking windward now and then, and the ranch dogs—always long haired, brown and black with friendly eyes—would sweep their tails around from a respectful distance. The ranches, scattered near places like Creston, Pozo, San Miguel, and San Ardo, stretched across burnt gold hills, the little ranch houses bent into themselves beneath a few dried-up cottonwoods or sycamores, some white oaks if the rancher's grandfather had settled early enough to choose his spot. Usually there would be kids, three or four ranging from diapers to hot-rod pickups, and like the friendly ranch dogs they would keep their distance. The cattle would hang close to the fences, eyeing the house and gray barn. In the sky, red-tailed hawks wheeled against a washed-out sun while ground squirrels whistled warnings from the grain stubble.

He would walk, steps measured as if the earth demanded measure, the willow fork held in both hands before him pointed at the ground like some kind of offering. We would follow a few yards behind with measured paces. Nearly always the wand would finally tremble, dip, and dance toward the dead wild oats, and he would stop to drive a stick into the ground or pile a few rock-dry clods in a cairn.

A displaced Mississippi Choctaw, half-breed, squat and reddish, blind in one eye, he would spit tobacco juice at the stick or cairn and turn back toward the house, feeling maybe the stirring of Yazoo mud from the river of his birth as if the water he never merely discovered, but drew all that way from a darker, damper world. Within a few days he would be back with his boss and they would drill a well at the spot he had marked. Not once did the water fail, but always it was hidden and secret, for that was the way of water in our part of California.

When I think now of growing up in that country, the southern end of the Salinas Valley, a single mountain range from the ocean, I remember first the great hidden water, the Salinas River, which ran out of the Santa Lucias and disappeared where the coastal mountains bent inland near San Luis Obispo. Dammed at its headwaters into a large reservoir where we caught bluegill and catfish, the river never had a chance. Past the spillway gorge, it sank into itself and became the largest subterranean river on the continent, a half-mile-wide swath of brush and sand and cottonwood with a current you could feel down there beneath your feet when you hunted the river bottom. As if a water witch yourself, you swayed at every step toward the stream below.

We lived first in withdrawn canyons in the Santa Lucias, miles up dirt roads into the creases of the Coast Range, where we kids squirmed through buck brush and plotted long hunts to the ocean. But there were no trails, and the manzanita would turn us back with what we thought must be the scent of the sea in our nostrils. Rattlesnakes, bears, and mountain lions lived back there. And stories of mythic wild boars drifted down from ranches to the north. In the spring the hills would shine with new grass and the dry creeks would run for a few brief weeks. We would hike across a ridge to ride wild horses belonging to a man who never knew that we rode them. In summer the grasses burned brown and the clumps of live oaks on the hillsides formed dark places in the distance.

Later we lived down in the valley on the caving banks of the river. At seven and nine years we had hunted with slingshots in the mountains, but at ten and twelve we owned rifles, .22s, and we stalked the dry river brush for quail and cottontails and the little brush rabbits that, like the pack rats, were everywhere. Now and then a deer would break ahead of us, crashing thickets like the bear himself. Great horned owls lived there and called in drumming voices, vague warnings of death somewhere. From the river bottom we pinged .22 slugs off new farm equipment gliding past on the flatcars of the Southern Pacific.

Once in a while we would return to Mississippi, as if my father's mixed blood sought a balance never found. Seven kids, a dog or two, canvas water bags swaying from fender and radiator, we drove into what I remember as the darkness of the Natchez Trace. In our two-room Mississippi cabin, daddy longlegs crawled across the tar-papered walls, and cotton fields surged close on three sides. Across the rutted road through a tangle of tree, brush, and vine, fragrant of rot and death, was the Yazoo River, a thick current cutting us off from the swamps that boomed and cracked all night from the other shore.

From the Yazoo we must have learned to feel water as a presence, a constant, a secret source of both dream and nightmare, perhaps as my father's Choctaw ancestors had. I remember it as I remember night. Always we would return to California after a few months, as much as a year. And it would be an emergence, for the Salinas was a daylight world of hot, white sand and bone-dry brush, where in the fall, red and gold leaves covered the sand and frost made silver lines from earth to sky. Here, death and decay seemed unrelated things. And here, I imagined the water as a clear, cold stream through white sand beneath my feet.

Only in the winter did the Salinas change. When the rains came pounding down out of the Coast Range, the river would rise from its bed to become a half-mile-wide terror, sweeping away chicken coops and misplaced barns; whatever had crept too near. Tricked each year into death, steelhead trout would dash upstream from the ocean, and almost immediately the flooding river would recede to a thin stream at the heart of the dry bed, then a few pools marked by the tracks of coons, then only sand again and the tails and bones of big fish.

When I think of growing up in California, I think always of the river. It seemed then that all life referred to the one hundred and twenty miles of sand and brush that twisted its way northward, an upside-down, backwards river that emptied into the Pacific near Monterey, a place I did not see till I was grown. As teenagers, my brother and I bought our own rifles, a .30-.30 and an ought-six, and we followed our father into the Coast Range after deer and wild boar. We acquired shotguns and walked the high coastal ridges for band-tail pigeon. We drove to fish the headwaters of the Nacimiento and the San Antonio Rivers. And from every ridgetop we saw, if not the river itself, then the long, slow course of the valley it had carved, the Salinas. Far across were the rolling Gabilan Mountains, more hawk hills than mountains, and on the valley bottom, ranches made squares of green and gold, with flashing windmills and tin roofs.

After school and during summers we worked on the ranches, hoeing sugar beets, building fences, bucking hay, working cattle (dehorning, castrating, branding, ear clipping, inoculating, all in what must have seemed a single horrific moment for the bawling calf). We would cross the river to drive at dawn through the dry country watching the clumps of live oak separate from the graying hillsides. Moving shadows would become deer that drifted from dark to dark. Years later, coming home from another state, I would time my drive so that I reached that country at daybreak to watch the oaks rise out of night and to smell the damp, dead grasses.

Snaking its way down through our little town was a creek. Dipping out of the Coast Range, sliding past chicken farms and country stores, it pooled in long, shadowed clefts beneath the shoulders of hills and dug its own miniature canyon as it passed by the high school, beneath U.S. 101, around the flanks of the county hospital, and on to the river, where it gathered in a final welling before sinking into the sand. En route it picked up the sweat and stink of a small town, the flotsam and jetsam of stunted aspirations, and along its course in tree shadow and root tangle, under cutbank and log, it hid small, dark trout we caught with hook and handline. From the creek came also steelhead trapped by a vanished river and great blimp-bellied suckers that hunkered close to the bottom, even a single outraged bullhead that I returned to its solitary pool. At the place where the chicken-processing plant disgorged a yellow stream into the creek, the trout grew fat and sluggish, easily caught. We learned every shading and wrinkle of the creek, not knowing then that it was on the edge already, its years numbered. I, more than anyone, fisher of tainted trout, kept what I thought of as a pact with the dying creek: as long as the water flows and the grass grows.

Up on Pine Mountain, not so much looming as leaning over the town of my younger years, a well-kept cemetery casts a wide shadow. From this cemetery one fine summer evening, a local youth exhumed his grandmother to drive about town with her draped over the hood of his car, an act so shocking no punishment could be brought to bear. Later, when I asked him why, he looked at me in wonder. "Didn't you ever want to do that?" he asked. That fall, after a bitter football loss, members of the high-school letterman's club kidnapped a bus full of rooters from a rival school, holding them briefly at gunpoint with threats of execution. The summer before, an acquaintance of mine had stolen a small plane and dive-bombed the town's hamburger stand with empty beer bottles. The town laughed. Later, he caught a Greyhound bus to Oregon, bought a shotgun in a small town, and killed himself. It was that kind of place also. Stagnant between Coast Range and river, the town, too, had subterranean currents, a hot-in-summer, cold-in-winter kind of submerged violence that rippled the surface again and again. Desires to exhume and punish grew strong. Escape was just around the corner.

Behind the cemetery, deep in a wrinkle of the mountain, was an older burial ground, the town's original graveyard, tumbled and hidden in long grasses and falling oaks. Parting the gray oat stalks to read the ancient stones, I felt as astonished back then as a Japanese soldier must have when he first heard the words of a Navajo code talker. Here was a language that pricked through time, millennia perhaps, with painful familiarity but one that remained inexorably remote.

A year ago, I drove back to the house nine of us had lived in on the banks of the river. The house was gone, and behind the empty lot the river had changed. Where there had been a wilderness of brush and cottonwoods there was now only a wide, empty channel gleaming like bone. Alfalfa fields swept coolly up from the opposite bank toward a modern ranch house. "Flood control," someone in the new Denny's restaurant told me later that afternoon. "Cleaned her out clear to San Miguel," he said.

13

Shared Blood

◆

New Mexico

My eldest daughter was two years old and intent on monkey bars so high above that they might have been the rungs of some heaven, when a little boy on the playground turned to her and said, in a voice as pure as mountain water, "Are you Japanese or Chinese?" My daughter, with her pale olive skin and almond-shaped green eyes, considered the little blond-haired boy who had been following her wistfully around the playground and finally replied, "I'm Elizabeth."

The little boy had evidently noticed the epicanthic folds that mark my daughter's eyes, what *Webster's New Collegiate Dictionary* defines as "a prolongation of a fold of the skin of the upper eyelid over the inner angle or both angles of the eye-called also *Mongolian fold*." This is the same characteristic that marks the eyes of many Native Americans, giving some of us a noticeably Asiatic cast. The same thing had happened to me throughout childhood, to such an extent that in fifth grade I finally gave in and proclaimed myself the great-nephew of Chiang-Kai-Shek, a name in the news a lot back then. The marbles-shooting, distance-spitting, sex-fabulationists I hung out with in fifth grade believed me. To my peers I became for a while the mixed-race descendent of an internationally prominent Nationalist Chinese leader, a position of some status. Not long afterwards, however, even more tired of the renewed ching-chong-chinaman baiting, I gave in to an even more perverse impulse and told an intimate friend—himself part Osage Indian and part Jewish—that in truth the freakishness of my slanted eyes was owing to a terrible birth trauma: a doctor had dragged me into the world with great pliers, pulling my eyes crooked in the process. Naturally my friend spread that bit of news with gusto. So long Nationalist China and hello handicap.

The truth, of course, as I knew well, was that my odd, slanty eyes were my inheritance from Cherokee and Choctaw grandmothers on both maternal and paternal sides, their hazel coloring the residue of Irish influence. But Indians were not cool back then the way they are now. To be part Indian was to invite war whoops on the playground and many scalping jokes. And our family's littered and fairly notorious poverty on the edge of our small town would have unquestionably been identified with being Indian, something I did not want. Bad enough to live where we did and how we did, with over-the-hill refrigerators and a couple of even further over-the-hill, cannibalized automobiles constantly in the yard. Bad enough to drive through town in a junker car crammed with nine kids and a father spitting tobacco juice on the nice streets of nice white people and to hear the inevitable "dollar's worth" in a definitely not-California accent when we stopped at the gas station. My Osage friend, a military brat whose father kept abreast of tribal politics and had survived the Bataan Death March (and of whom I still stand in awe today), knew we were Indian, of course, but the diabolical doctor with the big pliers made a much better story for everyone concerned; besides, my friend was part Indian, too, and his eyes were blue and round like everyone else's.

"I'm Elizabeth," my daughter replied in the kind of innocence we must all desire—the search for which, in fact, has driven Euramerica across a whole continent in a dire and pathological attempt to escape from history and reclaim a Garden innocence, to spring, as one of America's great writers put it, from our own Platonic conception of ourselves. It would be splendid if my daughter inhabited a world in which she could in fact be "Elizabeth" and not a cultural commodity of one sort or another that must be labeled and compartmentalized. Why must we be categorized by this invented thing called race or ethnicity?

What a strange concept: Mixedblood. As though the blood of human beings could fuse together in coitus somehow, yet not quite fuse, so that a human being might move from dark to dark with parallel streams running inside him or her. Although I have thought and written considerably about the mixedblood in American literature and American culture—and have done so in this present volume, in fact—perhaps paradoxically I have to think that on some crucial level it may be wrong in a profound ethical, moral, deeply human way to even conceive of such a thing. ("Suppose you should contradict yourself; what then?" says Emerson.)

I grew up being told I was part Cherokee, part Choctaw, part Irish, part Cajun, perhaps Welsh, too. What that meant, I came to know somehow, was that people before me, who in generational history had birthed me, had been both wanderers from far places and dreamers and warriors and storytellers in this place called America. Those people had accepted distance, dreams, magic, and difficulty into their lives the way I was supposed to accept the same into mine. They were not only Europeans shaken loose from whatever had once held them, but also Choctaw from what I was taught to call Mississippi (M-i-crooked-letter-crooked-letter-i-crooked-letter-crooked-letter-i-hump-back-humpback-i) and Cherokee from Oklahoma, the land of red men, what my mother's family called the Nation. And my brothers and sisters and I accepted very easily that inherited world, as well as our peripatetic life-style, the way we all accept the worlds our parents and grandparents create for us in their myriad stories and in the fabric of our real lives. When I returned from a backpacking trip in high school to find that my family had moved, leaving no forwarding address, I was not terribly surprised. We did things like that. Creditors had closed in. I found them two hundred miles away a month or so later, no hard feelings.

The night she died in my sister's home more than a thousand miles away, my mother came to me in a dream to say good-bye, an experience as real as any I have ever had. I awoke crying, mourning, and called my sister to confirm what I had already been told. And I paid careful attention when, more than a year later, my mother came twice again to speak to me in times of difficulty. Having grown up in a world of realized dreams and stories that wove those dreams into the tangle of our mixed lives, I was prepared for what others would call superstition, unprepared, in fact, to question in the slightest. Recently I described that experience to a younger brother and sister, only to find that they stared at me in amazement. The same thing had happened to them. My brother, serving seven years in a state penitentiary, had been crying in his cell bunk when our mother appeared and told him everything would be okay. Our sister had been at home. Our mother had come to each of us on the same night. What is real then? Is this where the bloods mix, the streams run parallel with separate and divisible banks? Do some dream real dreams and others lie fallow in their nights?

With what are we mixed? Too often, I think, we are pushed toward an ignorance of the other side, the other "other." Celtic in my case, and Cajun French. So that when little people came to my mother's dreams, there might have been the nagging question as to whether the little ones had come from her Irish or Cherokee roots, both of which told of such spirits. The three little men who came to her in a dream to foretell her stepfather's death most certainly arose from her Cherokee world, I think. Her little people were serious prophets of doom and death; they did not sound like the tricksterish hide-behinds of Choctaw stories or the mischievous leprechauns I had read about or seen in movies. And my grandmother's long dark hair that trailed along the floor, winding through those thick Mississippi swamps into my dreams yet today, wrapping my life in a time and place that still lives, was it French or Choctaw? And where, at what moment, in what darkness was engendered the love of an unidentifiable Frenchman estranged from home and family for a Choctaw woman—my grandmother's grandmother—whose dark skin and quick smile must have birthed memories of home and blood?

I want to know these things, but they are irretrievable, vanished in lost voices. I want to feel the quickening of pulse that Frenchman felt, so far from home and driven there by what must have been powerful forces, when he saw her. I know that feeling; it rushes through me. For the first experience must have been sight. And what of her, this

Choctaw woman? Did she see the Frenchman as a splinter of some force that was already overwhelming her people, a savior of death from death? Was he a shadowy reflection of those Spaniards who, two centuries earlier, had visited violence and astonishment upon the Choctaw before going away for generations that were left only with stories of alien death? Or could it have been a motion of hand and eye, a subtle movement of lips and arm, the ancient and completely human signals of procreation? Could I, born centuries earlier, have fought and perhaps died to save my people from the invaders, or would I have been the invader himself? Or, in the end, are the invader's wrath and the Native's desire merged into something new and defined as what the Chippewa writer Gerald Vizenor calls survivance?

I want to know these things, want to feel them in the torsion of my own bloods. My mother's grandfather was said (by my grandmother) to have been an "Indian Scout" in the "Territory." John Bailey, entered on the 1910 Oklahoma census as a Cherokee mixedblood. Married, so family story says, to a fullblood Cherokee woman named Edith with no last name. He is there, a mixedblood on the census and in the rolls and in recently discovered family photographs, but she is not. Who was he, this early product of miscegenation? How did he draw into his circumference this fullblood Cherokee woman? Who was she, this woman who must have been called from the fullblood's cabin and family stories to wed the mixedblood? We know that she disappeared as soon as my grandmother was born, most likely through death, but the trail ends there. There are no photographs, no papers, no birth certificates, death certificates, written records of her existence. For so many like my great-grandmother, erasure edged the outline of family and clan stories. In her dreams, I like to imagine, buzzard dipped his wings to wrinkle the earth while ravens swooped and trembled over-head and surely a red sun blanketed the east, red raven and redman watching and waiting, the bones of the people dancing beyond the next ridge.

The Chatah people, my father's distant relations, carried their bones from the west, so many they had to set down their load and rest, returning for more. And today, we still carry all those bones, sometimes so burdensome that any end, any termination is desired. Thus our young often leave us too soon, burdened not merely by history but by lives that are caricature: Redskins and Chiefs, Braves and Indians, Jeep Cherokees and Mazda Navajos.

Choctaw, Cherokee, Irish, French. Time and linear history have constructed such words as lines of demarcation, a kind of embargo of the blood—but we know better. Mixedbloods live in the ebbings of history. The full-moon tide of the future. Water lapping at the gravel and sandbar where spawning is possible, but the increasing siltation of clear-cut history a choking death.

For me, mixedblood means my father's dark skin and hair thicker and richer than my own, his difference from every other father I have known, his isolation and silence. My mother's compassion, the kind of resignation that comes from not one generation but generations of pain. Not professional victimization that we see too often, but simple understanding that life is difficult, love a gift pure and simple and often the only gift possible. The result of something called the Trail of Tears—The Trail Where They Cried—where one quarter of the Cherokee people died. And the Choctaws as well, on another long walk, dead by the thousands, though that is seldom mentioned. I imagine that: Children frozen to the ground each morning, mothers struggling to raise their faces from hair locked in ice while babies cry at the starved breast. At least four thousand Cherokees dead. Obviously many survived, but at what cost? Do we all bear this survivor's guilt that may be part of what drives even our best to self-destruct? For we know now that it is not just the dropouts and the terminal cases that end it, but painfully often those who are supposedly moving upward, mobile into American society, toward the American Dream. With what passes for success in sight, they terminate the process—with a bullet, drink, a wrecked car, a lost job, a class not completed, or whatever. For many, success means we leave family and relations, and often the only selves we know, behind. Authentic selves hang tattered on berry vines somewhere back there beside the trail, we think. America built that end, the Vanishing American, wove it into our red and white blood. Today, my family reads my books, stories, or essays with pride, pleased I think to find bits of themselves in printed words, and we call each other to chat about small things—the carburetor that just cannot be fixed, the big fish that got away—but we do not talk about what I do or how I live. The distance is so great that it becomes a kind of embarrassment.

And the Irishmen and Frenchmen who came to marry Cherokee and Choctaw wives—what drove those men from their family and shore? How did they end up at the edge of what they called civilization, married to darker women whose flesh told their stories?

We, my family, moved from Mississippi to California, from the rich decay of the Yazoo River to the golden hills of the golden state. My mother, grandmother, aunt, and uncle fled from Oklahoma and the Cherokee Nation to the shipyards of California. My father ran away from Mississippi to join the army at age fifteen. At twenty he was married to my mother, I was born, and we were all headed back to Mississippi. Sure, it is confusing and you lose track, but isn't that the way it is supposed to be? Mixedblood. *Isn't that concept the purest kind of ridiculous nonsense?* Implying the mixing of bloods as some kind of definition of cultural, human quantum. Shall we say *shared-blood* instead?[1] It doesn't sound right, does it?

In many ways it was not difficult growing up as a mixedblood. I know people want to feel the pain, to share the agony of those of us supposedly lost between worlds, neither Indian nor white, cultural castaways doomed to mutter ceaseless questions of identity and worth, but it was not that way. Except for odd eyes, I look white—the kind of white that makes Europeans assume I am Hungarian or Czech or Slovak or something from over *that* way, that made everyone when I traveled in South America assume I was from the country just over the nearest border. Passing was easy, something I did not really have to think about very much. The hard part was being poor in a small town where people knew everyone. Dirt poor, shit poor, offal poor, embarrassing poor. The kind of poor that brought neighbors to the door with pots of watery soup and tied an adolescent's guts into knots. But with nine children and a third-grade education, what could my father do? And with nine children and a third-grade education, what could my mother do? Work was not enough. Shame covered us like the green woolen army blankets we slept under and the commodity peanut butter, raisins, lard, canned "meat," rolled oats, and butter we gathered from the government each month to supplement the deer, rabbit, quail, fish, and mountains of potatoes and beans we consumed. Is this part of the way we define "mixedblood" identity? Was poverty the result of being part Indian? Was it the result of Mississippi whites who stole Choctaw homelands and denied Choctaw people the right to humanity? The result of white Americans so greedy for Cherokee and Choctaw land that they would enact a more brutal form of what in the former Yugoslavia has recently been called "ethnic cleansing"? Perhaps. Or perhaps it was more the end result of a merger of outcasts from both continent and tribe, for poverty knows no color. Maybe it was nothing more than the crosscut merger of marginalized and desperate people. Is the fact that my only two uncles by blood, maternal and paternal, were the victims of unsolved murders somehow related to their mixedblood lives? Such things are impossible to know, of course. But I do know, from many conversations with friends and acquaintances, that these are experiences common to Native American peoples, mixedblood or full.

The truth is that despite hardships not uncommon to many people of many different origins, despite starting to work in the bean fields alongside people called *braceros* when I was nine years old, mixedblood identity was not in itself painful. *Au contraire* (says my Cajun ancestor), it was, I believe, an important part of what kept us alive. We loved the stories of times and places so unlike where we were. We knew that lightning-struck trees were powerful, and we feared the owls that brought warnings of death. To hear the owl was to know death was near. To dream of a ghost was to invite death. To catch a fish with crushed black walnuts in a gunnysack was tradition. Although we often brushed the stories aside, or listened with one ear on a different channel (such as Wolfman Jack's radio program), I think the nine of us children blossomed with the mixed or shared blood, that we felt the earth in a special way and knew dreams as private and dear. We went into the night afraid yet protected, both feelings special, perhaps, to our mixedblood existence.

However, though it may not necessarily be painful, to be what is called a mixedblood is never to rest. One may opt for this side or that, but one is always balanced on a thin line between ways of knowing. A choice is there, in every day and moment. But only because cultures insist upon choice. Humanity is commonplace. A Frenchman or an Irishman is no less complex, no less human than a Choctaw or a Cherokee. Blend the four and you arrive at the place of your beginning: humanity. In between, however, one wrestles with choices. And America makes choice a difficult proposition for the Native American mixedblood because America loves Indians. America loves Indians so much it has tried to kill them to the last mother and child so that it might inhabit the empty skin. For Americans will never be at peace with this place; America will haunt its colonizers to their endless graves. The damp and desiccated earth will cast them off, no matter whose skin they wear. And to be mixedblood is to know that they are you, just as you are inescapably other.

Mixedbloods are fixed in a straitjacket of history, a metaphor not chosen lightly, for history attempts to bind the mixedblood into a certain and paradoxical schizophrenia. The mixedblood is not allowed ambiguity but only bifurcation, a breakdown in the signifying chain. The world has, from the point of view of the Indian or mixedblood, a most astonishing and often shocking investment in determining the singular definition of Indianness. One is Indian or one is not Indian. The mixedblood is forced to choose, to check a single box on every form. And the seminal bed, like that Spouter Inn conjugal place of Ishmael and Queequeg in *Moby-Dick*, is the clawing desire of white America to BE Indian. The Indian is desired, deeply and with a deadly, erotic earnestness, by Euramerica. What the Euramerican world wants is to capture and empty that space called Indian and to reinhabit it, becoming Indian. Only thusly, do they feel in their guts, can European Americans achieve a oneness with the invaded land, the land they are in the process of destroying with a ferocity truly unimaginable. America wants to dance with wolves and find the buffalo, but America has driven both to the precipice of extinction.

In-between does not cut it in the mixedblood world. Recently I watched part of a television program about a black man who was white. I came into the show late and missed the essential opening explanations. Therefore, all I know is that the white man I saw on television was really a black man, although there was nothing phenotypically black about him at all. He had been beaten as a child by a white mob for being black and showed the scars he bore to prove it. *What in the world is going on here?* Though the man looked for all the world white, he had been stoned for having black parents and thus being black. He was black, and white people had violently contested his right to be other than black. Now if that man were claiming to be Indian, the very same white people might be ridiculing him for his claims and stoning him until he admitted his whiteness. Some essentialist Indian people, too, would probably be picking up rocks to force the man toward whiteness.[2]

Clearly something is skewed here. If it takes only the most minute drop of "black" blood to make a person black, why must it take a preponderance of "Indian" blood—or a government number—to make a person a real Indian? Could we be dealing with a question of commodification? Could it be that white America bears a powerful residue of the old slave-owning sense that it is always most economically profitable to label a man or woman black if possible? A black person was once worth money to white America. And could it be that the same white America wants, deep, deep down in its colonial soul, to be Indian so desperately that such a quality becomes a bitterly contested value, a highly eroticized value, as the recent abominable movies *Dances With Wolves* and *Pocahontas* make painfully clear? America wants to strip itself bare, like Dunbar in *Dances With Wolves*, bathe in purifying baptismal waters, and confront—and in confronting possess—Indianness.

Mixedbloods in America inhabit an often hostile and bitterly contested realm. White America is intensely jealous of the mixedblood's claim to an essential place in this land, this beloved earth. White America feels its displacement, its not-at-homeness, and knows that it is very rapidly killing the only home left. Indian America, on the other hand, often bitterly resents the mixedblood's supposed ability to move between worlds, to reap a harvest from blood and shame. The mixedblood, it is often thought on both Indian and white sides, exploits Indianness in a way unavailable to others. What is ignored or forgotten is the price paid every step of the way, that has been paid by generations.

My brother and I hunted and trapped rabbits on mornings when red and gold leaves lay on the sand and sycamores stood like cold shadows, when the rains of the last winter had been forgotten and the new rains were the merest promise of the earth. We moved with thoughtless love across the frozen ground. We trapped in the old way our mother's brother had taught us, with traps made of hollow logs and figure-four triggers, and sometimes we even fished in the old way, grappling with hands or sinking crushed black walnuts into pools, contrary to every California law, not knowing that what we did was "Indian," thinking merely that it was human. We went to school, my older brother and I being the only two of the nine children to successfully negotiate high school, and, most strangely, I stumbled on in spite of every prediction—and despite dropping out several times—to a college education and a Ph.D.

To be mixedblood for me and my family meant not just difficulty, but a valuable sense of having descended from a people of whom we were proud. It meant possessing a limited knowledge different from that of our neighbors, just as anyone from a different land will know different things. We knew what the owls meant and we knew certain valuable plants that appeared each spring. Simultaneously, we children knew that somehow being who we were meant that our parents had virtually no way of supporting us and that my father would ride a bicycle twelve miles to work to stand for hours in water in a laundry—unable to afford either a working car or rubber boots—until his feet rotted and the flesh fell away when he removed his shoes at night.

Finally, however (and perhaps ironically), he found work as a water witch—a dowser—and enjoyed the luxury of walking the golden hills until his willow wand spoke, a skill not dependent even upon third grade. We knew that our mother's dreams would be shared with us and taken with utmost seriousness and that we would keep such things to ourselves, just as we held her stories close. We know now, as a large family, that being mixedbloods has somehow formed a foundation putting some of us in prison for a long time, some of us on welfare, and some of us in other, stranger parts of the world. We know that others, hearing and seeing us, may wonder and perhaps contest who we are and why we are. In the end, we know that we are a family with shared blood, history, dreams, stories, and love. We will live in liminal space, indeterminate latitudes, and in that we will share the fate of countless Americans. We know at some profound level that we inhabit the future while piecing together the past. We, I and my brothers and sisters—Betty, Gene, Linda, Judy, Troy, Juanita, Richard, and Brenda—shall go on. And like my daughter on that playground, our children, I hope, will continue in the face of questions that separate and divide to announce with confidence who they are.

4

Words, Wilderness, and Native America

14

Mapping, Naming, and the Power of Words

◆

In 1994 I was invited to give the opening address at an environmental writing conference called "The Art of the Wild" in Squaw Valley, California. I had been part of the faculty at the conference twice previously, and, despite very deep qualms about the name of the place, I enjoyed being there. Unlike most writing conferences, this one had not just a beautiful setting but also a shared subject beyond the desire to be a rich and famous writer: Everyone there was concerned in one way or another with the environment and with putting that concern into written language. Also, we had developed a fellowship program to bring young Native American writers to the conference, and the faculty had included such superb Indian writers and scholars as Luci Tapahonso, Gerald Vizenor, James Welch, and Edward Castillo. Despite my admiration for the conference, however, I tried to dodge the keynote invitation, for it had occurred to me not long before (a blasphemous thought for an academic) that I should actually have something to say when I talk to people, and my first thought was, what in the world could I say to a room full of writers. In addition, I knew that I would be in the midst of moving from Santa Cruz, California, to Tijeras, New Mexico, precisely during the time I should be thinking of something to say. But I like and admire Jack Hicks, the conference founder, and wish him to think well of me, so finally I accepted and said very truthfully that I was honored and flattered and other obsequious-sounding things we say at such times.

And then, while moving with my wife, two daughters, a dog, an octogenarian cat, and ten tropical fish from Santa Cruz to New Mexico, I had to think of something to say. A long day and night in Barstow, California, when our twelve-year-old VW Rabbit surprisingly broke down, dramatically increased my time for contemplation, but as much as I enjoy and admire the no-frills, straight-shooting character of Barstow, I found myself exceptionally dull-witted during my stay there. Perhaps it was the annual, world-famous Firecracker 200 or 300 Off-Road Vehicle Race in Barstow that weekend, featuring battalions of Hummers, or Hum-Vees as they called them during the so-called Gulf War, that distracted me. A dozen Hummers, each with its logo-shirted, very soft-bitten crew, shared our motel, one Hummer requiring two parking spaces. Despite owning an ancient Land Cruiser myself—a necessity for winter trips to the store—I detest almost all off-road vehicles, seeing them as mechanical extensions of the Euramerican manifest destiny that has nearly destroyed this continent. The thought of those three-yard-wide, all-terrain Hummer abominations tearing up the Mojave Desert was especially disturbing. I was not inspired to write about the art of the wild by my thirty-six-hour breakdown in Barstow.

Fortunately, a week in an empty house in the Manzano Mountains of New Mexico, waiting with my family, dog, cat, and ten dead fish for all of our possessions to arrive in a moving van a week behind schedule, gave me long hours for contemplation. With neither typewriter nor computer available, I began to record my deep thoughts on my youngest daughter's yellow notebook paper with my oldest daughter's fat black calligraphic pen, a combination I found extremely satisfying. I experienced, in fact, a kind of Proustian flashback in which I was reminded of the writing I had done in first and second grades when teachers gave me a fat brown pencil and a piece of thick beige paper with green lines—back when making words on paper was a new, exciting, and very difficult enterprise. In second grade, written—or even printed—words did not come easily. Each one seemed precious. In second grade, I breathed deeply, concentrated on the lovely architecture of letters, and tried unsuccessfully to stay between the lines—much as I did in preparing my talk for Art of the Wild. And in second grade I would sit uncountable hours on a hillside in the California Coast Range, hidden by tall wild oats, marveling with all the intensity a seven-year-old can muster at the sheer, inconceivable, gut-wrenching wonder of the natural world. The wondrous experience of that time included—as I noted above—digging a five-foot-deep cave in a hillside with my brother and finding at the bottom two arrowheads and a little white stone effigy, reminders of a more distant time and a people who had once inhabited that place. We naively collected the beautiful items, taking the doll to our mother as a gift. We thought it strange and disappointing that she "lost" the little carving almost immediately, and it was not until years later that I realized she had respectfully returned the figure to the soil from which it had come.

We were all there in Squaw Valley, I think, because we shared deep, or at least strong, feelings for two things: the word and the natural world. Our shared medium was written language, and our announced subject was something very loosely termed the Art of the Wild. By "wild" I assumed that we meant the natural world, not excluding humanity, that exists prior to and beyond our mechanical transformations of our environment.

In considering what art and wildness might mean to me, I remembered one evening in 1970 when I sat by a fire next to the Suiattle River in the North Cascade Mountains. I was working as part of a four-man trail crew in the Glacier Peak Wilderness, and we had spent that day grubbing out painfully steep switchbacks on the Miner's Ridge trail above our camp—ironically, of course, making the "wilderness" less wild, with the futile intention of keeping backpackers and horse-packers between the lines. The Cascades were experiencing a stupendously rare bout of sunshine that August, and we had been doing what loggers and trail crews called hoot-owling, getting up at three in the morning so that we could finish our eight hours before the worst heat struck the high country. During that particular day of hard, sweaty work with pulaskis and hazel hoes, one of our distinguished crew of three English majors and one M.A. in biology had paused and, posed against a backdrop of what seemed a thousand Cascade peaks, begun to quote Gary Snyder's wonderful haiku about switchbacks: "Turn, turn, / and again hard- / scrabble / steep travel a / head." That evening, our young and poetic souls borne aloft on the conjunction of wilderness and a slight after-dinner libation, we composed a fan letter to the poet of the day. "Dear Mr. Snyder," we wrote. "Us guys on the Milk Creek Trail Crew think your poetry is swell." We signed it MCTC and mailed it in the Darrington, Washington, post office at the end of that ten-day camp-out. Although we did not receive a reply, a few years later at a gathering in Davis, California, Gary Snyder swore to me that he not only remembered the letter but had responded to it. Since I for one was known and falsely suspected of being a no-good "Sahara Clubber" and Communist sympathizer at the Darrington Post Office, and Indians were not highly esteeemed in that redneck community to begin with, I have come to believe that Mr. Snyder's letter to us was intercepted and ceremonially desecrated by local interested parties.

I was not then but am now fully aware of certain hostility toward Snyder's poetry in Native American circles. He has been accused of something called "white shamanism" and of something like appropriation, and there may be some truth in the latter. However, we wrote our preposterous fan letter because we were collectively moved by Gary Snyder's poetry, for he had written about places we loved, had put into perfect language the rocks and trees and rivers and mountains we reveled and sweated in every day. He had written beautifully about grubbing trail and had written with admiration of the loggers and wranglers whom we admired hugely even though they suspected us of Communist tendencies. He had made us care for and about these places and people before we had ever seen or touched them, and he had done it with words that were real and hard wrought and never wasted. In our ranger district there were individuals who, upon being pressed, allowed as to how they actually remembered the Gary Snyder who had worked for the Forest Service in the North Cascades. They recalled that he was a "goddamned good worker," and there was simply no higher praise than that among those men and women. Fred Berry, a man who possessed a less than sunny disposition and the biggest biceps I had ever seen, even remembered running the ferry boat that took Jack Kerouac across a lake to the foot of Desolation Peak. Although none of these men seemed aware that Snyder and Kerouac were known in other parts of the world as writers, they remembered vividly how these world-famous men had worked. Kerouac, according to Fred Berry, was "the laziest sonofabitch I ever saw."

My talk was not intended to be a tribute to Gary Snyder, but it did not strike me then and does not strike me now as such a bad thing to do. For I can think of no writer who has realized the art of the wild as completely as has Snyder. When I was twenty-one years old, I could sit on an alpine ridge in the North Cascades and see Snyder Country, a wild and delicate landscape of young peaks, glaciated volcanoes, and waterfalls at every bend in the trail. A place so beautiful it could turn your soul inside out with a stroke of light. A place where men and women sweated and marked the land with an often violent kind of love. I could almost reach out and touch Glacier Peak, the astonishing white volcano up which Snyder had prodded and cajoled none other than Allen Ginsberg. And I could look north and see the rugged silhouette of Desolation Peak, where Snyder had contrived to place his city-slicker friend Jack Kerouac one summer, a summer that produced Kerouac's wonderful book, *Desolation Angels*.

In the summer of seventy-six, I was assigned the task of burning and eradicating all evidence of the White Pass Shelter, an ancient, three-sided log structure close to Glacier Peak, a job I did during a five-day snowstorm with truly impressive thoroughness. Only later, in reading *Earth House Hold*, did I realize that Snyder and Ginsberg had camped there and come across Snyder's description of the now-extinct log shelter as "inside like a primitive Japanese farmhouse."

The real subject of my talk at Squaw Valley that day, however, was not Gary Snyder or nostalgic remembrances of trail crew. What I had come to think about while taking notes on my daughter's yellow pad was the extraordinary power of words and our responsibility for using them with care. This is a fact of language that Native American people have always held close. According to Cherokee belief, for example, we can form and alter the world for good or bad with language, even with thought. The Glacier Peak Wilderness is a very real place in the state of Washington, and, like so much of the world, it is critically threatened by humanity's shortsighted inability to recognize our self-destructive folly. A multinational mining company, through a subsidiary, controls a patented claim in the middle of the wilderness at the end of the Miner's Ridge trail we poetic souls were grubbing that day in 1970. The company has plans to mine copper and molybdenum in the very center of the wilderness. Because of one of the enormous loopholes in the 1964 Wilderness Act, they have the right to push a road more than twenty miles into the center of the wilderness, put in a mill site, a townsite, a vast clear-cut for tailings, and so on. It is understatement to say that should they ever put their plans into action they will tear the heart out of the Glacier Peak Wilderness. I pirated copies of those plans from the Forest Service files, and I tried to tell a version of that story in a novel called *Wolfsong*. In doing so, I was conscious of the ambiguity of my own position. For I had participated in the mining company's ultimate goal: to exploit the wilderness. I had cut out windfalls and blasted rockslides to open trails and even installed what we called "wilderness shitters" for the convenience of backpackers; as a fire fighter I had been ferried to a lightning strike in one of the mining company's helicopters and had gratefully guzzled the miners' beer. Most unforgivably, I had felled a magnificent, centuries-old hemlock to make a bridge across a big creek that should never have been bridged.

I happen to be descended from a mix of Choctaw, Cherokee, Irish, and Cajun ancestors. Within all of these cultures the oral tradition runs strong. Stories, I learned very early, make the world knowable and inhabitable. Stories make the world, period. Whether they tell of Raven or Coyote imagining the world into complex being or start by telling us that in the beginning was the Word, and the Word was with God, stories arise from that essential and most human of needs— what the poet Wallace Stevens called that blessed rage for order, the Maker's rage to order words of the sea. Stories also arise out of our inescapable need to feel ourselves related to what John Steinbeck and Edward F. Ricketts, in *The Log from the Sea of Cortez*, called "the whole thing, known and unknowable."

Tyrants have always known the power of language and story. Silence a people's voices and you can conquer them. When Columbus arrived in this part of the world, one of his very first acts was to capture a handful of Taino natives and send them back to Spain. In a letter he explained to the Spanish monarchs, who had forbidden slavery in the so-called New World, that he was sending the Indians to Spain that they might be taught to speak. Clearly, when Columbus heard the Taino language, he did not hear speech. Just as clearly, one of the most common experiences for several generations of Native Americans is having been punished in school for speaking their native language.

Silence a people's stories and you erase a culture. To have graphic evidence of this phenomenon, all we have to do is look at a map. Mapping is, of course, an intensely political enterprise, an essential step toward appropriation and possession. Maps write the conquerors' stories over the stories of the conquered. At the center of the Glacier Peak Wilderness, for example, is the vastly beautiful mountain named on maps, most unimaginatively, Glacier Peak. We look at the peak and see glaciers, and the text of the mountain is laid bare. There are other names for the peak, however, one of which is Dakobed, a Salish word meaning something like Great Mother. The local Indian people, the Suiattle, look at Dakobed and see the place from which they came, the place where they were born, the mother earth. Their stories tell them that they are related in an ancient and crucial way to this magnificent peak. There is an important and invaluable message in this knowledge, for whereas a society may well mine the heart out of something called a natural resource, one does not violate one's mother. The future of that wilderness and, of course, the future of all life depends upon whose stories we listen to: the stories that tell us we are bound in a timeless and inextricable relationship with the earth which gives us life and sustains us, or the stories that tell us the earth is a resource to be exploited until it is used up.

On the day I gave my Art of the Wild talk, we writers were gathered in a beautiful Sierra valley to share ways of knowing and articulating the intangible thing we call the "wild." On maps the place where we had met is called Squaw Valley. Anthropologists—those people who study cultures—tell us that Native peoples, the people we call Washo, have lived in this area for perhaps 3,500 years. Given the way in which anthropologists' clocks are consistently being turned back—and the political investment Euramerica has in making Indians recent arrivals in the Americas—it is likely that these Native people have been there thousands of years longer. I do not know the indigenous name for that particular valley, but I have read that the Washo people who lived around Lake Tahoe called the lake, in an anthropologist's translation, "the life-sustaining water, the center of the world." I have also read that the Washos made special trips to hunt in that particular valley and to follow a trail that ran from there down to the Sacramento Valley to trade with other tribes. Whatever the Washo name for the place, it certainly would have called up particular values and stories for those who uttered it: stories of hunting, camping, exciting trading journeys, stories involving grandfathers and grandmothers, stories of love and, undoubtedly, warfare.

For Indian and non-Indian alike, the name Squaw Valley also comes laden with values and stories, the most universal of which is that evoked in the utterance "Squaw." The *Oxford English Dictionary* tells us that this is an eastern word of Algonquian origin, meaning wife or woman. Other authorities have argued that the word "squaw" is a corruption of the Iroquois word "otsiskwa," meaning "female sexual parts."

In the popular imagination—following centuries of appropriation and use by the invading Europeans—the word "squaw" is often received, and often meant, as derogatory and insulting, conjuring up stereotypes of an inferior race of women, a word popularized by invaders who saw Indian women as objects to be used and abused like the land itself. The frequency with which the word "squaw" has been applied to land forms underscores this corrupt association. White men who cohabited with Indian women were often damned as "Squaw-Men." Squaw Valley is a legacy of the gold rushers and homesteaders who, in only two decades between 1848 and 1870, were responsible for murdering over fifty thousand Native Americans in California alone.

While I would never pretend to speak for Native American people, I know from conversations that the Native American writers who came to the Art of the Wild conference did so with more than a little sense of irony and some doubt. As one participant from a south-western tribal community put it succinctly in her application letter, "That valley needs a new name." But we came there nonetheless, because we shared an urgent sense that the future of all people and, most inescapably, the continued existence of this earth as a habitation for our children and their children depends upon the stories we tell and the words we use. Traditional Native American stories tell us that words are powerful and sacred, that words bring into being and compel and order the world. Words are powerful creators, and they can be powerful destroyers.

I doubt that we would have much success in attempting to change the name of Squaw Valley, famous site of the Winter Olympics. Too much money depends upon the valley's name recognition world wide. Perhaps we should be thankful that elsewhere in the United States, at least, people are successfully fighting to change such names as Squaw Peak in Phoenix; Squaw Lake, a town in Minnesota; and Squaw Butte in Burns, Oregon. However, every time we see the name Squaw Valley on a brochure or utter it in conversation, we should be uncomfortably reminded of the power of language. In myriad ways, of course, we all participate in both the destruction and preservation of the world. To gather in such a beautiful place, with such inspirational company and purpose, beneath ravaged ski slopes and signs reading "Squaw Valley," places us all in that too-familiar bind of complicity and opposition. It is a position that should remind us at every moment of the invaluable significance of what we do as writers and the forces—both internal and external—arrayed against art that would truly be of and for the "wild."

15

Burning the Shelter

◆

In the center of the Glacier Peak Wilderness in northern Washington a magnificent, fully glaciated white volcano rises over a stunningly beautiful region of the North Cascades. On maps, the mountain is called Glacier Peak. As noted above, however, to the Salishan people who have always lived in this part of the Cascades, the mountain is Dakobed, the place of emergence. For the better part of a century a small, three-sided log shelter stood in a place called White Pass just below one shoulder of the great mountain, tucked securely into a meadow between thick stands of mountain hemlock and alpine fir.

In the early fall of seventy-six, while working as a seasonal ranger for the U.S. Forest Service, I drew the task of burning the White Pass shelter. After all those years, the shelter roof had collapsed like a broken bird wing under the weight of winter snow, and the time was right for fire and replanting. It was part of a Forest Service plan to remove all human-made objects from wilderness areas, a plan of which I heartily approved. So I backpacked eleven miles to the pass and set up camp, and for five days, while a bitter early storm sent snow driving horizontally out of the north, I dismantled the shelter and burned the old logs, piling and burning and piling and burning until nothing remained. The antique, hand-forged spikes that had held the shelter together I put into gunnysacks and cached to be packed out later by mule. I spaded up the earth beaten hard for nearly a century by boot and hoof, and transplanted plugs of vegetation from hidden spots on the nearby ridge.

At the end of those five days not a trace of the shelter remained, and I felt good, very smug in fact, about returning the White Pass meadow to its "original" state. As I packed up my camp, the snow-storm had subsided to a few flurries and a chill that felt bone deep with the promise of winter. My season was almost over, and as I started the steep hike down to the trail head my mind was on the cold months I would be spending in sunny Arizona.

A half-mile from the pass I saw the two old women. At first they were dark, hunched forms far down on the last long switchback up the snowy ridge. But as we drew closer to one another I began to feel a growing amazement that, by the time we were face-to-face, had become awe. Almost swallowed up in their baggy wool pants, heavy sweaters, and parkas, silver braids hanging below thick wool caps, they seemed ancient, each weighted with at least seventy years as well as a small backpack. They paused every few steps to lean on their staffs and look out over the North Fork drainage below, a deep, heavily forested river valley that rose on the far side to the glaciers and saw-toothed black granite of the Monte Cristo Range. And they smiled hugely upon seeing me, clearly surprised and delighted to find another person in the mountains at such a time.

We stood and chatted for a moment, and as I did with all back-packers, I reluctantly asked them where they were going. The snow quickened a little, obscuring the view, as they told me that they were going to White Pass.

"Our father built a little house up here," one of them said, "when he worked for the Forest Service like you. Way back before we was born."

"We been coming up here each year since we was little," the other added. "Except last year when Sarah was not well enough."

"A long time ago, this was all our land," the one called Sarah said. "All Indi'n land everywhere you can see. Our people had houses up in the mountains, for gathering berries every year."

As they took turns speaking, the smiles never leaving their faces, I wanted to excuse myself, to edge around these elders and flee to the trail head and my car, drive back to the district station and keep going south. I wanted to say, "I'm Indian, too. Choctaw from Mississippi; Cherokee from Oklahoma"—as if mixed blood could pardon me for what I had done. Instead, I said, "The shelter is gone." Cravenly I added, "It was crushed by snow, so I was sent up to burn it. It's gone now."

I expected outrage, anger, sadness, but instead the sisters continued to smile at me, their smiles changing only slightly. They had a plastic tarp and would stay dry, they said, because a person always had to be prepared in the mountains. They would put up their tarp inside the hemlock grove above the meadow, and the scaly hemlock branches would turn back the snow. They forgave me without saying it—my ignorance and my part in the long pattern of loss that they knew so well.

Hiking out those eleven miles, as the snow of the high country became a drumming rain in the forests below, I had long hours to ponder my encounter with the sisters. Gradually, almost painfully, I began to understand that what I called "wilderness" was an absurdity, nothing more than a figment of the European imagination. An "absolute fake." Before the European invasion, there was no wilderness in North America; there was only the fertile continent where people lived in a hard-learned balance with the natural world. In embracing a philosophy that saw the White Pass shelter—and all traces of humanity—as a shameful stain upon the "pure" wilderness, I had succumbed to a five-hundred-year-old pattern of deadly thinking that separates us from the natural world. This is not to say that what we call wilderness today does not need careful safe-guarding. I believe that White Pass really is better off now that the shelter does not serve as a magnet to backpackers and horsepackers who compact the soil, disturb and kill the wildlife, cut down centuries-old trees for firewood, and leave their litter strewn about. And I believe the man who built the shelter would agree. But despite this unfortunate reality, the global environmental crisis that sends species into extinction daily and threatens to destroy all life surely has its roots in the Western pattern of thought that sees humanity and "wilderness" as mutually exclusive.

In old-growth forests in the North Cascades, deep inside an official Wilderness Area, I have come upon faint traces of log shelters built by Suiattle and Upper Skagit people for berry harvesting a century or more ago—just as the sisters said. Those human-made structures were as natural a part of the Cascade ecosystem as the burrows of marmots in the steep scree slopes. Our Native ancestors all over this continent lived within a complex web of relations with the natural world, and in doing so they assumed a responsibility for their world that contemporary Americans cannot even imagine. Unless Americans, and all human beings, can learn to imagine themselves as intimately and inextricably related to every aspect of the world they inhabit, with the extraordinary responsibilities such relationship entails—unless they can learn what the indigenous peoples of the Americas knew and often still know—the earth simply will not survive. A few square miles of something called wilderness will become the sign of failure everywhere.

"Everywhere There Was Life"

How Native Americans Can Save the World

◆

Since I began this book with the discovery of America, it seems somehow appropriate to rediscover America in the final chapter, with a look at how five hundred years of colonization (replete with what we can call, without exaggeration, genocide, ethnocide, and ecocide) have left our home. A "discovery" that sought extractable resources to begin with and ended up discovering beings called "Indians" is bound to have had enormous impact on both the earth and its inhabitants. Because this is an absurdly broad and ambitious subject for a literature specialist such as myself, I will open on safe ground citing passages from works by three Native American authors: D'Arcy McNickle, N. Scott Momaday, and Luther Standing Bear.

McNickle, of mixed Cree ancestry but adopted into the Flathead or Confederated Salish-Kootenai Tribe of Montana, began his final novel, *Wind from an Enemy Sky*, in 1936, completing it near the end of his life and having it published posthumously in 1979. In the intervening years, McNickle published other fiction as well as historical, political, and anthropological works and became a leader in the national Native American community. *Wind from an Enemy Sky* is about a conflict between a Native American tribe called the Little Elk people and the Euramericans who have come to turn the Indians into farmers. A dam has been built to harness a free running stream sacred to the Indian people and provide irrigation for white farmers and ranchers in the valley below. When Bull, the chief of the Little Elk tribe, learns of the dam, he is shocked that the white people have, in his words, "killed the water." "A stream has its life," he explains. "It starts from many small springs and from the snows, it brings them all together. It flows over rocks, washing them smooth and round. It feeds small bushes and large trees. It provides for the needs of fish, muskrat and beaver, the kingfisher, and the little bugs that skip on the surface. Were the animals and the trees asked to give their consent to this death?" (24). Bull's attitude is a very important indicator of how indigenous Native Americans have traditionally conceived of their relationship with the environment, in contrast to a Western European world view. The relationship Bull articulates is one marked by reciprocity and equality; it is not the attitude of a "discoverer" searching for extractable wealth.

Luther Standing Bear, a member of the Lakota Tribe, wrote of the Native American world view in his book *Land of the Spotted Eagle*, explaining that for the Indian, "There was no such thing as emptiness in the world. Even in the sky there were no vacant places. Everywhere there was life, visible and invisible, and every object possessed something that would be good for us to have also—even to the very stones. . . . Even without human companionship one was never alone. The world teemed with life and wisdom; there was no complete solitude for the Lakota" (14). Finally, in his splendid mixed-genre masterpiece, *The Way to Rainy Mountain*, published in 1969, the Kiowa author N. Scott Momaday tells a brief vignette about his grandfather, Mammedaty, and a mole:

> . . . . something had always bothered Mammedaty, a small aggravation that was never quite out of mind, like a name on the tip of his tongue. He had always wondered how it is that the mound of earth which a mole makes around the opening of its burrow is so fine. It is nearly as fine as powder, and it seems almost to have been sifted. One day Mammedaty was sitting quietly when a mole came out of the earth. Its cheeks were puffed out as if it had been a squirrel packing nuts. It looked all around for a moment, then blew the fine dark earth out of its mouth. And this it did again and again, until there was a ring of black, powdery earth on the ground. That was a strange and meaningful thing to see. It meant that Mammedaty had got possession of a powerful medicine. (73)

Amidst the more lyrical and moving prose of Momaday's book, this is an odd little story, and it should lead us to ask at least two questions: What kind of powerful medicine is Momaday talking about? And how did his grandfather gain possession of it?

These three passages tell us a great deal about the epistemologies of Native Americans, and I will come back to each of them shortly. But first I would like to try to put them into something of a social and historical context.

It has long been fashionable for Euramericans and Native Americans alike—but more so for Euramericans since theirs has for five hundred years been the dominant discourse on this continent— to speak and write of American Indians as something like genetically predetermined environmentalists. The iconographic moment for this romantic referent may be the image, familiar to North Americans from an environmental television commercial, of the alleged Indian actor Iron Eyes Cody with a cosmetic tear running down his cheek as he paddles his canoe across a polluted stream. In the past few years, however, a group of brave and daring revisionist cultural historians have sought to show this environmentalist image for what they think it is: historically and culturally inaccurate romanticism. Making the irrefutable point that all human beings leave the marks of their existence upon the landscape, these revisionists have gone so far as to argue that in fact Native Americans' ancestors were responsible during the Pleistocene era for exterminating the "megafauna" of this continent with extraordinary efficiency, wiping out with their deadly obsidian, flint, and chirt spears and arrows the millions of mega-bison, mammoths, sloths, armadillos, and so on that once roamed this new world paradise. The picture we are given is one of wholesale and wanton decimation by our ancestors, an extermination program that makes even the white man's slaughter of the passenger pigeon and buffalo look like child's play, especially considering that relatively small numbers of Paleo-Indians were supposedly using stone weapons to exterminate enormous herds of gargantuan animals and doing so apparently for the fun of it, since they would truly have to have been giants of the earth to eat all that megafauna.

Ten years ago, a writer for *USA Today* (who confessed to being "an admirer of Indians") challenged what he called the "popular concept that Native Americans are inherent conservationists because of their traditional beliefs." "I am not attempting to challenge the assertion that they were living in relative harmony with their natural environment," he adds; "I am rejecting the notion that it is their values which caused them to do so. . . . it should be pointed out that most American Indians did alter their environments in very significant ways, intentionally or not." Having apparently read a bit of revisionist eco-history, if not writings by actual Indians such as those quoted above, this journalist explains with authority that "early Native Americans were so proficient with their well-fashioned stone-tipped spears and co-operative hunting techniques that, in a few thousand years, they may have helped eliminate their most important food source." Indians, he declares with an exclamation point, "commonly dammed streams, quarried for stone, tilled the soil, and even littered!" (Layng, 56–57). Heaven save us, we feel in reading this, from Pleistocene litterers. If only McNickle, Luther Standing Bear, or Momaday had known this about their ancestors, perhaps they would have written and spoken differently.

Another bold, non-Native revisionist, writing for *U.S. News & World Report*, declares, "New archeological findings suggest that, far from living in perfect harmony with nature, prehistoric civilizations dealt major and sometimes fatal blows to their natural surroundings" (Dudiansky, 75–76). As his most damning example, he points out that the Anasazis, the ancient inhabitants of the southwestern U.S., deforested the area around Chaco Canyon in what is now New Mexico. Considering that Pueblo Bonito, the largest of seventy-five townsites in Chaco, was itself four stories high with eight hundred rooms, and that among the thousands of wooden beams built into these magnificent stone structures many are estimated to have averaged six hundred pounds each and to have been hand carried from between twenty-five and fifty miles, the writer's conjecture is not hard to believe. The Chaco culture, it should also be pointed out, not only cut and carried trees but also built a complex system of roads stretching hundreds of miles in all directions from the canyon, roads still visible today, and carved an intricate, ingenious drainage and irrigation system into the granite and sandstone rock above the canyon. These litterers and deforesters even went so far as to leave graffiti—still visible today—on the rocks.

It is a simple fact that just as the Incas did in Peru and people have done everywhere on earth, the Chacoan culture modified their environment to make living there less difficult, and such information should shock no one. What the writer fails to point out, however, is that the Chacoan people did not in fact deal a "fatal" blow to their natural surroundings. For whatever reason, the Anasazis abandoned Chaco Canyon around 1200 A.D. and moved not very far away, most likely to become the Pueblo cultures still thriving throughout the Southwest as we approach the year 2000. Today, Chaco Canyon is in fact a vital ecosystem, though admittedly an altered one, and Indian people still populate the high desert and mountain reaches all around the canyon, just as descendants of the Incas still live in the towns and utilize the roads, aqueducts, and farming terraces of their ancestors.

Clearly, the Anasazis did not do fatal damage to their environment, for if that were true then we would not today see tens of thousands of Californians and New Yorkers streaming into New Mexico to live in Santa Fe and Taos in chic, expensive homes often built as much as possible to imitate the architecture invented by the Anasazi and Pueblo peoples. Similarly, scattered across the Southwest, most particularly in northern New Mexico, are remainders of elaborate irrigation systems as well as reminders that the Anasazis were sophisticated farmers whose "pebble-mulch" gardens, along with myriad other adaptations to the environment, allowed them to live in a difficult region as a farming as well as hunting and gathering people. Studies have shown that nearly a thousand years later "the water-conserving pebble mulch is still in place, stimulating more vigorous plant growth in the native shortgrasses growing on the gardens when compared to grasses growing on non-mulched soil" (Lightfoot, 116). Even writers who seek to endorse the ecological world view of indigenous Americans can exhibit a strange timidity and confusion in doing so, as when in an essay published originally in Spanish, Raúl Valadez Azúa praises Mesoamerican Indian ecology as a model for modern civilizations but apologizes by admitting that his essay "does not seek to associate the level of scientific knowledge of the Mesoamerican culture with that of contemporary science, nor does it pretend to demonstrate that they planned, in a rational sense, the way in which natural resources should be used" (53).

I would like to challenge a couple of the points I have just quoted. First of all, it would seem self-evident that a people cannot continue to inhabit a region for millennia while doing fatal damage, and that, in fact, those same people would have necessarily developed a traditional world view and a "planned" use of natural resources passed from one generation to another that would allow them to live in balance with their environment if they did not intend to build ships to "discover" Europe or the Far East. Second, can we really have the arrogance to believe that we know more about the world than did Mesoamerican peoples or our Pleistocene ancestors? Obviously we know different kinds of things about the world, knowledge that we like to call "science," but just as obviously we have lost an incalculable quantity of knowledge of the same natural world that our "science" is in the process of destroying, knowledge held by our predecessors in this land. The question is clearly one of difference, not quantity or quality. I want to argue that in fact, contrary to what the writer for *USA Today* says, Native Americans are very much "inherent conservationists because of their traditional beliefs." As the Lakota author Vine Deloria, Jr., has written, "The task of the tribal religion, if such a religion can be said to have a task, is to determine the proper relationship that the people of the tribe must have with other living beings" (*God Is Red*, 102). We should add, as Luther Standing Bear suggested, that "other living beings" includes every aspect of the universe we inhabit, from animals and trees to rivers and stones.

No one who is not exceptionally naive would argue that the Pre-Columbian inhabitants of this continent left no imprint upon their environment. From the engineering and artistic wonders of the Incas, Mayans, and Aztecs to the extraordinary architecture of Chaco Canyon and such imposing constructions as the Choctaws' sacred mound called Nanih Waiya, Native Americans left their marks. From the stone fish dams of the eastern United States to the roads and irrigation systems in both northern and southern hemispheres and, more significantly perhaps, the open forests and grasslands across North America, signs of indigenous alteration of the environment are far more abundant than Europeans long realized. In Missouri today, one can easily come across one of the so-called "thong" trees created by the early Native inhabitants of that region. These hardwoods, centuries old, were bent and tied into significant shapes as saplings to mark the directions to important places, and today, like metaphors for so much of our contemporary ignorance, they still point the way to places on the earth the importance of which no one understands. But it does not take such elaborate signs to show us the Native imprint upon the continent. Indian people routinely used fire to keep forests open, to maintain valuable meadows, to alter their world in a large way.

According to one study, "little or no natural landscape" existed in southern California at the time the Spanish first arrived there. The author of the study assumes, of course, that humanity is not a "natural" part of the landscape; though herbivores grazing and thus altering the landscape is natural, human interaction with and imprint upon the same landscape is unnatural. This displacement of humanity from nature points to perhaps the most profound cause of human-kind's destructive relationship with our environment. The study goes on to note that in place of the climax or old chaparral growth that would have been "natural," early Spanish reports "describe grass, oak-park grasslands, limited chaparral, and areas with plants so even and regular they looked planted, all the product of human management to provide food"; and that "In addition to the well known acorn, mesquite, and agave, a now extinct grass seed may have been developed into a semi-domesticate. . . . This grass was harvested by cutting and gathering stalks into sheaves. . . . After harvest, the stubble was burned, a section at a time as it dried. Burning was followed by broadcasting seeds for next year's crop. Food resource trees were planted," including acorn oaks, palms, manzanita, ceonothus, and wild roses (Shipek, 298). Obviously, indigenous inhabitants of what is now California had learned how to live, and live well, with their environment. They had not marked portions of it off as untouchable "wilderness," thus leaving the rest to be despoiled; rather, they had developed a sophisticated, holistic understanding of the ecosystems they inhabited and applied that understanding successfully.

Historian Richard White, in a published conversation with William Cronon, says, "I remember reading a Sierra Club book which claimed that Indians had moved over the face of the land and when they left you couldn't tell they'd ever been there. Actually, this idea demeans Indians." Cronon replies: "Fundamentally, it's an ahistorical view. It says not only that the land never changed—wilderness was always in this condition—but that the people who lived upon it had no history, and existed outside of time. They were natural." And Cronon adds: "The great arrogance of Western civilization in the industrial and postindustrial eras has been to imagine human beings existing some-how apart from the earth . . . when in fact all history is a long-standing dialogue between human beings and the earth" (Cronon and White, 20, 25).

Being in a position, I think, to accept the fact that the original Americans, like all human beings throughout time, did indeed impact their environments, and that in fact the whole concept of "wilder-ness"—that space defined in the U.S. Wilderness Act of 1964 as being forever "untrammeled by man"—is a romantic European notion, we have to recognize nonetheless that Native Americans managed to live on this continent for many thousands of years without destroying it, poisoning it, or making it uninhabitable. In just five hundred years, Western man has come close to accomplishing that apocalypse. Let us now return to our Native American writers, beginning with McNickle.

When he sees the dam, McNickle's Indian character, Bull, describes a world in which all is interrelated, in which every action affects every aspect of the ecosystem. In Bull's world view, one cannot build a dam and stop or alter the flow of a stream without altering the entire world of which that stream is a part. When he says, "Were the animals and the trees asked to give their consent to this death?" Bull is suggesting what White and Cronon agree to call a "social" relationship between the Indian and the natural world and what other observers of Native American cultures have called "reciprocity." This concept I interpret as arising from the self-evident fact that everything in existence is dependent upon and related to everything else and, while one cannot live without having impact upon one's environment and being impacted by that environment, it is essential that one acknowledge this interdependence and act accordingly. Momaday has defined the Native American "ethic with respect to the physical world" as "a matter of reciprocal appropriation: appropriations in which man invests himself in the landscape, and at the same time incorporates the landscape into his own most fundamental experience. . . . this appropriation is primarily a matter of imagination. . . . And it is that act of the imagination, that moral act of the imagination, which I think constitutes his understanding of the world." Momaday adds, "I think his attitude toward the landscape has been formulated over a long period of time, and the length of time itself suggests an evolutionary process perhaps instead of a purely rational and decisive experience" ("Native American Attitudes to the Environment," 80).

Studies of tribal people living in the Amazon region suggest the same kind of relationship with and conception of the natural world that Momaday describes. In an essay titled "The Amazon: Divergent Evolution and Divergent Views," researcher Joyce Marcus describes one Amazonian tribal conception of the world as "families in place." In this conception, all members of the animal world, including humans, have their own spaces. "The absolute dominion of each group in its "sitting place"—its boundedness—must be respected. Bounded groups may trade or transact across the social and spatial boundaries that separate and define them. Such exchanges—reciprocities—are carefully followed and calculated, with numerous words to describe types of payments." Marcus defines the relationship as one of equality and notes that "reciprocity" is the mode of boundary crossing. "Breaching the rules creates imbalance and requires retaliation. The numbers of both humans and [animals] are seen as finite and precarious, locked into a carefully monitored exchange relationship" (452).

McNickle's Bull is responding to the white man's dam from such a position. The Euramerican dam builders saw the earth as a nonliving resource to be exploited for short-term human profit, rather than the extension of themselves that it logically is. "Were the animals and trees asked to give their consent?" is thus a profound question, one that cuts to the heart of our planet's future.

McNickle's message is that we inhabit a world that is ecosystemic and not egosystemic, a world in which everything is interrelated and humanity is connected with the natural world through social relationship. Luther Standing Bear's message is very similar. "There was no such thing as emptiness in the world," Standing Bear wrote. "Everywhere there was life, visible and invisible. . . . the world teemed with life and wisdom; there was no complete solitude for the Lakota." Standing Bear, a Lakota youth of great wisdom and resilience, had gone forth into the white world and survived to become an Indian man capable of reporting on his explorations much as did Lewis and Clark from the other side of the coin. Standing Bear's message is that for the Indian the world is rich and full, every niche inhabited, and every inhabitant a relative to value and respect. Unlike the Western European, in a traditional world view the Indian is not removed from and superior to nature but rather an essential part of that complex of relationships we call environment.

If McNickle and Standing Bear seem to be reinforcing the world's conventional image of the Indian as the ultimate ecologist, what is the message of N. Scott Momaday's homely little story of his grandfather and the mole? I would suggest that the "strange and meaningful thing" that Mammedaty saw, the thing that meant he "had got possession of a powerful medicine," was nothing more than an excruciatingly close and patient observation of the world he inhabited. This, Momaday, suggests, is where the power of vision and of life comes from: the greatest possible intimacy and communication with the world one inhabits. Only in this way does a people gain the knowledge that enables not just a culture but a world to survive. It is a moral vision and a holy one, truly a vision of great medicine.

It seems to many of us poised on the verge of a new millennium that wisdom such as that articulated by these Native writers must be heeded. It is convenient, as Vine Deloria has recently pointed out in his darkly hilarious book, *Red Earth, White Lies*, to try to "smear the American Indians as even worse ecologists than our present industrialists" (10). However, as Deloria also argues persuasively, it is not very easy to make such smear tactics stick. Deloria compares indictments of Native Americans for exterminating big-game animals during the Pleistocene era to a scholarly "southern lynching," and he provides very persuasive evidence to support his position. He does not really have to go to any great lengths to point out the absurdity of such positions, quoting Robert Bakker, for example, to the effect that "once they got going, our primordial forefathers cut a wide swath through both the Old World and the New, exterminating dozens of big species of mammal—mammoths, mastodons, sabre-toothed cats, giant ground sloths. . . . And they killed tortoises" (113). (They littered and killed tortoises. Clearly, our indigenous ancestors would stop at nothing.) Deloria quotes a 1990 essay by Paul Martin that provides the following quaint scenario:

> Once upon a time 12,000 years ago, a small band of people physically very like us and speaking a common language trekked farther east than anyone had ever gone before. . . . In autumn they followed their prey-mammoth, bison, and caribou—to wintering grounds. Helped in the hunt by opportunistic wolves or wolfish dogs, the hunters were expert at locating and tracking game, at killing it in excess of their needs, at butchering the carcass, and preserving the meat. . . . At 60° below, they dressed in warm furs and slept in bearskin bags. . . . By sharing food, there was always more than enough to eat and large animals were easily killed just for the fun of it, although wise elders spoke against this. . . .
>
> Spreading southward, the unwitting [?] explorers found that they were in a hunter's paradise, a Garden of Eden vastly rich in resources of the kind they were so expert in hunting. Some of the animals they discovered were new to their experience and some of these, three great ground sloths, were slow-moving and extraordinarily easy to dispatch. The children of the hunters could use them for target practice. (124–25)

We should note that Indians never have been very good at listening to wise elders (and what is one to make of such a concept as "opportunistic wolves"?), although Martin is polite enough to agree that these small-minded slaughterers were "physically very like us." Deloria has great fun with what he calls Martin's "dreadfully silly scientific scenario," explaining that "On their arrival in Alaska, we are asked to believe, an incredible blood lust appeared and Paleo-Indians changed their hunting techniques in order to slaughter herds of mammoth, bison [and] armadillos . . . with great efficiency." He points out that because by the age of ten most Indian children traditionally have certain adult responsibilities, the children "who were knocking off the ground sloths must have been between five and nine years old. Since some of these ground sloths were the size of modern adult giraffes, we can conclude that these hunters' children were among the more precocious and ambitious youngsters any society has ever raised" (127). Deloria has even more fun dismantling published theories of migration to and from Asia through the Bering Straits.

It would be a great deal of entertainment, and certainly more fun, to continue quoting from Deloria's sardonic deconstruction of accepted "scientific" views of Native Americans, including the Bering Strait "ice-bridge" theory, but the fact is that we are dealing with quite serious issues here. As Deloria says, "Some people are offended by the idea that many people believe . . . Indians were more concerned and thoughtful ecologists than modern industrial users. Advocating the extinction theory is a good way to support continued despoliation of the environment by suggesting that at no time were human beings careful of the lands upon which they lived" (112–13).

Let us consider briefly a few details about the state of our planet and the contexts and conditions of indigenous peoples around the globe. We can begin right here in the United States, where both the environment and the native populations are facing dire times and increasing pressures under a Republican-controlled congress determined to roll back as many environmental gains as possible in favor of big business. We all know that the economies, cultures, and populations of indigenous peoples throughout the Americas were originally decimated by the European invasion, with population declines estimated at 75 percent or more since 1492. Yet today, indigenous Americans continue to inhabit some of the most resource-rich areas on the globe while remaining the most impoverished of the earth's inhabitants. In the contemporary United States, according to *Greenpeace,*

Though only one percent of the United States population is indigenous, they are the single largest land holders in the country after the federal government. Yet they [the Indians] suffer the lowest standard of living, the highest rate of unemployment (higher than 50%), and the worst poverty of any ethnic group in the United States. Sovereign Indian lands are now viewed as a potential dumping ground for industrial poisons, a region to be stripped of all natural resources, and a proving ground for the industrialized nations' nuclear weapons. (1)

By 1992, the date of this *Greenpeace* essay, "Over 650 nuclear weapons [had] been detonated at the Nevada Test Site by both the U.S. and British governments on Western Shoshone sacred land, in apparent violation of the 1863 Treaty of Ruby Valley and ancestral land rights." The essay goes on to point out that "Nearly 100 percent of all uranium used in the production of nuclear weapons by the U.S. government is extracted from Indian lands using Native workers" (1). Uranium extraction has resulted, according to another source, in more than one thousand open and abandoned uranium mines on Indian land today, with no federal effort to clean up the sites that leak deadly radon gases and spread radioactive dust through Indian country. In his 1994 book, *If You Poison Us*, Peter H. Eichstaedt likens these abandoned mines to the "smallpox-infected blankets that the government issued to thousands of . . . Indians in the nineteenth century" (xi). Ironically, while many contemporary Americans express grave concern for the moral damage casino-style gambling may do to the noble Indian, no one except Indians seems interested in the cancers, stillbirths, and birth defects resulting from these ignored uranium sites. Also, more darkly ironic is the fact that tribal leaders have been implicated in this poisonous exploitation. Donald A. Grinde and Bruce E. Johnson, in *Ecoside of Native America*, point out that Peter McDonald, chairman of the Navajo tribe during the seventies and eighties, actively promoted such "resource development" and that "rents and royalties paid by the coal mining companies flowed directly to his tribal government." Called "MacDollar" by Navajos who suffered from the destructive mining, McDonald "lived in a luxurious ranch house, drove a Lincoln Continental," and collected an annual salary more than thirty times the average per capita income on the reservation. Obviously, greed can strike anywhere, and being born Indian does not make one an automatic environmentalist.[1]

Native American reservations are indeed viewed as the most convenient dumping grounds for nuclear and toxic waste, the U.S. Department of Energy having approached, with some success, "nearly every Indian nation, offering millions of dollars, if the nation would provide above-ground storage of nuclear waste" (*Greenpeace*, 1). With unemployment on reservations often ranging as high as 80 percent, it is difficult for Native American communities to resist the lure of such deadly profit, and several have not resisted. In 1989, according to an editorial in the *Multinational Monitor* for September 1992, "Colorado-based Waste Tech Incorporated, a subsidiary of Amoco, approached Dilkon, an isolated Arizona Navajo community with a 72 percent unemployment rate. Waste Tech proposed taking over one hundred acres of Navajo land to build an incinerator for burning hazardous waste and a landfill for burying its toxic ash. In exchange, the company promised 175 jobs, a new hospital and a $100,000 signing bonus." While it looked as though Waste Tech would succeed, a Navajo group called Citizens Against Ruining Our Environment (CARE) organized to force the cancellation of the Waste Tech proposal, but other Native communities have not been so fortunate (5).

It would be easy to go on with the bad news about coal strip-mining, oil extraction, clear-cut logging, and other disastrous environmental practices on and near Native American lands, including the U.S. Senate's recent attempt to give away more than 20 million acres of Utah canyonlands to national and international extractive industries in something called the Utah Public Lands Act of 1995. But the list of such destructive land grabs for deadly short-term profit quickly becomes redundant.

And conditions are certainly not better in many places outside of the United States. In the South Pacific, for example, France has recently conducted a round of nuclear tests undertaken despite widespread outrage not only from Pacific Islanders but from people throughout the world. Ninety-five United Nations states endorsed a resolution condemning the French government's proposal for renewed testing, but France went ahead with testing under the Mururoa atoll, an atoll discovered in 1979 by Jacques Cousteau to have already been fractured and polluted with radioactive poisons from earlier French tests. The French Minister for Overseas Territories, Jean-Jacques de Peretti, arrogantly compared the test site to a French bathroom, declaring, "The 12-mile zone is a bit as if you were in the bathroom and you said, I'm taking my bath and I don't want anyone to come in. You wouldn't be happy if somebody did. It is the same for us."[2] What is truly "the same for us" is that the indigenous inhabitants of the South Pacific, like indigenous peoples all over the globe, have little or no control over the fates of their environments or families in the face of such colonial power mongering, and all of us will eventually and inexorably be touched by the poisons released into the sea by such tests. Did anyone, we might wonder, ask permission of the fish and the coral reefs?

In South America, U.S. and multinational corporations are wreaking havoc in perhaps the world's richest biological zone. Ecuador's Oriente, for example, a 32-million-acre area in the Upper Amazon Basin, is estimated to be "one of the most biologically rich zones on the planet, where a single acre of land can contain up to a hundred different species of trees—five times the amount in the temperate rain forests of the Pacific Northwest. This basin nurtures more than twenty thousand plant species and provides a habitat for hundreds of varieties of rare fish, reptiles, birds, and mammals." The 600,000-acre Yasuni National Park in the Oriente has been declared by UNESCO to be a "world biospheric reserve" (Cooper, 40).

According to the article from which the above information is taken, "over the past twenty years, after discovering a crude petroleum bonanza, . . . companies, led by U.S.-based Texaco, have super-imposed a grid of more than a dozen 500,000-acre geometric drilling blocks over the Amazon. . . . [By 1992], a tenth of the Ecuadorian Amazon [had] been consumed directly by the oil companies." This same essay points out that in 1992 three million acres in the Amazon region remained "under active oil exploration" (41).

We are talking here about the life of the planet. The Amazon River "disgorges 20% of all fresh water entering the world's oceans," with the "known total of species in the Amazon region [exceeding] 100,000" (Marcus, 396). More than two thousand species of fish have been recorded in the Amazon, almost four times as many as are found in the Congo, the second biologically richest river in the world. Meanwhile, in the United States, "80 million acres of Alaskan off-shore oil lease sales lie in waters surrounding the primarily Native coastal villages whose traditional subsistence base is threatened by the inevitable spills, habitat destruction and disturbance of the industry" (*Greenpeace*, 1).

Currently, indigenous peoples are estimated to include fifteen thousand cultures and six thousand languages. The area of the earth occupied by indigenous peoples is calculated at 12 to 19 percent. While 12 to 19 percent may not seem like much, according to *USA Today*, native cultures "remain day-to-day stewards of an area of the globe larger than all the world's national parks and nature reserves put together." This same publication reports that Brazil is reputed to have lost "87 tribes in the first half of this century alone"; that half of the world's 6,000 languages will disappear within a century; and that "Far from a vestige of the colonial past, the extinction of cultures has accelerated in this century as the modern economy has scoured the globe for resources and markets." The writers note that

> Native peoples' homelands encompass many of the planet's last tracts of wilderness—ecosystems that shelter millions of endangered species, buffer the global climate, and regulate hydrological cycles. . . . [and that] Even without considering questions of human rights and the intrinsic value of cultures, indigenous survival is a matter of crucial importance. We in the world's dominant cultures simply can not sustain the Earth's ecological health without the help of the world's endangered cultures.

Finally, this report concludes: "When the Indians vanish, the rest will follow."[3] In an essay from *OMNI Magazine*, Stephen Mills—wisely trying to hit the dominant cultures where it hurts—suggests that "Perhaps the most compelling and widely cited argument for safeguarding indigenous environments (and hence their human inhabitants) is the environments' unequaled abundance and diversity of medicinal plants" (Mills, 82–83). Another 1994 article notes the massacre in Brazil in 1993 of "two dozen Yanomami Indians" as their lands were plundered by illegal gold-diggers and concludes with a statement worth quoting at length:

> Many indigenous groups live in areas that contain much of the world's biodiversity and are threatened with destruction. Plant and animal species are estimated to become extinct due to natural processes at a rate of between one and ten a year; but human activity and the parallel destruction of habitat cause between 10 thousand and 150 thousand species to die off annually, a rate unmatched in biological history at least since the age of the dinosaurs. Some experts predict that at the current rate of deforestation, up to 25 percent of all species on earth may disappear by the middle of the next century.
>
> This environmental destruction threatens the survival of native peoples dependent upon their immediate habitat and imperils the gene pool important for propagating food crops. It also undermines the ecological balance. Because the fate of indigenous peoples directly affects the stewardship of the environment, their well-being affects us all. With reason, one writer has called them "the miner's canary for the twentieth century."

This is not a trivial subject, certainly. The same essay adds, "Some 80 percent of the world's population depends on traditional knowledge for its primary health care. As many as 25 percent of prescriptions in the United States contain natural products extracted from plants, even though less than one percent of the more than 265 thousand known plant species has been tested for medical purposes, or even assayed for chemical composition." And the essay quotes Harvard ethno-biologist Richard Schultes, who explains what should be obvious to all of us:

> The accomplishments of indigenous peoples in learning plant pro-perties is a result of a long and intimate association with, and utter dependence on, their ambient vegetation. This native knowledge war-rants careful and critical attention on the part of modern scientific efforts. If phytochemists must randomly investigate the constituents of

biological effects of 80,000 species of Amazonian plants, the task may never be finished. Concentrating first on those species that people have lived and experimented with for millennia offers a short cut to the discovery of new medically or industrially useful compounds.

Finally, this essay concludes that "The protection of traditional knowledge is, unfortunately, a race against time. Scientists fear that an immense undocumented repository of ecological, biological, and pharmacological knowledge may be lost unless the cultures that generated it are also protected. Nearly half of the planet's tropical rain forests have been destroyed in the last four decades, as have many of the cultures of the peoples who inhabited them. In Brazil one tribe has disappeared each year of this century" (Andersen, 143–50). Far from taking the lead in preserving indigenous cultures and endangered bioregions of the earth, the United States remains one of many villains in the global scenario. At the June 1993 human rights summit in Vienna, "the U.S. delegation did not even have a position paper ready for discussion on human rights" (Andersen, 154).

We have all gotten somewhat hardened to the ceaseless stream of terrifying and depressing environmental news, and it seems redundant to simply parrot that same tune. However, if we are to survive not just as indigenous cultures but as a species inhabiting a living planet, we had better pay attention to what Indian people such as McNickle, Standing Bear, and Momaday have to say. We cannot continue with malignant arrogance to consider the earth and its nonhuman elements simply a resource to be exploited, and we cannot continue to dismiss the traditional knowledge of indigenous peoples. Vine Deloria speculates that "perhaps only 10 percent of the information that Indians possess is presently in print and available for discussion," and says, "There is strong doctrinal bias against giving any Indian accounts credence—simply because the source is Indian." Deloria cites a panel at the American Association for the Advancement of Science annual meeting in 1992 that explored a new field called "zoopharmacognosy," a term coined to describe the medicinal use of plants by animals. A *Newsweek Magazine* article about the panel "quoted Harvard ethnobotanist Shawn Sigstedt suggesting that bears may have taught the Navajos to use a species of *Ligusticum* plant, just as [the Navajos] had claimed!" Deloria very rightly finds both humor and astonishment in the pretense of such scientific discovery, explaining that "For Western peoples, the announcement of zoopharmacognosy may be an exciting breakthrough on the frontiers of science, but getting information from birds and animals regarding plants is an absurdly self-evident proposition for American Indians" (*Red Earth*, 11, 159, 59).

Ultimately, we have to realize, along with Luther Standing Bear, that there is no emptiness in this world unless we create it, and that when that happens not only does our environment become more fragile, but we are forever cut off from a part of our inheritance as living beings in a richly interconnected web of life. Extinction, as the bumper sticker says, is forever. We must learn to ask the trees and stones for permission to take them into our lives for our survival, and we have to lay ourselves close to the earth for a long, patient time in order, along with N. Scott Momaday's grandfather, actually to see the powerful reality that is before us and part of us. Such closeness of vision, reciprocity, and respect are powerful medicines, the only medicines that may, perhaps, save humanity from itself. This is a lesson Native Americans and all indigenous peoples really do have to teach, and it is time the world began listening carefully.

Notes

Preface

1. See my afterword to Gerald Vizenor, *Bearheart: The Heirship Chronicles* (Minneapolis: University of Minnesota Press, 1990).

2. I owe my exposure to this great novel to Professor Jack Hicks at the University of California, Davis. Always a visionary, Professor Hicks not only recognized the brilliance of Welch's novel but actually invited the author to the university, a rare instance of action and wisdom combined.

Chapter 1

1. See James A. Clifton, "Simon Pokagon's Sandbar: Potawatomi Claims to Chicago's Lakefront," *Michigan History* 71, no. 5 (1987): 14.

2. Frederick Jackson Turner, "The Frontier in American History." In *American Issues: Volume One, The Social Record*, ed. Willard Thorpe, et al. (Chicago: J. B. Lippincott Co., 1941), p. 662. For a discussion of "Indians" and "hyperreality," see Gerald Vizenor, *Manifest Manners: Postindian Warriors of Survivance* (Hanover, N.H.: Wesleyan University Press/University Press of New England, 1991), p. 9ff.

Chapter 2

1. See Louis Owens, *Other Destinies: Understanding the American Indian Novel* (Norman: University of Oklahoma Press, 1992), p. 78.

2. See John Ashton, "Tempest in a Tepee," *Westward, Denver News and Arts Weekly* 7, no. 12: 1–2, 15.

3. See Owens, *Other Destinies*, p. 43.

4. When I have asked Navajo friends and students to be specific, for example, in their criticisms of Tony Hillerman—who is deeply resented by some, though not all, Navajos—their responses have invariably been that he is inaccurate and misleading in his representations of their complex culture. Not once has a primary criticism been simply that he is not Navajo or even Indian.

5. A fine example of a reader who has done just that is to be found in Chris LaLonde, "Trickster, Trickster Discourse, and Identity in Louis Owens' *Wolfsong*," *Studies in American Indian Literature* 7, no. 1 (Spring 1995): 27–42.

Chapter 3

1. Quoted in Vizenor, *Manifest Manners*, p. 9.

2. The first known novel by a Native American author is *The Life and Adventures of Joaquin Murieta*, by the half-Cherokee writer John Rollin Ridge, published in 1854. The first known novel by a Native American woman is mixedblood Creek author Alice Callahan's *Wynema*, published in 1891, a work only recently rediscovered by critics of Native American literature. Ridge's work is discussed in my book *Other Destinies*. For a discussion of *Wynema*, see A. LaVonne Brown Ruoff, "Justice for Indians and Women: The Protest Fiction of Alice Callahan and Pauline Johnson," *World Literature Today* 66, no. 2 (Spring 1992): 249–55.

Chapter 5

1. Quoted in Vizenor, *Manifest Manners*, p. 10.

2. Quoted in Krupat, *Ethnocriticism*, pp. 84, 89.

3. Quoted in Krupat, *Ethnocriticism*, p. 5.

4. Quoted in Owens, *Other Destinies*, p. 233.

5. In his most recently published study, Krupat breaks a bit of new ground with his examination of what he calls "Ratio- and Natio-" in Vizenor's *Heirs of Columbus* and his analysis of autobiographical writing in Vizenor's *Dead Voices*. Still, Krupat has great difficulty with what he sees as contradictions in Vizenor's messages, while Vizenor would undoubtedly reply that contradictions require terminal absolutes, which are the contrary

of trickster discourse. See Arnold Krupat, *The Turn to the Native: Studies in Criticism and Culture* (Lincoln: University of Nebraska Press, 1996).

Chapter 6

1. See Owens, *Other Destinies*, pp. 90–127.

2. "Aboriginal" is defined by *Webster's New Collegiate Dictionary* as "being the first of its kind present in a region and *often primitive in comparison with more advanced types.*" *Webster's New Collegiate Dictionary* (Springfield, Mass.: G. & C. Merriam Co., 1973), emphasis added.

3. For more complete discussion see Owens, *Other Destinies*, pp. 93–117.

4. For a thorough discussion of the questing hero in this novel according to Pueblo and Navajo tradition, see Susan Scarberry-Garcia, *Landmarks of Healing: A Study of House Made of Dawn.*

5. See, for example, Owens, *Other Destinies*, pp. 90–127.

6. "Selling Myself By Arturo Islas." Islas Papers, Special Collections, Stanford University Library.

7. James D. Houston, conversation with Louis Owens, January 3, 1997.

8. See Owens, *Other Destinies*, pp. 272–73.

9. Personal correspondence, Marlon Sherman to Louis Owens, March 31, 1996.

10. Internet posting, Sherman Alexie as "lester@mail1.halcyon.com," April 19, 1997. ("lester" was the self-confessed "psuedonym" [*sic*] used by Alexie for his Internet exchanges.)

11. Personal correspondence, Sherman to Owens, March 31, 1996.

12. Internet posting, lester@mail1.halcyon.com, April 12, 1997.

13. See William Faulkner's "Red Leaves," *Absalom, Absalom!*, and the appendix to the Modern Library Edition of *The Sound and the Fury.*

Chapter 7

1. See Owens, *Other Destinies*, pp. 225–54.

2. "Trickster Discourse: Comic Holotropes and Language Games," unpublished paper presented by Gerald Vizenor at the School of American Research in Santa Fe, New Mexico, June 1986. In the prologue to his third novel, Vizenor omitted this definition and wrote instead: "The trickster is comic nature in a language game, not a real person or 'being' in the ontological sense. Tribal tricksters are embodied in imagination and liberate the mind; an

androgyny, she would repudiate translations and imposed representations, as he would bare the contradictions of the striptease." "Tricksters and Transvaluations," in *The Trickster of Liberty: Tribal Heirs to a Wild Baronage* (Minneapolis: University of Minnesota Press, 1988), p. x.

3. Vizenor, "Trickster Discourse," p. 4.

4. Warwick Wadlington, *The Confidence Game in American Literature*, quoted in the epigraph to Vizenor, *The Trickster of Liberty*.

5. Alan Velie was the first critic to recognize Vizenor's poststructuralist methodology and to point out the central thread in Vizenor's writing: "In this work, Vizenor . . . tries to celebrate the unique status of the mixedbloods—to reverse the prejudice that has plagued them, to make a hero of the half-breed." Alan Velie, *Four American Indian Literary Masters: N. Scott Momaday, James Welch, Leslie Marmon Silko, and Gerald Vizenor* (Norman: University of Oklahoma Press, 1982), p. 138. Velie has followed this pioneering introduction to Vizenor's work with a second essay examining the trickster elements in Vizenor's fiction: "The Trickster Novel," in *Narrative Chance: Postmodern Discourse on Native American Indian Literatures*, ed. Gerald Vizenor (Albuquerque: University of New Mexico Press, 1989), pp. 121–39. In one of the first book-length studies of American Indian literature, Kenneth Lincoln's *Native American Renaissance* (Berkeley: University of California Press, 1983), Vizenor receives only two lines of attention. In contrast, A. LaVonne Brown Ruoff has published extensive (mostly bibliographical) work on Vizenor in two essays: "Gerald Vizenor: Compassionate Trickster," *Studies in American Indian Literature* 9, no. 2 (1985): 52–63; and "Woodland Word Warrior: An Introduction to the Works of Gerald Vizenor," *MELUS* 13, no. 1–2 (Spring–Summer 1986): 13–43.

6. According to William Warren, writing in 1885, "The No-ka or Bear family are more numerous than any of the other clans of the Ojibways, forming fully one-sixth of the entire tribe. . . . It is a general saying, and an observable fact, amongst their fellows, that the Bear clan resemble the animal that forms their Totem in disposition. They are ill-tempered and fond of fighting, and consequently they are noted as ever having kept the tribe in difficulty and war with other tribes." *History of the Ojibway People*, p. 49. Bearheart, whose totem is the bear, is somewhat ill-tempered in his response to the AIM radicals and, through his novel, to American culture, but, like Proude, he assumes the role of trickster and uses laughter as his weapon in his war against hypocrisy and "terminal creeds."

Chapter 8

1. Ford's fondness for Navajo actors may explain the fact that the Mexican vaquero who introduces Edwards to Scar greets the Comanche with the Navajo greeting of *Yatahey*, while Scar refers to Edwards as *bilagaana*, the Navajo word for white man.

Chapter 9

1. In an extraordinarily bitter and racist attack upon Native Americans in general, which he published in the guise of a review of Costner's film, Wayne Michael Sarf also critiques Dunbar and the wolf: "Fixing up his post, Dunbar finds his intellectual equal—a wolf too stupid to fear man at a time when both Indians and whites routinely shot or poisoned them." About the shooting of Two Socks, Sarf says, "Dunbar's loss is natural selection's gain. . . ." Wayne Michael Sarf, "Oscar Eaten by Wolves." *Film Comment*, 27, no. 6 (1991): 63, 69.

2. Philip Zaleski, "Balancing the Scales in a Hollywood Epic." *Parabola* 16, no. 2 (1991): 91. See also Peter Seixas, "Confronting the Moral Frames of Popular Film: Young People Respond to Historical Revisionism." *American Journal of Education* 102 (May 1994): 261–83, in which Seixas compares the two films.

3. Quoted in Ward Churchill, *Fantasies of the Master Race: Literature, Cinema, and the Colonization of American Indians* (Monroe: Common Courage Press, 1992), p. 231.

4. Blake repeatedly refers to Dunbar in this fashion, culminating in the Lakotas' attitude toward him after he saves them from the Pawnee: "No one came forward to declare him a god, but in the life of these people he was the next best thing," *Dances With Wolves*, p. 270.

5. In 1763 Jeffrey Amherst, an English military leader, suggested spreading smallpox among tribes by means of infected blankets, declaring, "You will do well to try to inoculate the Indians by means of blankets," a tactic that was, in fact, used with deadly results. James Welch, *Killing Custer: The Battle of the Little Bighorn and the Fate of the Plains Indians* (New York: W. W. Norton and Co., 1994), p. 33.

6. David Seals has pointed out that "the filmically perfect village of tipis *Wolves* shows . . . is perched on a Belle Fourche River that is undrinkable and polluted from gold mine tailings." David Seals, "The New Custerism." *The Nation* 252, no. 18 (May 13, 1991): 638.

7. It is most interesting to note that in Blake's novel, Dunbar and his new wife remain with the Comanches. Dunbar's transformation is completed as Ten Bears tells him, "The one called Loo Ten Nant is not here. In this lodge they will only find a Comanche warrior, a good Comanche warrior and his wife." The novel ends with the dire warning: "The good times of that summer were the last they would have. Their time was running out and would soon be gone forever." *Dances With Wolves*, pp. 312–13.

8. In the United States, "real" Indians are expected to be enrolled like domestic pets and given an identity number by the federal government. Indian artists are required to produce these federal documents of authenticity upon demand; failure to possess such documents when selling "Indian" art can result in enormous fines and even prison sentences.

Chapter 10

1. A revised version of this chapter was delivered as the annual Oklahoma Lecture in the Humanities in Oklahoma City, February 28, 1997. After delivering that talk, I made a trip to spend time with my older sister, who had very recently been diagnosed with cancer, and with our brothers and sisters who had also gathered. During the visit, my older sister brought out a turn-of-the-century photo album and a box of ancient photographs none of us had seen before. They were pictures of our Cherokee, white, and mixedblood ancestors in Oklahoma and the Territory, photographs our mother had left us in a box that had not been opened until that time. With the opening of the box and photo album, a whole world seemed to open for us. For the first time we saw a picture of our mother's mother as a child, our grandmother's father, aunt, and grandmother, and much more.

2. Until I had a recent conversation with my older sister, I had thought that all three children had been given to the same share cropper. I learned, however, that the three were divided up to different families, only to be reunited with one another because of death and brutal child abuse. As I write in "Motion of Fire and Form," in this book, they were removed from that final family after seven years because of the death of the husband of that childless couple. Thus even our oral stories keep evolving as we talk together and learn more. A year from now the stories I tell here may have evolved yet further as I continue to learn about the past, and that past increasingly informs the present.

3. Gerald Vizenor, *Fugitive Poses: Native American Indian Scenes of Absence and Presence* (Lincoln: The University of Nebraska Press, forthcoming).

4. It was, in fact, only two months prior to this writing that I first saw this collection of family pictures.

5. In Kenneth Rosen, *Voices of the Rainbow* (New York: Viking Press, 1975), p. 230.

Chapter 13

1. I have borrowed this powerful phrase and concept from Erika Aigner-Varoz, who coined it in conversation with me concerning her own "mestizaje" heritage. I am grateful for the loan.

2. I have since learned that the man in question is Gregory Williams, dean of the Ohio State University law school in Columbus. He discovered his "Blackness" when he "learned that the black cook at his father's restaurant was his grandmother." *Albuquerque Journal*, April 24, 1997, D2.

Chapter 16

1. Donald A. Grinde and Bruce E. Johansen, *Ecocide of Native America: Environmental Destruction of Indian Lands and Peoples* (Santa Fe: Clear Light Publishers, 1995), pp. 125, 128.

2. *Ka Leo O Hawai'i*, February 19, 1996, p. 3. When, during a trip to France, I confronted a French official with these facts, her response was, "But we're not doing that anymore"—as if the results of such tests ended when the last test was conducted.

3. "Native People's Survival Crucial for Environment," *USA Today*, 121 (April 1993): 15.

References

Alexie, Sherman. *Indian Killer*. New York: Atlantic Monthly Press, 1996.
———. *The Lone Ranger and Tonto Fistfight in Heaven*. New York: Atlantic Monthly Press, 1993.
———. *Reservation Blues*. New York: Atlantic Monthly Press, 1995.
"America's Killing Ground." *Multinational Monitor* (September 1992): 5.
Andersen, Edwin Martin. "Chiapas, Indigenous Rights, and the Coming Fourth World Revolution." *SAIS Review* (summer/fall 1994): 141–57.
Anderson, Kat, and Gary Paul Nabhan. "Gardeners in Eden." *Wilderness* 55, no. 194 (fall 1991): 27–30.
Appleford, Robert. "Coming Out from Behind the Rocks: Constructs of the Indian in Recent U.S. and Canadian Cinema." *American Indian Culture and Research Journal* 19, no. 1 (1995): 97–118.
Ashcroft, Bill; Gareth Griffiths; and Helen Tiffin. *The Empire Writes Back: Theory and Practice in Post-Colonial Literatures*. London and New York: Routledge, 1989.
Azúa, M. en C. Raúl Valadez. "The Man-Fauna Relationship in Mesoamerica Before and After the Europeans." *Diogenes* 159 (winter 1992): 51–56.
Baker, Houston A., Jr. "Introduction to Multiculturalism: The Task of Literary Representation in the Twenty-First Century." *Profession* (1993): 5.
Bakhtin, Mikhail. *The Dialogic Imagination: Four Essays by M. M. Bakhtin*. Edited by Michael Holquist. Translated by Caryl Emerson and Michael Holquist. Austin: University of Texas Press, 1981.
Barthes, Roland. *Critical Essays*. Translated by Richard Howard. Evanston, Ill.: Northwestern University Press, 1972.

Baum, Dan. "Sacred Places." *Mother Jones* 17, no. 2 (1992): 32–39.

Bird, Gloria. "The Exaggeration of Despair in Sherman Alexie's Reservation Blues." *Wicazo Sa Review* (fall 1995): 47–52.

Blake, Michael. *Dances With Wolves*. New York: Ballantine, 1988.

Booth, Annie L., and Harvey M. Jacobs. "Ties That Bind: Native American Beliefs as a Foundation for Environmental Consciousness." *Environmental Ethics* 12, no. 1 (1990): 27–43.

Bowden, Larry R. "Dances with Wolves." *Cross Currents* 41, no. 3 (fall 1991): 391–96.

Bowers, Neil, and Charles L. P. Silet. "An Interview with Gerald Vizenor." *MELUS* 8 (1981): 41–49.

Bruchac, Joseph. "The Families Gathered Together." *Parabola* (winter 1993): 37–39.

———, ed. *The Next World: Poems by Third World Americans*. Trumansburg, N.Y.: The Crossing Press, 1978.

Butzer, Karl W. "No Eden in the New World." *Nature* 362, no. 4 (March 1993): 15–17.

Callahan, Alice. *Wynema: A Child of the Forest*. Chicago: Smith, 1891.

Carlson, Paul H. "Indian Agriculture, Changing Subsistence Patterns, and the Environment on the Southern Great Plains." *Agricultural History* 66, no. 2 (1992): 52–65.

Castillo, Edward D. "Review of Dances With Wolves." *Film Quarterly* 44, no. 4 (1991): 14–23.

Churchill, Ward. *Fantasies of the Master Race: Literature, Cinema, and the Colonization of American Indians*. Monroe, Maine: Common Courage Press, 1992.

Clifton, James A. "Simon Pokagon's Sandbar: Potawatomi Claims to Chicago's Lakefront." *Michigan History* 71, no. 5 (1987): 12–17.

Coates, Peter. "Chances with Wolves: Renaturing Western History." *Journal of American Studies* 28 (1994): 241–54.

Colson, Charles. "Dances With Wolves in Sheep's Clothing." *Christianity Today* 36, no. 5 (1992): 72.

Columbus, Christopher. *The Diario of Christopher Columbus's First Voyage to America 1492–1493*. Abstracted by Fray Bartolomé de las Casas. Transcribed and translated into English with notes and a concordance of the Spanish by Oliver Dunn and James E. Kelley, Jr. Norman: University of Oklahoma Press, 1989.

Cook-Lynn, Elizabeth. "American Indian Intellectualism and the New Indian Story." *American Indian Quarterly* 20, no. 1 (winter 1996): 57–76.

Cooper, Marc. "Crude." *Mother Jones* 17, no. 2 (March–April 1992): 39–47, 75–76.

Cronon, William, and Richard White. "Indians in the Land." *American Heritage* 37, no. 5 (August–September 1986): 19–25.

Crow, Charles L. Review of *Wolfsong*. *Western American Literature* 27, no. 4 (1992): 386–87.

Curan, William D. "'Nightland' Predictable Crime in Desert Setting." *The Star Newspaper*, Chicago Heights, Ill., August 22, 1996, 23.

Deloria, Vine, Jr. *God Is Red*. New York: Grosset & Dunlap, 1973.

———. *Red Earth, White Lies: Native Americans and the Myth of Scientific Fact*. New York: Scribners, 1995.

Dorney, Cheryl, and John R. Dorney. "An Unusual Oak Savanna in Northeastern Wisconsin: The Effect of Indian-Caused Fire." *The American Midland Naturalist* 122 (1989): 103–109.

Dudiansky, Stephen. "The trees fell—and so did the people." *U.S. News and World Report* (February 9, 1987): 75–76.

Dufour, Darna L. "Use of Tropical Rainforests by Native Amazonians." *BioScience* 40, no. 9 (October 1990): 653–59.

Eichstaedt, Peter H. *If You Poison Us*. Santa Fe: Red Crane Books, 1994.

"Five Hundred Years of Plunder." *Greenpeace: A Quarterly Publication Dedicated to Building Environmental Awareness and Activism* (October/November/December 1992): 1–2.

Flores, Dan. "Bison Ecology and Bison Diplomacy: The Southern Plains from 1800 to 1850." *The Journal of American History* 78, no. 2 (September 1991): 465–85.

Gates, Henry Louis, Jr. "Beyond the Culture Wars: Identity in Dialogue." *Profession* 93 (1993): 6–11.

———. *Black Literature and Literary Theory*. London: Methuen, 1984.

Godoy, Ricardo. "The Effects of Rural Education on the Use of the Tropical Rain Forest by the Sumu Indians of Nicaragua: Possible Pathways, Qualitative Findings, and Policy Questions." *Human Organization* 53, no. 3 (fall 1994): 233–44.

Gray, Andrew. "Indegenous Peoples and the Marketing of the Rainforest." *The Ecologist* 20, no. 6 (November/December 1990): 223–27.

Greenpeace: A Quarterly Publication Dedicated to Building Environmental Awareness and Activism (October/November/December 1992).

Grenier, Richard. "Indian Love Call." *Commentary* 91, no. 3 (March 1991): 47–51.

Grinde, Donald A., and Bruce E. Johansen. *Ecocide of Native America: Environmental Destruction of Indian Lands and Peoples*. SantaFe: Clear Light Publishers, 1995.

Harlow, Barbara. *Resistance Literature*. New York: Methuen, 1987.

Harvey, David. *The Condition of Postmodernity: An Inquiry into the Origins of Cultural Change*. Cambridge: Basil Blackwell, 1989.

Hinckley, Ted C. "Vanishing Truth and Western History." *Journal of the West* 31, no. 1 (1992): 3–4.

Hymes, Dell. "In Vain I Tried to Tell You." *Essays in Native American Ethnopoetics*. Philadelphia: University of Pennsylvania Press, 1981.

Jahner, Elaine. "A Critical Approach to American Indian Literature." In *Studies in American Indian Literature*, edited by Paula Gunn Allen. New York: Modern Language Association, 1983.

Ka Leo O Hawai'i, February 29, 1996, p. 3.

Kincaid, James R. "Who Gets to Tell Their Stories?" *The New York Times Book Review*, May 3, 1992, 1, 24–29.

Krupat, Arnold. *Ethnocriticism: Ethnography, History, Literature*. Berkeley: University of California Press, 1992.

———. "Scholarship and Native American Studies: A Response to Daniel Littlefield, Jr." *American Studies* 33 (fall 1993): 108–109.

———. *The Turn to the Native: Studies in Criticism and Culture*. Lincoln: University of Nebraska Press, 1996.

———. *The Voice in the Margin: Native American Literature and the Canon*. Berkeley: University of California Press, 1989.

LaDuke, Winona. "Native Environmentalism." *Earth Island Journal* (summer 1993): 35–36.

———. "Recovering the Land." *Environmental Action* (fall 1993): 15–16.

La Flesche, Francis. *Ke-ma-ha: The Omaha Stories of Francis La Flesche*, edited by James W. Parins and Daniel F. Littlefield, Jr. Lincoln: University of Nebraska Press, 1995.

LaLonde, Chris. "Trickster, Trickster Discourse, and Identity in Louis Owens' *Wolfsong*." *Studies in American Indian Literature* 7, no. 1 (spring 1995): 27–42.

Landau, Diane, ed. *Dances With Wolves: The Illustrated Story of the Epic Film*. New York: Newmarket Press, 1990.

Layng, Anthony. "American Indians: Adapting to Change." *USA Today* 115 (September 1986): 56–59.

Lightfoot, Dale. "The Cultural Ecology of Puebloan Pebble-Mulch Gardens." *Human Ecology* 21, no. 2 (1993): 115–43.

Lincoln, Kenneth. *Native American Renaissance*. Berkeley: University of California Press, 1983.

Louis, Adrian C. *Skins*. New York: Crown Publishers, 1995.

McFarland, Ron, ed. *James Welch*. Lewiston, Idaho: Confluence Press, 1986.

McGovern, Dan. *The Campo Indian Landfill War: The Fight for Gold in California's Garbage*. Norman: University of Oklahoma Press, 1995.

McNickle, D'Arcy. *The Surrounded*. 1936. Reprint, Albuquerque: University of New Mexico Press, 1978.

———. *Wind from an Enemy Sky*. New York: Harper & Row, 1978.

Marcus, Joyce. "The Amazon: Divergent Evolution and Divergent Views." *National Geographic Research & Exploration* 10, no. 4 (1994): 385–476.

Melville, Herman. *Moby-Dick*. New York: W. W. Norton, 1967.

Mills, Stephen. "Last Chance for First Peoples." *OMNI Magazine* 17, no. 6 (1995): 63–64, 82–86.

Momaday, N. Scott. *House Made of Dawn*. New York: Harper & Row, 1968.

———. "Native American Attitudes to the Environment." In *Seeing With a Native Eye: Essays on Native American Religion*, edited by Walter Holden Capps, 79–85. New York: Harper & Row, 1976.

———. *The Way to Rainy Mountain*. Albuquerque: University of New Mexico Press, 1969.

Morrison, Toni. *Playing in the Dark: Whiteness and the Literary Imagination*. Cambridge: Harvard University Press, 1992.

Mourning Dove. *Cogewea, the Half-Blood: A Depiction of the Great Montana Cattle Range*. With notes and biographical sketch by Lucullus Virgil McWhorter. Boston: Four Seas Co., 1927. Reprint with introduction by Dexter Fisher, Lincoln: University of Nebraska Press, 1981.

Murray, David. *Forked Tongues: Speech, Writing and Representation in North American Indian Texts*. Bloomington: Indiana University Press, 1990.

"Native American Chic." *U.S. News and World Report* (December 31, 1990/ January 7, 1991): 71.

"Native People's Survival Crucial for Environment." *USA Today* 121 (April 1993): 15.

Newman, Charles. *The Post-Modern Aura: The Art of Fiction in an Age of Inflation*. Evanston: Northwestern University Press, 1985.

O'Dell, Rice. "Alaska: A Frontier Dividend." *Environment* 28, no. 7 (summer 1986): 11–15, 34–37.

Owens, Louis. *Bone Game*. Norman: Univesity of Oklahoma Press, 1994.

———. *Nightland*. New York: Dutton Signet, 1996.

———. "N. Scott Momaday." In *This is About Vision: Interviews with Southwestern Writers*, edited by John F. Crawford, William Balassi, and Annie Esteroy. Albuquerque: University of New Mexico Press, 1990.

———. *Other Destinies: Understanding the American Indian Novel*. Norman: University of Oklahoma Press, 1992.

———. *The Sharpest Sight*. Norman: University of Oklahoma Press, 1991.

———. *Wolfsong*. 1991. Reprint, Norman: University of Oklahoma Press, 1994.

Pratt, Mary Louise. *Imperial Eyes: Travel Writing and Transculturation*. London and New York: Routledge, 1992.

Ridge, John Rollin. *The Life and Adventures of Joaquin Murieta, The Celebrated California Bandit*. 1854. Reprint with introduction by Joseph Henry Jackson, Norman: University of Oklahoma Press, 1977.

Ruoff, A. LaVonne Brown. "Gerald Vizenor: Compassionate Trickster." *Studies in American Indian Literature* 9, no. 2 (1985): 52–63.

———. "Justice for Indians and Women: The Protest Fiction of Alice Callahan and Pauline Johnson." *World Literature Today* 66, no. 2 (spring 1992), 249–55.

———. "Woodland Word Warrior: An Introduction to the Works of Gerald Vizenor," *MELUS* 13, nos. 1–2 (spring–summer 1986): 13–43.

Said, Edward. *Culture and Imperialism*. New York: Knopf, 1993.

———. *The Politics of Dispossession: The Struggle for Palestinian Self-Determination, 1969–1994*. New York: Pantheon Books, 1994.

Saldívar, Ramón. *Chicano Narrative: The Dialectics of Difference*. Madison: University of Wisconsin Press, 1990.

Sarf, Wayne Michael. "Oscar Eaten by Wolves." *Film Comment* 27, no. 6 (1991): 62–70.

Scarberry-Garcia, Susan. *Landmarks of Healing: A Study of "House Made of Dawn."* Albuquerque: University of New Mexico Press, 1990.

Schruers, Fred. "Kevin Costner." *Rolling Stone* 592 (November 29, 1990): 55–60, 125–26.

Schubnell, Matthias. *N. Scott Momaday: The Cultural and Literary Background*. Norman: University of Oklahoma Press, 1985.

Seabrook, Jeremy. "The Nature of Wealth." *New Statesman and Society* 6, no. 273 (October 1993): 26–27.

Seals, David. "The New Custerism." *The Nation* 252, no. 18 (May 13, 1991): 634–39.

Seixas, Peter. "Confronting the Moral Frames of Popular Film: Young People Respond to Historical Revisionism." *American Journal of Education* 102 (May 1994): 261–85.

Shipek, Florence C. "A Native American Adaptation to Drought: The Kumeyaay as Seen in the San Diego Mission Records 1770–1798." *Ethnohistory* 28, no. 4 (fall 1981): 295–312.

Shoots the Ghost (Marlon Sherman). "Good Indians Live, Bad Indians Die: A Critique of Dances with Wolves." In *Multicultural America: A Resource Book for Teachers of Humanities and American Studies*, edited by Betty E. M. Chmaj. Lanham, N.Y.: University Press of America, 1993: 231–33.

Silko, Leslie Marmon. "Here's an Odd Artifact for the Fairy-Tale Shelf." *Impact Magazine Review of Books, Albuquerque Journal*, October 17, 1986, 10.

Smith, Barbara Hernstein. "Contingencies of Value." In *Canons*, edited by Robert von Hallberg. Chicago: University of Chicago Press, 1984.

Standing Bear, Luther. *Land of the Spotted Eagle*. Lincoln: University of Nebraska Press, 1933.

Stewart, Susan. "The State of Cultural Theory and the Future of Literary Form." *Profession* 93 (1993): 12–15.

Stone, Edward T. "Columbus and Genocide." *American Heritage* 26, no. 6 (1975): 76.

Szasz, Margaret Connell, ed. *Between Indian and White Worlds: The Culture Broker*. Norman: University of Oklahoma Press, 1994.

Trosper, L. Ronald. "Traditional American Indian Economic Policy." *American Indian Culture and Research Journal* 19, no. 1 (1995): 65–95.

Turner, Frederick Jackson. "The Frontier in American History." In *American Issues, Volume One, The Social Record*, edited by Willard Thorpe, et al., 661–74. Chicago: J. B. Lippincott Co., 1941.

Velie, Alan. *Four American Indian Literary Masters: N. Scott Momaday, James Welch, Leslie Marmon Silko, and Gerald Vizenor*. Norman: University of Oklahoma Press, 1982.

———. "The Trickster Novel." In *Narrative Chance: Postmodern Discourse on Native American Indian Literatures*, edited by Gerald Vizenor, pp. 121–39. Albuquerque: University of New Mexico Press, 1989.

Vizenor, Gerald. *Bearheart: The Heirship Chronicles*. Minneapolis: University of Minnesota Press, 1990.

———. "Crows Written on the Poplars." In *I Tell You Now: Autobiographical Essays by Native American Writers*, edited by Brian Swann and Arnold Krupat, pp. 99–110. Lincoln: University of Nebraska Press, 1987.

————. *Darkness in Saint Louis Bearheart*. Minneapolis: Truck Press, 1978. Reprinted in a new edition as *Bearheart: The Heirship Chronicles*, with an afterword by Louis Owens. Minneapolis: University of Minnesota Press, 1990.

————. *Earthdivers: Tribal Narratives on Mixed Descent*. Minneapolis: University of Minnesota Press, 1981.

————. *Fugitive Poses: Native American Indian Scenes of Absence and Presence*. Lincoln: The University of Nebraska Press, forthcoming.

————. *Manifest Manners: Postindian Warriors of Survivance*. Hanover, N.H.: Wesleyan University Press/University Press of New England, 1991.

————. "Socioacupuncture: Mythic Reversals and the Striptease." In *The American Indian and the Problem of History*, edited by Calvin Martin, 180–91. New York: Oxford University Press, 1987.

————. *The Trickster of Liberty: Tribal Heirs to a Wild Baronage*. Minneapolis: University of Minnesota Press, 1988.

Warren, William. *History of the Ojibway People*. Minnesota Historical Society, 1885. Reprint, Saint Paul: Minnesota Historical Society, 1984.

Welch, James. *Fools Crow*. New York: Viking Press, 1986.

————. *Killing Custer: The Battle of the Little Bighorn and the Fate of the Plains Indians*. New York: W.W. Norton and Co., 1994.

Young, Robert. *White Mythologies: Writing History and the West*. London: Routledge, 1990.

Zaleski, Philip. "Balancing the Scales in a Hollywood Epic." *Parabola* 16, no. 2 (1991): 89–93.

Index

—◆—